The 6-step program for a happier, healthier body, for life

Get Lean, Stay Lean

DR JOANNA McMILLAN

MURDOCH BOOKS
SYDNEY · LONDON

Roast veggie salad with pomegranate dressing (see page 95)

Contents

Introduction

It is now the norm across much of the world to be fat. This is despite a multi-million-dollar slimming industry comprising special supplements, home delivery meal offerings, meal replacement shakes, diet clubs, exercise programs, diets galore and numerous weight loss programs. So what on earth is going wrong? Could there possibly be room for another book on the subject?

I firmly believe the answer is yes. Not because the advice in this book is the latest scientific breakthrough or the newest fad diet to hit the headlines, but precisely because it doesn't offer a quick fix. This book will not give you a beach body in 10 days. But keep reading because what it will give you instead is far more valuable. What you will find here are the skills, the knowledge and the inspiration to make the real changes required to your diet and lifestyle, in order to achieve lasting, permanent results.

Get Lean, Stay Lean is not a program with an end date—it's a way of life. It's not about being perfect or becoming some sort of health evangelist. It's a do-able, realistic, joyful and delicious way of living life that aligns with great health, vitality and weight control.

There is no doubt it's hard to be a healthy weight in the modern world—it is what experts call an 'obesogenic environment'. We are surrounded by an abundance of food, with many of the cheapest options the worst for us, and we make some 200 decisions regarding food every single day. Our activity levels have dropped substantially and exercise is now rarely part and parcel of everyday life; we have to buck against our nature to reserve energy and instead choose to be active. Our work lives are often more demanding on our time, while stress levels go through the roof. All of this takes a toll on our

sleep patterns, and the fact that sleep clinics are popping up everywhere is testament to the fact that this is now a common problem.

You might think it's all in your genes and therefore you can't do anything about your body shape. But the good news is that genes are not necessarily your destiny and they are certainly not set in stone. The hot new research area is epigenetics. Although you have been given a set of genes from your biological parents, you do have some control. Epigenetics shows us that genes are like a dimmer light switch—they can be switched on or off, or ramped up or down—and the controllers are your diet and lifestyle choices.

We know that the diet and lifestyle of your parents, and even your grandparents, affects your expression of genes—your epigenetics. But while there is clearly nothing you can do about this, the uplifting part of this story is that you can still exert an influence through the choices you make. For those of you who have, or are planning on having, a family, you also affect your children. That has to be a major motivator to turning your lifestyle around. You have the opportunity to affect the health of future generations.

But back to you. Through the six steps of *Get Lean, Stay Lean* you'll learn how to reboot your body's computer. By adopting certain dietary and lifestyle changes, you really can change the way your body works for the better. You can make yourself better at burning fat, better at controlling your appetite, better at controlling blood glucose and insulin levels, better at exercising, and better at performing at work while still having the energy you need to enjoy life at home. Ultimately you will have a healthier, happier body … for life.

Genes are like a dimmer light switch—they can be switched on or off, or ramped up or down.

Part 1

The 6 steps to

Get Lean, Stay Lean

The 6 steps

The problem with most popular diets or the latest exercise regimen is that they don't consider a holistic approach to health and wellbeing. A short-sighted goal of weight loss over a few weeks isn't going to help you with long-term weight control, let alone your total body health.

In contrast, there are six key steps to the *Get Lean* lifestyle and I think of these as the pillars that hold your healthy lifestyle together.

These are food, drink, exercise, activity, stress and sleep—and importantly they are built on a foundation of joy. Because at the end of the day we are pleasure seekers, and when we enjoy what we do, we seek to do it more!

Understanding and giving attention to each of these areas of your life will ensure you are getting optimal results that last. These form the basis of the six-step program.

The 6 steps centring on joy

The 6 Steps at a glance

STEP 1. FOOD

Eat delicious food that nourishes your body in appropriate portions to lose body fat if you need to, or stay lean if you are already a healthy body composition. The Dr Joanna Plate is your guide to creating a healthy meal whether you are at home or ordering from a menu, while your Daily Blocks guide you towards the portion control you need to reach your goals. (More on both these concepts a little later on.)

STEP 2. DRINK

Drink water as your main drink to stay well hydrated. You can also enjoy coffee and tea, with milk if you like, but without added sugar. Veggie-based smoothies are also fabulous additions to your daily menu plan to boost your intake of plant foods. Soft drinks and juices are out—you don't need those extra kilojoules and it's much better to get them from whole foods. If you enjoy an alcoholic drink, then you still can. Just try to stick to no more than two a day, particularly while actively trying to get lean.

STEP 3. EXERCISE

Exercise is a non-negotiable factor for long-term good health and weight control. It changes the way your body works, making you a better fat burner and, with a little extra muscle, you'll burn more kilojoules even at rest. Aim for a minimum of a 30-minute walk every day and add two to three more formal exercise sessions into your week—such as fitness classes, yoga, pilates, dancing, cycling or running.

STEP 4. ACTIVITY

Aside from the formal exercise you do, how active you are for the rest of the day also matters. Count up how many hours you sit on an average day. Especially if you work at a desk, you'll be amazed how these add up. Set yourself goals to break up sitting times, so that you never sit for more than a couple of hours without a break for at least a few minutes of activity. If your office has a standing desk, use it for some of the time; stand on the bus or train; stand when you are on a long phone call; walk on escalators and grab other opportunities for movement.

STEP 5. STRESS

If you're stressed to the max, it's almost impossible to get any of the other steps of *Get Lean, Stay Lean* right. Stress can lead you to sleep badly; you're then tired so skip your exercise. Many find they turn to food, often unhealthy food, when stressed, while elevated levels of stress hormones direct your body to lay down those extra kilojoules as fat around your middle—the worst kind of fat for health. Others may find they turn to alcohol to blunt a stressful day. Learning how to manage your stress more effectively really can make a major difference to your ability to get and stay lean. Take action to manage your stress levels and seek help if you need it.

STEP 6. SLEEP

Being tired all the time erodes your ability to eat well, move more and manage your stress. Aim for seven to eight hours sleep on most nights and you'll be amazed how much better you look, feel and perform.

If you're tossing and turning in the night or you struggle to get to sleep, think about what sleep researchers call 'sleep hygiene'. This includes things like going to bed and getting up at roughly the same time, avoiding caffeine after lunchtime, having at least two hours before bed without food, avoiding more than one or two alcoholic drinks, and having no screen time (especially tablets and smartphones) for an hour before bed—try reading a book or having a bath instead to help you wind down.

Joy

The foundation to all of this is joy. This isn't meant in a flippant way; that somehow we have to be happy with every moment of our lives. Of course this is not possible and life at times is tough. During those hard times a focus on getting lean or even being healthy may seem far from your mind. But importantly what research has shown is that when healthy habits are well established we tend to default to them, even during the most stressful, rough patches.

So aside from the truly tough times, give joy some priority. Do something every day that makes you happy. It can be as simple as having a coffee with a friend or having half an hour to yourself in the bath with the door locked to a demanding family. Seek joy in preparing a new recipe (you'll find plenty of inspiration in the recipe section of this book), having an evening walk with your partner or reading a good book in bed instead of staying up late watching TV. Moments of joy are just as important with *Get Lean, Stay Lean* as the food you eat or the minutes of exercise you clock up.

So give each of the six areas some thought and decide which ones you need to give some priority to. Set weekly goals to align with your chosen areas and pay attention to the knock-on effect this has on strengthening your entire *Get Lean, Stay Lean* approach. You just might be surprised at the results.

Now let's look at each of the six steps in more detail, before learning how to pull them all together to build your new healthy *Get Lean, Stay Lean* lifestyle.

STEP 1: FOOD

Food is, of course, key to weight control, but also to your overall health and wellbeing. If you're already lean, that doesn't mean you can sit back and rest on your laurels and eat whatever you like!

Knowledge continues to grow in science and research, linking what, how and when we eat with how we feel today, but also how our bodies age and our health fares decades into the future. Eating well reduces the risk of several chronic diseases, including type 2 diabetes, heart disease, stroke and several types of cancer. However, unless you have had some sort of health scare, these things are probably not the key motivators driving your food choices today.

So, instead, motivate yourself with the more immediate effects. If you eat well, you have more energy, your skin is brighter, your hair glossier, your eyes clearer, your brain sparkier, your mood happier, and it is easier to control your appetite and your weight. Focus on these tangible benefits to help stay on track.

So what is a healthy diet? If you're confused about this, then you're not alone. But the truth is that good nutrition is not as complicated as it's often made out.

This is my overarching philosophy for food: Eat delicious, real food that nourishes your body, in appropriate portions to lose body fat if you need to, or to stay lean if you currently have a healthy body composition (that means healthy levels of body fat and good levels of muscle).

Real food means food that is close to the way nature intended. This is food that is full of

Phytochemicals and zoochemicals

Phytochemicals are the chemicals found in plants that are of benefit to us, such as antioxidants.

Zoochemicals are the chemicals found in animal foods that are of benefit to us, such as lutein and zeaxanthin in eggs.

beneficial nutrients, phytochemicals and zoochemicals, which our bodies need to function at their best.

Real food is vegetables, fruit, nuts, seeds, wholegrains, legumes, seafood, meat, dairy, eggs and certain foods made directly from these, such as extra virgin olive oil (the juice squeezed from olives) or tofu (made from soy beans).

This doesn't mean no processed foods at all. I keep hearing people say that processed food is bad. But this is a far too simplistic statement. Processing can, in fact, be beneficial for certain foods. Processing tomatoes to make tomato paste, for example, not only gives us a food with a conveniently long shelf life, it also dramatically increases the levels of the powerful antioxidant lycopene. Legumes and most wholegrains cannot be consumed raw, but our ancestors were smart enough to work out how to prepare and cook them in order for us to benefit from their nutritional offering. Cooking is itself a form of processing, and this gave our ancestors a survival advantage. They learned that cooking makes some foods safer to eat, while making others easier to digest and garner good nutrition.

Many processed foods actually make it easier to achieve a healthy diet. If we're smart we can use modern technologies and food processing techniques to help us, while avoiding the health disaster that comes from many modern, highly processed foods. Check out the shopping list on

page 18 to be clear about the best foods to stock your kitchen.

What I'm suggesting is not a set diet, and a real strength of *Get Lean, Stay Lean* is that it gives you the flexibility to build your own unique diet that is right for you. This is based on your genetics, any allergies or intolerances you might have, your likes and dislikes, your culture and upbringing, your religious, spiritual or moral beliefs, and the foods that are available to you in your area. All of these factors are equally important and hence what is right for me may not suit you, and vice versa. There's no one diet that fits all, and that's why flexibility is key.

You can choose to be a vegan or vegetarian. You may need to avoid lactose due to an intolerance, or shellfish due to an allergy. You may avoid pork on religious grounds or have strict rules on not combining dairy foods with meat. You may simply dislike salmon, and if you really hate kale I promise it's not essential for a healthy diet! All of your personal reasons for making certain food choices can, and should, be taken into account so that you create a healthy menu plan that works for you, forever.

So instead of giving you a diet, I give you a template for fabulously healthy eating. This is the Dr Joanna Plate. It's your guide to creating a healthy meal, whether you're at home or eating out. If you have this template in your mind at most meals, you are 80 per cent there towards achieving a healthy diet.

How much you eat is also clearly important, particularly if you have body fat to lose. This is where your Daily Blocks come in. They guide you towards the portion control you need to reach your goals. For the purposes of this book, I give you four example energy levels. These are the levels suitable for most women and men looking to get lean or to stay lean.

Custard filo tart with caramelised figs
(see page 201)

The Dr Joanna Plate

Diets usually fail because they don't give you autonomy. You need flexibility and choice in selecting what to eat, while having the framework and knowledge you need to create a healthy menu plan. That's where the Dr Joanna Plate comes in. It's a brilliant tool to use when creating a meal at home, or ordering in a restaurant or café. With a simple '1, 2, 3, 4' thought process you have a plant-rich, fibre-rich, low GI meal with the right balance of protein, carbohydrate and fat.

I want you to be as healthy as you can possibly be. This means you need to ensure you're getting all of the nutrients and phytochemicals your body needs, as well as using up your fat stores. The aim of the Dr Joanna Plate, therefore, is to maximise nutrient density while lowering energy density.

Dr Joanna Plate portions

1. PLANTS
Mostly non-starchy veggies with a little fruit

2. PROTEIN
Seafood, meat, dairy, eggs, legumes—including soy

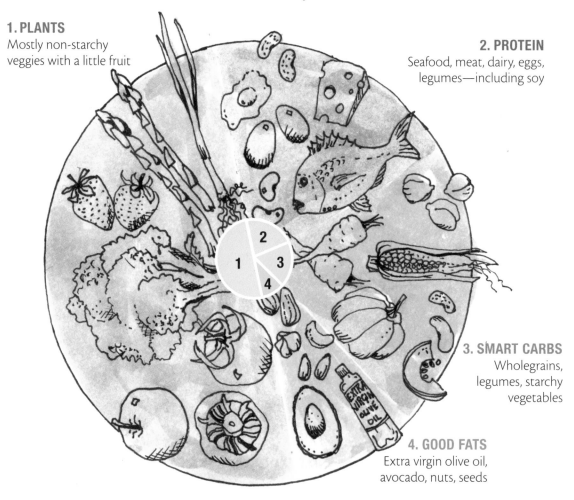

3. SMART CARBS
Wholegrains, legumes, starchy vegetables

4. GOOD FATS
Extra virgin olive oil, avocado, nuts, seeds

1. PLANTS

Fill 50 per cent of your plate with non-starchy vegetables and/or fruit. These provide volume and filling power for not many kilojoules, and they are packed with nutrients, fibre and phytochemicals our bodies need. With a low energy density and high nutrient density, they are worthy of the biggest space. Veggies are the one food type that you can pretty much eat as much of as you like. These should be the heroes of the plate, with fruit playing a smaller role—two to three pieces a day is about right for most people.

2. PROTEIN

Fill roughly 25 per cent of your plate with a protein-rich food. High protein diets have been immensely popular in recent years, and there is indeed good evidence that a good protein intake can help you to not only get lean, but stay lean.

However, it needn't be at the expense of good quality carbohydrates, nor should you eat unlimited amounts of protein. It will help your appetite control to spread your protein intake out over the day, rather than eating a huge amount at dinner. Applying the Dr Joanna Plate at each meal will help you to do just that.

Bear in mind that the majority of your carbs will also provide some protein and so by balancing your plate you will end up with a high protein, reduced carb, low GI, moderate but healthy fat eating plan.

Protein-rich foods include meat, poultry, fish and other seafood, eggs, dairy, tofu and legumes. The best quality choices are lean cuts of meat

Cheese

Cheese is often thought of as a fattening food. That's a shame as it's one of the best foods to boost your calcium intake, and provides high quality protein. While once demonised for its saturated fat content, recent research has shown that cheese doesn't have a detrimental effect on cholesterol profiles—neither do milk or yoghurt. Furthermore, all dairy foods have been shown to help with improving body composition— losing body fat and maintaining or gaining lean muscle. Nevertheless, full fat varieties are energy dense, so we don't need much of them. Watch your portion sizes to gain all the benefits without overdoing the kilojoules.

(look for grass-fed and/or free-range), game meats such as venison or kangaroo, sustainable fish and other seafood, free-range or organic eggs, milk, natural yoghurt, tofu, tempeh, beans, chickpeas and lentils.

You'll see that legumes are listed in both the proteins and carbs in the diagram to the left. If you're a vegan or vegetarian, count legumes as one of your proteins and you will want to combine them with a carb, such as a wholegrain, to meet your protein needs. For those who eat animal sources of protein, you will usually count legumes as one of your carbs. The exception being if you have a vegetarian meal, which I encourage you to do at least once a week, when you can happily include legumes as your protein.

Eating cheese boosts your calcium intake, and provides high quality protein.

3. SMART CARBS

Fill 15 to 20 per cent of your plate with smart carbs. Contrary to many popular diets today, you don't need to cut out all carbs to get lean. In fact, doing so may well be detrimental to your long-term health and vitality.

For starters I want you to have the energy to exercise, and carbohydrate is a major fuel for exercise. It also feeds the brain (30 per cent of the glucose circulating in your bloodstream is used by the brain) and other cells around the body. These foods are also major sources of fibre in the diet, and good levels of fibre are crucial for good gut health and encouraging the growth of beneficial bacteria in the colon.

I'm not totally against low carb diets as they have certainly been shown to be an effective option, at least in the short term. However, most people find them very hard to stick with long term and that leads to unsustainable results.

My own PhD research was in the area of high protein and low GI diets for fat loss and reduction of cardiovascular disease risk. My results (and research by others in recent years) send a clear message that it is the type of carb-rich foods that you choose to eat that is important. Refined grain products (just think of those based on white flour), those with a low nutrient density and/or those with high levels of added refined sugars are the problem. I strongly recommend cutting out or strictly limiting these products. But do include what I call smart carbs,

using your Daily Blocks (see page 55) as a guide to appropriate portion size.

Carbohydrate-rich foods are grains, corn, starchy vegetables, legumes and any food made from these. Smart carbs include wholegrains such as rolled oats, brown rice*, freekeh, barley, wholegrain pasta, soba (buckwheat) noodles, wholegrain low GI breakfast cereals, wholegrain bread (especially traditional sourdough); pseudo-grains, such as quinoa; whole corn (fresh, frozen or tinned); sweet potatoes*, yam or taro, small waxy potatoes*; lentils, dried beans, chickpeas (tinned is fine) and peas. Note: Pumpkin (winter squash) and butternut pumpkin (squash) really don't have much carbohydrate and therefore I just include them as vegetables.

* These choices are not always low GI, but being minimally processed, or completely unprocessed and having a host of other nutritional benefits makes them good choices nonetheless. Just watch the portion size.

4. GOOD FATS

Fill five to 10 per cent of your plate with good fats. Gone are the days of fat phobia! We need good fats, such as those found in nuts, seeds, avocado and extra virgin olive oil. What we don't need are highly processed modern fatty foods.

Fat is energy-dense stuff, so your portion size of foods rich in fat is smaller. However, I'm not in favour of low fat diets. Fat provides essential nutrients, it is necessary to absorb certain antioxidants and so, for example, by adding an

Smart carbs versus bad carbs

'Smart' carbs are carb-rich foods that deliver stacks of nutrition, have good levels of phytochemicals, are fibre-rich and/or have a low GI. They are usually foods that have been minimally processed, or processed intact as in the case of wholegrains; and are associated with better health and weight control in scientific studies.

'Bad' carbs are those carb-rich foods that are high in refined starch and/or refined sugars. They are less nutritious (sometimes offering nothing or little more than carbohydrate), are low in fibre, lack the phytochemicals found in whole plant foods, and are often moreish, making them easy to over-consume. These are foods that have been associated with poorer health outcomes and/or weight control in scientific studies.

extra virgin olive oil–based dressing to your salad you absorb more of the antioxidants from vegetables, as well as adding those present in the oil itself. Just as importantly, it provides taste, flavour and palatability to foods. You'll find you eat far more veggies when they taste good! Remembering the foundation of joy principle—your meals have to taste delicious if you're to keep this eating pattern up for life.

Fat also slows stomach emptying and therefore plays a role in slowing down the digestion process. This in turn slows the absorption of carbohydrates in the meal—effectively lowering the GI—and helps you to feel more satisfied for longer afterwards.

So fat gets a smaller, but no less important, space on the plate. A drizzle of extra virgin olive oil, some mashed avocado, a sprinkle of nuts and seeds, or a dollop of hummus are all great healthy examples.

The best choices are nuts and cold pressed nut oils, seeds, avocado and avocado oil, olives and extra virgin olive oil, tahini and hummus. I don't really like margarines or butter, and would far rather you use avocado or hummus in sandwiches and wraps, or brush your bread with extra virgin olive oil. However, a little butter, coconut oil and animal fats higher in monounsaturated fats, such as duck fat, are also okay for occasional use.

A FINAL NOTE

While we have a special slice on the Dr Joanna Plate for good fats, there are also fats appearing with food choices from other parts of the plate. These are the fats naturally present in oily fish (especially important), eggs, dairy—including cheese—healthy meat choices and in smaller amounts in many other foods we consume, including oats and other wholegrains. Most foods contain a mixture of macronutrients and for these it's impossible to classify them as a carb, protein or fat. The correct terminology is

Macronutrients and micronutrients

The term macronutrient literally means 'big nutrient'. These are the nutrients that provide us with energy (kilojoules). The three macronutrients are protein, carbohydrate and fat. Since alcohol also delivers kilojoules, it is sometimes called the fourth macronutrient, although clearly it is not essential and therefore not a 'nutrient' in the same way as the other macronutrients.

The term micronutrient literally means 'small nutrient'. These are the vitamins and minerals our bodies require to function, but they do not give us any energy.

to refer to carb-rich, protein-rich or fat-rich foods. The plate is my means of making things super easy for you and is meant only as a guide for creating healthy, balanced meals.

Hence, the lines between the fats, carbs and proteins are not set in stone. The most important factor is that you choose wholesome minimally processed foods, and then ensure you half fill the plate with plants.

The remaining half is more flexible, depending on the meal, your likes and dislikes, what you are doing and the other meals in the day. If you have just finished a pretty tough cardio workout you probably need a few extra carbs to restock your body's stores. Conversely, after a sedentary day at the office you could drop the carb from dinner and just have a light meal of fish with salad. Or perhaps you had a large steak while out for lunch and feel like a lighter vegetarian supper—this is likely to have more carbs and fewer proteins. All these options are fine so long as you have stuck to your block allocations of each for the day as a whole.

Good foods for the Dr Joanna Plate

1. PLANTS

Leafy greens and cruciferous vegetables—such as spinach, silverbeet (Swiss chard), witlof (chicory), lettuce, broccoli, cauliflower, kale, brussels sprouts, cabbage, cavolo nero (Tuscan cabbage), Asian greens, watercress, rocket (arugula)

Alliums—onions, garlic, French shallots, leeks, spring onions (scallions)

Fungi—button, field, oyster, shiitake and all other varieties of mushrooms

Capsicum (peppers) and chilli

Asparagus

Beetroot (beets), carrots, turnip

Pumpkin (winter squash) and butternut pumpkin (squash)

Tomatoes

Other fruit—such as berries, apples, pears, pomegranate, grapefruit, grapes, cherries, mango, pineapple, papaya, star fruit, passionfruit, bananas, oranges, mangosteen, plums, kiwi fruit

Herbs and spices—such as parsley, basil, coriander (cilantro), mint, oregano, tarragon, cumin, cardamom, paprika, spice mixes

2. PROTEINS

Fish*—including salmon, trout, barramundi, snapper, ling, perch, cod, sardines, tuna, mackerel ... the list is endless, but do look for sustainable seafood varieties

Other seafood*—oysters, mussels, clams (vongole), prawns (shrimp), octopus, crab, squid and all types of crustaceans and shellfish

Quality fresh red meat—look for non-marbled meat, grass-fed is a good indicator—beef, lamb and free-range pork

Game meats—venison, kangaroo, buffalo, wild boar, emu, ostrich, crocodile

Although we count these as our protein-rich food on the plate, fish and other seafood are also the best sources of the long chain omega-3 fats we need for good health. Oily fish, including salmon, trout, mackerel and sardines, are especially rich. Unless you are vegetarian or vegan, include at least two seafood meals a week.

Poultry—chicken, turkey and duck— look for free-range or organic

Eggs—look for free-range or organic

Dairy—milk, yoghurt, cheese

Soy—soy milk, tofu, tempeh, soy beans

Other legumes—chickpeas, dried beans, lentils

3. SMART CARBS

Legumes—chickpeas, dried beans, lentils

Wholegrains—rolled or steel cut oats, barley, freekeh, brown rice**, farro, teff, millet

Pseudo-grains—quinoa, amaranth, buckwheat

Wholegrain products—wholegrain bread, crackers and wraps, wholegrain pasta

Starchy vegetables – sweet potatoes**, taro, yam, parsnip and choose small potatoes in their skins**

*** These options are not always low GI, but they are nutritious and therefore worthy of inclusion.*

4. GOOD FATS

Extra virgin olive oil—I recommend this as your pantry staple for cooking and dressings.

Avocado and avocado oil

Nuts of all types—including almonds, Brazil nuts, cashews, macadamias, pistachios, pine nuts, peanuts, pecans, walnuts

Nut butters—preferably made yourself from quality nuts with no nasty additives, or good quality bought

Seeds—sunflower, pepitas (pumpkin seeds), poppy, sesame, flaxseed (linseed), chia

Tahini and hummus

How can vegetables and fruit help you get lean?

While there remain some controversies in human nutrition, one aspect that nearly all experts agree on is that humans thrive best on a plant-based diet. Whether or not you also eat animal foods, making the bulk of foods on your plate plant foods is helpful to get lean, to stay lean and to boost your long-term health.

Using the Dr Joanna Plate for most meals will ensure you achieve this. In fact, about 75 per cent of the plate is plant food. For simplicity's sake we're only calling veggies and fruit 'plant food', but your smart carbs are also plant foods, as are your good fats and some protein foods. Choose to be vegan and you can make your entire Dr Joanna Plate plant food. Vegetables and fruit have been deliberately separated out to command the biggest section of the plate, however, and here's why:

- The volume of food on our plate is crucial for helping us to feel full and satisfied after eating. When your stomach swells with the contents of a meal, stretch receptors in the stomach wall send messages to the brain to signal the stomach is filling and, once full, we feel sated and consequently stop eating. Vegetables and fruit have lots of volume for relatively few kilojoules— they have a low energy density. In short, they fill up our stomachs for very few kilojoules.

- Although low in kilojoules, vegetables and fruit are rich in micronutrients and phytochemicals. These are essential for nourishing the body, allowing you to function at your best, keep your immune system strong and optimally protect your body from oxidative damage that takes its toll, especially as we age.

- Vegetables and fruit generally contain lots of water—in part this is why they have such low kilojoules for their volume. This water content contributes to your hydration status, potentially stopping you from turning to kilojoule-containing drinks.

How can protein help you get lean?

Proteins are essentially what we are made of. Our hair, nails, skin, muscle, organs and all cells in the body are constructed with proteins. They are used to mend damaged tissue, grow new tissue and repair muscle tissue after you exercise to make new cells to replace old ones, and are used in many of the body's biochemical processes.

We also use proteins for energy when there is not enough carbohydrate or fat around. When we eat more protein than our body needs, or can burn as fuel, it can be converted to fat for storage. So remember, protein is not a magic bullet to getting lean—it still contributes kilojoules and can be over-consumed.

That said, higher protein diets have been shown in research to be helpful not just to lose body fat, but to keep it off. Ensuring a good protein intake can also help to ensure you maintain or build muscle—exactly what we want for long-term health and weight control. Here's how:

- Protein is the most satiating of the three major macronutrients—the others being carbohydrate and fat. When you include a decent serve of protein in your meal you tend to feel more satisfied and stop eating earlier and/or delay the return of hunger.

- There is evidence to suggest that we keep eating until our requirements for protein are met—this is called the Protein Leverage Hypothesis. A typical Western diet is often low in protein through the day, when lots of simple carbs and fatty meals are consumed. But, come dinner, a huge amount of protein is taken in—considering that a 200 g (7 oz) steak contains about 50 g of protein. Spreading your protein intake across all meals ensures you meet your protein requirements earlier in the day. This in turn can help to curb your appetite so that you end up eating less overall.

Protein is not a magic bullet to getting lean—it still contributes kilojoules and can be over-consumed.

- Protein takes more energy to digest and metabolise in the body than either carbohydrate or fat. In other words, we use up a few extra kilojoules dealing with a high protein meal, compared to a similar carb- or fat-rich meal.
- By tucking into a quality protein-rich food, you potentially reduce your intake of other less nutritious foods, such as refined carbs.

We don't, however, need to eat bucket-loads of protein to gain the benefits.

I also recommend that you skip the fancy protein powders, high protein bars and other manufactured, highly processed foods. Why go down the same wrong road we did previously with low fat foods? Where we once saw a 'low fat' label as a licence to eat as much as we liked, I see this happening with the 'high protein, low carb' claim. Heavily processed food is not what we should be eating—period. It doesn't matter the levels of protein, carb or fat, it's still highly processed. One caveat—protein shakes do have a place in sports nutrition and can be a convenient way of ensuring you get your protein immediately after a strength-training workout. But for many I see at the gym, downing enormous protein shakes post workout, they are simply giving themselves unnecessary extra kilojoules.

Why not have a milk- or yoghurt-based smoothie instead, or simply eat a balanced meal? My preference is to opt for the many fabulous naturally protein-rich foods we have on offer and include at least one at each meal.

Finally, following a higher protein menu plan need not be at the expense of good quality carbs—your smart carbs. Get Lean, Stay Lean guides you towards achieving a high protein, reduced carbohydrate, low GI diet containing plenty of healthy fats.

Why seafood is a particularly good protein choice

Seafood is a pretty perfect choice for the protein section of your plate. All types are high in protein, but additionally they are fabulous sources of many nutrients including:

- Long chain omega-3 fats (DHA, EPA and DPA). These are crucial for brain health, are anti-inflammatory throughout the body, are important for eye health (they protect against macular degeneration), are beneficial for heart health and may even protect against some forms of cancer. The highest levels are found in oily fish, including salmon, trout, mackerel, sardines, tuna, herring and kingfish.
- Niacin and other B group vitamins required for energy metabolism.
- Iodine, an essential component of thyroid hormones that are key regulators of your metabolism.
- Iron for healthy red blood cells and oxygen transport.
- Zinc, essential for many metabolic processes and a strong immune system.
- Small quantities of folate, essential in the production of DNA and new cells in the body.
- Potassium, needed to maintain healthy blood pressure, phosphorus, for strong bones and teeth, and magnesium needed for proper nerve and muscle function and heart health. Particularly for those who don't eat dairy products, fish with edible soft bones (such as tinned salmon and sardines), oysters, prawns (shrimp) and scallops become valuable sources of calcium.

PROTEIN IN FOODS ON THE DR JOANNA PLATE

Our physiological requirement for protein, expressed as grams of protein per kilogram of body weight, is about 0.75 g for women and about 0.84 g for men. It does increase once you reach the age of 70 to 0.94 g for women and 1.07 g for men. On average, this means adult women need about 46 g a day and 57 g for women 70 plus, while men need 64 g a day and 81 g for 70 plus years of age.

To give you an idea of what you need to eat to reach these levels, the table to the right provides the protein levels in various foods. You'll see that the foods we count as smart carbs or good fats often deliver good amounts of protein, too.

It's not at all difficult to meet our physiological requirement for protein and very few people in developed countries are going short. However, for appetite, weight control and optimal body composition, eating more protein than this may be beneficial. Unless you have a specific medical condition that requires you to limit your protein (a kidney disorder for example) it is perfectly safe to eat up to 2 g of protein per kilogram of your ideal body weight.

On *Get Lean, Stay Lean*, rather than focusing on the absolute amount of protein, I recommend you spread your protein intake out over the day to optimise the benefits. For example, you may have eggs with breakfast, chicken at lunch and fish for dinner, with nuts and yoghurt as snacks. There is no need for you to count your grams of protein—using the Dr Joanna Plate as your template for meals will ensure you achieve good protein distribution across the day.

Protein in foods

FOOD	PROTEIN
ANIMAL FOODS	
100 g (3½ oz) raw meat, poultry or seafood	20–22 g
2 eggs	12 g
200 g (7 oz) natural yoghurt	12 g
250 ml (9 fl oz/1 cup) milk	9 g
30 g (1 oz) cheese	8 g
LEGUMES	
100 g (3½ oz) tofu	12 g
220 g (7¾ oz) tinned baked beans in tomato sauce (ketchup)	11 g
250 ml (9 fl oz/1 cup) soy milk	9 g
100 g (3½ oz) cooked green or brown lentils	10 g
100 g (3½ oz) tinned soy beans	9 g
30 g (1 oz) peanuts*	7 g
100 g (3½ oz) tinned mixed beans	6 g
GRAINS AND PSEUDOGRAINS	
2 slices of wholegrain bread	10 g
190 g (6¾ oz/1 cup) cooked quinoa	8 g
155 g (5½ oz/1 cup) cooked pasta	8 g
40 g (1½ oz/½ cup) rolled (porridge) oats	5 g
185 g (6½ oz/1 cup) cooked brown rice	5 g
NUTS AND SEEDS	
30 g (1 oz) pepitas (pumpkin seeds)	9 g
30 g (1 oz) sunflower seeds	8 g
30 g (1 oz) almonds	6 g
30 g (1 oz) mixed nuts	5 g

* Note that peanuts are actually a legume, although nutritionally they are more like tree nuts. For the Dr Joanna Plate I therefore count them with nuts and seeds as a good fat.

Spread your protein intake out over the day to optimise the benefits.

How can carbs help you get lean?

Get Lean, Stay Lean is not weight loss at any cost. It's about developing the kind of healthy diet and lifestyle that makes you look and feel great today, while giving you the best chance of optimum health in the future. That's why I recommend a balanced approach—you can still achieve the benefits of a high protein diet, while consuming smart carbs to give you the fibre, energy and nutrients your body needs.

For some people cutting out carbs has undoubtedly helped them to lose weight. If you think about it, following a low carb diet means no biscuits, no cake, no soft drinks, no confectionary, no moreish fluffy white bread, no potato chips and no big bowls of pasta with rich creamy sauce. So really, it's a no brainer that you'd lose weight.

Unfortunately, what can happen with very low carb diets is that you just don't function at your best, you'll find it hard to do any sort of intense exercise, and such diets can be very hard to stick to long term. They can lead to symptoms such as bad breath, a foggy brain, irritation, an inability to concentrate and constipation. Admittedly, there is evidence that you can adapt to such a diet over several months, but I'm yet to see convincing long-term evidence of the benefits. There are also valid concerns about the effect on gut health in particular. It's very hard to meet your fibre requirements without

carbohydrate-containing foods, plus low fibre and high fat both alter the bacteria living in your gut in undesirable ways. I therefore favour a more moderate approach where a broader selection of foods can be consumed.

Not all carbohydrates are equal, and they do not affect your body in the same way.

Wholegrains and legumes have been associated with a whole host of healthy benefits, including heart health, gut health and weight control. Don't lump all carbs together as fattening, but instead focus on the quality and quantity of the carb-rich foods you consume. We need carbohydrates to exercise at any intensity. I want you to be exercising regularly as part of your *Get Lean, Stay Lean* lifestyle and without the right carbs you won't have the energy to do this.

Carbs in your diet will be used to replenish your body's carb stores—called glycogen—that are stored in your liver and muscles. Only when these stores are full and your overall energy needs are met will carbs be converted to fat.

So fuel your body with what it needs. Very active people will need more carbs, while sedentary office workers will need less—but they also need less fuel overall. By using the Dr Joanna Plate as your guide to creating healthy menu plans you'll hit the right balance of carbs in your diet to *Get Lean, Stay Lean*.

Following a low GI diet reduces your risk of heart disease, type 2 diabetes and can help you to lose body fat.

Controlling your blood glucose

One of the key differences between various carbohydrate-containing foods is how they affect your blood glucose levels. This is where the glycaemic index (or GI) is a useful tool.

The GI ranks foods according to their measured effect on blood glucose levels when compared gram for gram of carbohydrate. While research in this area will continue for years to come, it is already clear that following a high GI diet is detrimental to both health and weight control, while following a low GI diet reduces your risk of heart disease, type 2 diabetes and can help you to lose body fat.

In short, a high GI food, such as white jasmine rice, is broken down and absorbed quickly, producing a large and rapid rise in your blood glucose levels. This in turn forces your body to produce a correspondingly large amount of the hormone insulin.

Insulin's job is to get the glucose, as well as incoming fat and protein from the meal, out of the blood and up into the cells where they are needed. Meanwhile insulin also 'instructs' fat cells to stop releasing stored fat into the bloodstream for use as fuel and store what is coming in.

This is all a normal part of metabolism, indeed without insulin we wouldn't be able to survive. After a strength-training workout you actually want an insulin rise as this is what drives the uptake of amino acids (from protein) into

Blood glucose effects from high versus low GI foods

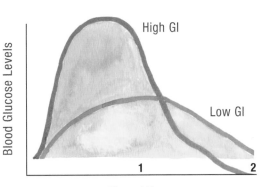

For the same amount of carbohydrate, low GI foods produce smaller blood glucose responses, without the rapid decline that stimulates appetite.

Low GI foods need less insulin to be dealt with. This reduces the insulin demand on the body—and chronically high blood insulin levels are themselves damaging—allowing for improved fat metabolism.

muscle and stimulates the process of repair and the synthesis of new muscle.

The problem comes when there is too much insulin around, too much of the time. Such a situation would make it hard for the body to burn fat effectively and, slowly over time, a net gain in body fat would occur.

Metabolism and metabolic rate

Metabolism is really just the chemical processes that go on in your body to allow it to function. It includes turning incoming food into energy to fuel body cells, to make new cells from skin cells to new muscle, to power our brains, keep our hearts pumping, give us energy to exercise, and to break down tissues such as glycogen, body fat and muscle when energy is required.

Metabolic rate is the rate at which your body uses energy. The idea that some of us have a slow metabolic rate is not true. There are small differences between people, but it's almost entirely explained by incidental exercise (such as fidgeting), heat production, diet and, importantly, the level of muscle—muscle uses far more energy even at rest than fat. To boost your metabolic rate—move!

In addition, the more rapid fall in blood glucose after eating a high GI meal, with a dip one-and-a-half to two hours after a meal, stimulates us to eat again. Studies have now shown that low GI foods are more filling and keep you full for longer thereby helping you to eat less.

Many nutrition scientists now believe that the predominance of high GI foods in our diet—especially in the last 50 or so years—is a major contributor to overweight and obesity.

Our bodies are designed to run on both carbohydrate and fat, and glucose must be kept at a certain level in the bloodstream for our bodies to function. The key therefore is to provide your body with a slow steady stream of incoming carbohydrate after eating, avoiding large rapid influxes which overload the system. Choosing low GI foods in appropriate quantities helps you to do just that.

However, the GI is not the only consideration, so be careful not to be fooled by the marketing of some food products claiming to be low GI. Ice cream is low GI but it doesn't make it a smart carb! There is even a type of sugar that is marketed as low GI, and clearly these types of products are misleading.

Instead, look at the big picture and consider the whole nutrition package of the food. Smart carbs are those that offer bags of nutrition—be it fibre, high levels of vitamins and minerals, phytochemicals such as antioxidants—and the best of these also have a low GI. Most minimally processed wholegrains, legumes and starchy vegetables in their skins tick most, if not all, of these boxes.

How to make the smart carb choice

POTATOES

If you're a potato fan, I take heart. I grew up on a diet of meat, potatoes and two to three veg. Unfortunately, the varieties most commonly cultivated have been chosen to give us the type of potato that makes good mash or chips, are easy to grow and harvest, and are, inadvertently, high in GI. It doesn't mean you have to avoid them—just choose those likely or known to have a lower GI and then watch your portion size and how often you have them. Here's how:

- Opt for small potatoes, with the skin. They are closer to the wild potatoes we used to eat and correspondingly have a lower GI.

- Use them cold in a potato salad as this increases the level of resistant starch, while decreasing the level of available carbohydrate.

- Skip the mash and fries, especially in restaurants, as you'll be much more likely to overeat these and you have no control over the type of fat added.

- Make your own potato chips at home, keeping the skins on and cutting into chip shapes, tossing in extra virgin olive oil and baking in a hot oven.

- Make your own mash by mixing potatoes in their skins with other veggies such as parsnips, cauliflower, sweet potato and carrot.

- In place of potatoes regularly, try eating more legumes—a terrific source of plant protein, fibre, folate and many more nutrients than potatoes.

BREAKFAST CEREALS

Breakfast cereals have had a bad rap of late. Some of this is justified as many have a high GI and/or have high levels of added sugar. However, the breakfast cereal companies have been seriously pulling up their socks and there are now many good options. This is great news as they are a convenient, quick and easy breakfast choice. Furthermore, recent research has been very positive showing that breakfast cereal eaters have a lower risk of being overweight, have better intakes of many vitamins and minerals, and there are further benefits, particularly for gut health, from consuming wholegrain cereals.

So here's how to incorporate breakfast cereal into your *Get Lean, Stay Lean* menu plan:

- Choose high fibre cereals made from wholegrains. In particular look for those higher in soluble fibre from oats, psyllium, legumes, or where the wholegrains are more intact.
- Muesli made with no added refined sugar, or better yet you can make your own. You'll find a few of my muesli recipes in the breakfast chapter.
- Use the Dr Joanna Plate to get the portion right and team with plenty of fruit, protein (in the form of milk, natural yoghurt or soy milk) and a handful of nuts and/or seeds for good fats.

Quinoa porridge with rhubarb, pear and toasted coconut (see page 63)

BREAD

Once considered a staple food for most households, bread is now unfairly thrown into the same basket with all the other carb-rich foods. But if you think about it, we have been eating bread for thousands of years but have only gotten fat in the last 50 or so. Can we really blame bread? It's ridiculous to lump bread into the same category as cakes, biscuits, pastries and other energy-dense, less nutritious baked goods. Bread is made from a relatively high protein wheat and therefore is a significant source of protein, as well as providing a range of nutrients including the B group vitamins we need to turn our food into energy. Most importantly, provided you pick the best options, bread is a key source of fibre. Cereal fibre seems to be particularly protective against colon cancer. So the key with bread is quality and quantity.

Here are your choices:

- Best choices—wholegrain varieties. These are made from the intact grain so that all the fibre and nutrients found in the outer layers of the grain are included. Opt for traditionally made breads, such as sourdough or stoneground, as these tend to have a lower GI. Rye breads may have particular digestive benefits.

- Okay choices—wholemeal varieties. These have the fibre portion of the grain added back to the flour after processing. As a result, they tend to have a higher GI than wholegrain. Multigrain breads can be okay and some do have a lower GI if they contain enough soluble fibre, however, most are simply white flour mixed with some wholegrain or intact grains.

- Skip or strictly limit—white breads made without any additional fibre added. These are made with white flour, which is high in refined starch and therefore have a high GI. If you must have white bread, opt for those with added fibre or sourdough loaves as these have a lower GI.

PASTA

If you like wholemeal pasta, then this is a terrific choice. They are full of fibre and the nutrients found in the outer part of the intact grain. However, if you really can't get used to it, even the traditional varieties made from durum wheat are in fact low GI.

This is due to the physical structure, and the fact that pasta is relatively high in protein (more than double rice). Where we go wrong is in the quantity and what goes with it. Keep your portion to less than a quarter of the plate, team with a protein-rich food and loads of veg and it's a *Get Lean, Stay Lean* winning meal.

Is sugar toxic?

Sugars are the simplest types of carbohydrates and they serve as the building blocks for other carbohydrates. Starch, for example, is just long chains of glucose units. In plants, sugars and starch are their energy store and are used to fuel the plant's growth and reproduction. Plants are our major source of both sugars and starch.

When we eat plant foods, we break down the sugars and starches to their simplest sugars—the monosaccharides (these are the building blocks of all other sugars and starches) of which the most important is glucose. This is the sugar that runs in our blood and fuels cells all over the body from the brain to our working muscles. Since both sugar and fat are essential fuels in our bodies, it's wrong, scientifically, to say that sugar is toxic.

What's interesting, however, is that in nature almost all of these carbohydrates—so both sugar and starch—occur alongside fibre and a whole bunch of different nutrients. When we eat these plants whole we benefit from this complete nutritional package.

The sugar you can buy at the supermarket is a different thing. In this case the sugars are extracted from the plant and refined so that only the sugars remain (or occasionally with minute amounts of nutrients if not completely refined to white sugar). The fibre and all the other nutrients found in the plant are discarded.

This sugar is then added ubiquitously to many modern processed foods and drinks. In this case the sugar is adding kilojoules to the product without any accompanying nutrients. A little sugar added to an overall healthy product can still deliver a nutritious meal. The major problem is with the products with lots of added sugar (or starch for that matter). Such products tend to have a high energy density—packing in the kilojoules per mouthful—but a low nutrient density. We are hard-wired from our hunter-gatherer days to seek out energy-dense food and sweet food is a sign of valuable carbohydrates. We therefore have a tendency to overeat them.

Products with high levels of added sugars are clearly not helpful for weight control or health. Eating too many will almost inevitably lead to becoming over-fat but under-nourished.

You don't need to give up all sugar. A healthy diet can include the odd slice of cake or whatever your sweet treat of choice is. Just not every day and if you're in an active phase of getting lean be stricter with cutting back on added sugars. You just don't have room in a reduced kilojoule menu plan to fit in foods that offer little nutrition.

On the other hand, do enjoy whole fruit, or a little dried fruit (provided you watch the portion size) for nature's sweet treat. You'll find a

Types of sugars

There is now a dizzying array of sugars on the market with many touting themselves as healthier. These include coconut nectar/sugar, brown rice malt syrup, panela, evaporated cane juice and agave. There is also widespread confusion with some using the term sugar only to apply to table sugar (sucrose). This is scientific nonsense. These different types of sugar are just sugars extracted from different plants. Some are less refined than others, but really this is splitting hairs; don't be fooled by the marketing, and recognise these all as added sugars we need to limit if we want to have optimal health.

Honey and maple syrup are two sugars I do tend to favour as they are the least refined and have some evidence of medicinal use. Indeed, honey was part of a true paleo diet—evidence of our ancestral sweet tooth. Nevertheless, these are also added sugars and we should use cautiously. A drizzle on your porridge or to sweeten a wholegrain muffin is fine—pouring over white flour pancakes is clearly not helpful for weight or blood glucose control!

few delicious sweet treat recipes in this book where I've kept added sugars to a minimum, or used foods with naturally present sugars to sweeten them. Do remember even these are not intended to be everyday foods, but to be enjoyed and savoured on occasion when you truly feel like something sweet.

A healthy diet can include the odd slice of cake or whatever your sweet treat of choice is. Just not every day.

Crunchy gluten-free muesli (see page 69)

Low or full fat dairy?

Dairy foods, except butter, are terrific sources of protein and they are all low GI. This is one of the reasons they have been shown to be advantageous for weight control—they help boost lean mass while losing body fat when part of a reduced kilojoule diet.

New research suggests that full fat milk and other dairy may well be much better for us. This probably seems like yet another flip in nutritional wisdom, so let's take a closer look at what is going on.

Well, if you changed nothing else in your diet but swapped whole milk for skim, you'd reduce your kilojoules and benefit weight control. However, if you felt hungrier as a result of the switch, resulting in you eating more of other foods, then the change would not be beneficial—particularly if the additional foods were low fat, but high in refined carbs instead. Full fat

dairy on the other hand may promote better satiety, there may be components in the fat that are beneficial, or it may just be that those opting for full fat dairy are eating more whole foods in general and less 'fat-modified' diet foods. The bottom line though, is that full fat dairy is more energy dense so you need to watch your portion size, while low fat dairy is not a green light to eat more.

My recommendation is to opt for one you prefer the taste of! Personally, I prefer skim milk but I always have full fat cheese and choose to get more of my fats from my other 'good fats' on the plate. With *Get Lean, Stay Lean* just alter the portion size accordingly such that a block of full cream milk is 185 ml (6 fl oz/ ¾ cup) while a block of skim milk is 250 ml (9 fl oz/ 1 cup).

How can good fats help you get lean?

The low fat message has dominated dietary advice in the last few decades, but it has spectacularly failed in curbing our collective waistlines.

One of the major reasons for this is that with a blinkered view of nutrition focusing solely on fat, we inadvertently replaced it with carbs, and usually highly refined (and therefore high GI) carbs at that. Just think of all those low fat cookies, ice cream, snack bars and so on. These low fat and fat-free products are often just as energy dense as the original products they replaced, while also giving us a green card to eat as much as we liked—'fat-free' was interpreted by the low fat dieter as 'kilojoule-free' and consumed in abandon.

Today we understand much more about how choosing the right fats can actually help us to get and stay lean as well as boost our health and vitality. Here's how:

- Fat slows down digestion—in particular the time it takes for food to leave the stomach and enter the small intestine. With food still in your stomach you dampen appetite cues, while at the same time slowing down the digestion and absorption of the nutrients, including the carbohydrates, from the small intestine. In short this means fat helps to lower the GI of a meal.
- Fat makes food tasty. It transmits flavours to tastebuds and improves the mouthfeel of the food. When we enjoy and feel satisfied with our meal, we are less inclined to be looking for 'a little something else' a short time later.
- Fat contains the fat soluble vitamins A, D, E and K, but it's also necessary for the absorption of numerous phytochemicals. You actually need some fat present to absorb all those wonderful antioxidants found in your salad, for example.
- By eating a little more fat and reducing your carbohydrate intake, you help to make your body a better fat burner.

- Many natural fat-rich foods are also packed with numerous other nutrients and phytochemicals that benefit our health. Nuts are a great example. Once shunned for their energy density, we now know that a handful a day dramatically reduces heart disease risk and actually helps with body weight control.

So what are the best fats to consume? There are essentially three main types of fat: saturated, monounsaturated and polyunsaturated. Although there is a mixture of all different fats in any one food, we tend to label them according to the one that predominates. Let's understand a little more about each of these fat families.

SATURATED FAT

For decades, saturated fats have been thought of as the baddies. However, in recent years this has been questioned, particularly with respect towards the association with heart disease. The confusion may have arisen at least in part, from pooling all saturated fats together when in fact there are many with different effects in the body.

We know from clinical trials that some of the saturated fats raise blood LDL 'bad' cholesterol, while others don't. For example, a saturated fat called stearic acid, dominant in dark chocolate, seems to have a neutral effect on blood cholesterol, while lauric, myristic and palmitic acids all raise both LDL 'bad' cholesterol and HDL 'good' cholesterol.

The other problem is we eat foods, not individual nutrients like saturated fat, alone. Different saturated fat–containing foods have different effects within the body. Consuming saturated fat from a piece of cheese is not the same as consuming it from a commercial party pie or a meat-lover's pizza. Eating a steak is not the same as eating a processed hot dog. You get the idea.

The bottom line is that despite the current controversies surrounding saturated fats, there is no evidence that a high saturated fat diet is good for us.

However, that doesn't mean total avoidance of saturated fats. Focusing on foods rather than nutrients is the best way of getting the balance right. So cut down on pastries, biscuits, cakes, crisps/chips (regardless of the fat they are fried in) and processed meats. These not only contain saturated fats but the undoubtedly harmful trans fats, not to mention preservatives, salt, sugar and whatever other undesirable additives are in such highly processed foods.

TRANS FAT

Trans fats do not occur to any great extent in nature. They are produced during food processing when an oil, which is liquid at room temperature, undergoes a chemical process called hydrogenation to make it more solid. In effect, this is trying to make it behave more like a saturated fat but the end result is far worse for us. There is no doubt that they are implicated in the development of heart disease. The evidence is so strong against trans fats that many places, including New York City, have put policies in place to ban them in food completely. Trans fats are found in fast foods where oils are heated repeatedly, some commercial pies, pastries, biscuits and cakes, or any product where you see 'hydrogenated vegetable oil' in the ingredients list. That's your red flag to put the product back.

MONOUNSATURATED FAT

Monounsaturated fats dominate in olive oil, avocado and most nuts including peanuts, cashews, hazelnuts, macadamias, pecans, pistachios and almonds. Eggs are not usually labelled as monounsaturated fat sources, yet it is the dominant fat in them, providing about half of the fat present.

Interestingly, although animal fats tend to be assumed to be all saturated fat, duck fat is actually half monounsaturated fat and is lower in saturated fat than most other animal fats.

In general, fats and oils that are rich in monounsaturated fats are good fats to eat. The Mediterranean diet has a large body of solid evidence showing that this dietary pattern, rich in monounsaturated fat, reduces the risk of heart disease, type 2 diabetes and many cancers.

Cholesterol

Although the common perception is that cholesterol is bad, it is in fact the most common type of steroid in the body and is essential for the functioning of nearly every cell. It is also required in the production of bile salts (to digest dietary fat), several hormones and vitamin D. Because it is such a necessary component of metabolism, we make most of our cholesterol in the liver, while a smaller amount comes from animal foods in our diet.

The bad-boy image of cholesterol comes from the associations of blood cholesterol and the development of atherosclerosis (narrowing of the arteries). Cholesterol is carried in the blood by a type of protein and these particles are called 'lipoproteins'. Low-density lipoproteins (LDL) carry cholesterol from the liver to cells around the body, while high-density lipoproteins (HDL) collect excess cholesterol and return it to the liver. High levels of LDL cholesterol has been associated with an increased risk of heart disease as it is prone to damage from oxidation, leading to the cholesterol being deposited in plaques on the artery walls. In contrast, high levels of HDL cholesterol seem to be protective, because they can pick up the excess cholesterol and return it to the liver.

Your doctor will therefore look for low LDL and high HDL as being more important than a total cholesterol value. Newer tests can now also measure oxidised LDL or the LDL particle size as these may be better measures of risk. However, these are not yet routinely available.

When used in place of refined carbohydrates, such as all those 'diet' low fat snacks and foods made from white flour, they do an excellent job of raising HDL (good) cholesterol while modestly reducing LDL (bad) cholesterol—exactly the direction of change we want.

There is even some evidence that mono-unsaturated fats are less likely to be stored around your middle. Swapping saturated fats and refined carbs for monounsaturated fats may even help you to shift the fat in this area of your body.

They are also far more stable in cooking than the polyunsaturated fats, making them less likely to form harmful fats at high heat or to go rancid in storage. Those Mediterranean countries have much right in their diet and I follow their example and make extra virgin olive oil my pantry staple.

Spanish seafood stew (see page 129)

The Mediterranean diet

The traditional Mediterranean diet stands out as one of the healthiest in the world. In scientific studies it has been associated with a lower risk of cardiovascular disease (stroke and heart disease), several types of cancer, type 2 diabetes, Parkinson's and Alzheimer's diseases.

When it comes to weight control the Mediterranean diet also provides solid evidence in support of eating good fats. Extra virgin olive oil is one of the diet's staples, along with plentiful amounts of nuts, seeds, avocado and omega-3-rich seafood. Despite (or perhaps as a result of) this relatively high fat intake, the diet has been associated with weight loss and, importantly, reduces the deposition of fat around the middle—the most dangerous fat for health.

Aside from the types of fat there are many other health benefits of this diet. It is also characterised by large amounts of vegetables, herbs and spices, fruit, legumes and wholegrains. Mediterraneans tend to eat seafood, poultry and eggs regularly, but have red meat less often. They enjoy moderate amounts of dairy foods, principally as cheese and yoghurt. Bread is a staple food, but rather than slathering it in butter, they dip it in extra virgin olive oil. They enjoy a glass of wine, but don't binge drink. And just as significantly, they place importance on mealtimes, taking time out of the day to sit at the table and enjoy the meal with family or friends.

You can see that this is all very similar to *Get Lean, Stay Lean* and thankfully it's a pretty delicious way to live!

Extra virgin olive oil – a true superfood

Extra virgin olive oil is totally different from the refined oils that dominate supermarket shelves. It is, quite simply, the juice of olives and on account of its numerous health benefits it really does earn its right to be called a superfood. This is why I follow the lead of the Mediterranean diet and include it specifically on the Dr Joanna Plate and you'll find it used ubiquitously in my recipes.

So what is it about extra virgin olive oil that makes it so special?

- The principle fat present is a monounsaturated fat called oleic acid. Aside from the benefits already outlined for monounsaturated fats, a compound produced in the gut when we digest oleic acid plays a role in triggering satiety. In turn this reduces appetite and helps you to eat less for the rest of the day.

- European studies have shown that including extra virgin olive oil in your diet can reduce blood pressure, increase HDL cholesterol, reduce oxidised (damaged) LDL cholesterol, reduce triglycerides, reduce inflammation and improve blood glucose control.

- These effects are not just due to the type of fat. Extra virgin olive oil is a rich source of numerous phytochemicals, including antioxidants, that play a role in protecting body cells from damage. For example, squalene, a phytochemical uniquely high in extra virgin olive oil, concentrates in the skin where it plays a role in protecting skin cells from sun damage.

- The peppery taste of extra virgin olive oil comes from the presence of a phytochemical called oleocanthal. This has an anti-inflammatory effect in the body, working in much the same way as a low dose of ibuprofen, making it helpful in managing inflammatory conditions such as osteoarthritis. Oleocanthal has also been shown to protect neurons in the brain and this may be the mechanism by which extra virgin olive oil–rich diets reduce the risk of brain diseases such as Parkinson's and Alzheimer's.

One myth that needs to be busted once and for all concerns cooking. You can, and indeed should, cook with extra virgin olive oil. The monounsaturated fats are stable, plus the antioxidants present protect the fats from damage. In fact, the latest evidence shows that cooking vegetables in extra virgin olive oil raises the numbers of total antioxidants present. It seems that the oil adds its own antioxidants, but also increases the numbers of antioxidants released and absorbed from the veggies.

POLYUNSATURATED FAT

Polyunsaturated fats can be divided into two groups:

- Omega-6s—these predominate in seeds, seed oils such as sunflower oil, and some nuts including walnuts and Brazil nuts.
- Omega-3s—these are found primarily in oily fish and seafood, with smaller amounts present in eggs, grass-fed meats and game meats. Some plant foods, including chia, flaxseed (also called linseed) and walnuts also provide omega-3s, however an important point I'll expand on shortly is that these are short chain as opposed to the long chain omega-3s found in fish.

Polyunsaturated fats include the essential fatty acids that we must eat because we cannot make them in our body. There are in fact only two; linoleic acid (in the omega-6 family) and alpha-linolenic acid (in the omega-3 family). We need to get these two fats from the foods we eat. All of the other omega-6 and omega-3 fats can be made from these and so are not, strictly speaking, essential.

However, if the body is swamped with omega-6 this prevents the body from being able to make enough omega-3s. Furthermore, there is a limit to our capacity to make the long chain omega-3s and due to genetic differences some of us are better at this than others. For this reason, for optimal health it is best to ensure a good intake of the long chain omega-3 directly from food (or from supplements), while avoiding an excessive intake of omega-6s.

When polyunsaturated fats replace saturated fats they lower LDL cholesterol and raise HDL cholesterol. This is why most countries' health recommendations have advised using vegetable oils in place of animal fats. Recently this has come under scrutiny from some researchers. The trouble is that polyunsaturated fats are far less stable than other fats and this makes them prone to oxidative damage, both in the bottle of oil and once in your body.

In their defence, most foods high in poly-unsaturated fats are also high in vitamin E, which helps to protect them. However, the truth is that seed oils are a new addition to the human diet, they are heavily processed and refined using chemicals, heat and/or high pressure. This destroys many of the nutrients present in the whole seed—vitamin E is usually added back to the resulting oil to help protect it.

Added to the fact that consuming too many omega-6 fats makes it hard for us to get sufficient omega-3s, I am not a fan of such oils. I strongly recommend you use whole seeds (or pastes such as tahini) in your menu plan, but avoid using the refined oils made from them.

The exceptions are cold pressed chia and flaxseed oils, as these do provide valuable plant omega-3s, and cold pressed sesame oil as you use this in small amounts as a key flavour for traditional Asian cooking. To help protect these oils, buy them in small dark bottles and once opened keep them in the fridge.

A closer look at omega-3s

The long chain omega-3s (principally DHA and EPA) are the really good guys and the ones most of us lack. They have many benefits in the body, including:

- They are important in both preventing and managing cardiovascular disease.
- They have an anti-inflammatory effect in the body. This has many benefits, including playing a role in maintaining healthy joints. High dose supplements may help to manage the symptoms of arthritis.
- DHA is especially important for optimal brain function and crucial for brain. development in infants and children
- They can reduce your need for asthma medication and may also help to prevent asthma.
- They are involved in the healthy functioning of the eye and may protect against macular degeneration, a major cause of blindness.
- They play an important role in maintaining a strong immune system and more recent research even suggests they may reduce the risk of some cancers.

To ensure you get an optimal amount of omega-3 fats, aim to include oily fish or seafood at least twice a week, include the plant sources regularly and take a good quality fish oil supplement daily. Vegetarians and vegans should include plenty of plant sources of omega-3 and take an algal sourced supplement as well.

I strongly recommend you use whole seeds (or pastes such as tahini) in your menu plan, but avoid using the refined oils made from them.

STEP 2: DRINK

If you're confused over what, when and how much to drink, you're not alone. We are bombarded with almost as many choices on the drinks menu as we are with food.

The questions I am asked all the time include: How much water do I need to drink? Are juices a healthy option? Is diet soft drink okay? Should I be cutting out coffee? Can green tea help me to get lean? Can I enjoy a glass of wine or a beer as part of a healthy lifestyle?

So let's tackle the question of what and how much we drink to give you a clear understanding as to how this pillar of Get Lean, Stay Lean can help or hinder your progress towards your health and wellbeing goals.

Maintaining hydration

Up to two-thirds of the body is water—this equates to 42 litres (11 gal) of water in a 70 kg (154 lb) person! Water is absolutely crucial to the functions and metabolism of the body and while we can survive several weeks without food, without water we wouldn't survive beyond a few days.

Despite this, many of us don't drink enough to maintain adequate hydration. It seems that we are not very good at interpreting thirst signals and by the time we register that we are thirsty, we may already be mildly, but significantly dehydrated.

Some of the symptoms of dehydration include headaches, fatigue, low energy, dry

Fluid balance

Fluid balance in your body is determined by:

Water intake from food and drinks—water losses from urine, faeces, sweat and evaporation from the skin and through the lungs.

Water and getting lean

There is no doubt that water is best as your primary drink. When you are thirsty go for water, have a glass of water with your meals and on average try to have a glass every hour through the day. Water has no kilojoules, no undesirable additives, and serves the purpose of hydration.

However, there is nothing magical about water that will help you to burn fat. Drinking more water will only help you to lose weight if it is replacing kilojoules contained in other drinks or food.

What drinking water can do is help you to eat less, simply by filling you up a little. Often we reach for food when in fact we are thirsty, and so by drinking little and often, you can help to keep hunger pangs at bay.

mouth and/or bad breath, irritability and a reduced ability to exercise. Since these symptoms are very general and could be attributed to a number of things, it's easy to overlook your hydration status.

If you are mildly, but chronically, dehydrated you may also find you are susceptible to frequent urinary tract infections. Going to the bathroom less often means more concentrated urine in your bladder and creates a fertile breeding ground for bacteria. By upping your fluid intake, you not only reduce the concentration of your urine, but you also flush out the urinary tract more often, preventing the bacteria from travelling up to your bladder.

As a general guide most adult women need about 2 litres (70 fl oz/8 cups) of fluids a day and adult men around 2.5 litres (87 fl oz/10 cups). But you may need much more on days where you exercise, for instance. Fortunately, determining whether you are drinking enough is easy—simply check the colour of your urine.

What about other drinks?

It's not only water that can contribute to hydration. All drinks, including tea and coffee, contribute to fluid balance. Although caffeine itself is a diuretic, this would only be dehydrating if you were to down several espressos. All drinks, therefore, add to your net fluid intake. However, what you choose to drink also has a significant effect on your health and weight control.

TEA

There are numerous health benefits associated with tea. Much of the research has focused on green tea—and certainly there is some evidence that green tea can boost fat burning—but in fact all teas are rich in different antioxidants and have potential benefit. These include plain old black tea, white tea, green tea and oolong.

Essentially, you can drink as much tea as you like, provided you take it with no sugar and either straight or with only a splash of milk.

Herbal teas do not offer the same health benefits as they lack the antioxidant compounds found in real tea. However, they are caffeine free and contribute to your fluid intake for hydration purposes. Some also have other benefits, such as chamomile tea in assisting sleep.

COFFEE

Despite the mud slung at coffee, not much of it sticks. Just like tea, coffee contains antioxidants and there is much research showing health benefits, including a lower risk of type 2 diabetes.

However, coffee does have higher caffeine levels than tea. Remember that caffeine can affect not just your ability to fall asleep, but the quality of your sleep, too. Coffee can also irritate the gut. If you're struggling with reflux or have a sensitive gut, try reducing your coffee intake to see if it helps.

For most people coffee is absolutely fine and can even help with fat burning. In fact, it's a terrific drink to have immediately before your workout. It helps to release fatty acids from your adipose tissue ready for burning, increases your concentration and alertness, and these factors combined can help you to put more into exercise.

If you love your coffee, then you can happily include it in your *Get Lean, Stay Lean* diet. I do advise you to take it black or with milk (but watch the portion size) and without any added sugar or flavoured syrups.

Coffee is a terrific drink to have immediately before your workout.

Beetroot, apple and ginger smoothie (page 219)

VITAMIN-ENRICHED WATERS

Don't be fooled by the marketing of these drinks. Read the nutrition panel and you'll find that most have some form of sugar added, sometimes just as much as in soft drinks. Adding a few vitamins and/or minerals does not a health drink make!

Obtain your nutrients from real foods and drinks or, where needed, take a reputable supplement that gives you a controlled dose.

ENERGY DRINKS

Energy drinks are generally devoid of nutrients and have high levels of added sugar and caffeine. Remember that 'energy' is just kilojoules, and what you are really after is vitality. You will only get this from eating nutritious foods, combined with following your *Get Lean, Stay Lean* lifestyle, and not from a caffeine sugar hit. Give these drinks a wide berth.

FRUIT JUICE

Fruit juice is struggling to hang on to its once healthy image and for good reason. Most fruit juices have just as many kilojoules and sugar as soft drinks. It's true that the sugar is naturally present in the fruit, while refined sugars are added to soft drinks. However, drinking juice is not the same as eating the fruit whole.

Be especially careful with juice bars. These may seem bursting with health from the outside, but reading the kilojoules and sugar content of the typical serves shows a different picture. Most do have healthy options available—go for veggie-based smoothies, which retain the fibre, and use just a little whole fruit to sweeten. You can of course make these at home, but I do favour using a powerful blender such as a Vitamix over a juicer. The latter removes the pulp and therefore much of the fibre, while blending retains all the nutrients and fibre—try My go-to green smoothie recipe on page 224.

SOFT DRINKS

Soft drinks are a disaster for your health and wellbeing. They add unnecessary kilojoules and far too much added sugar (up to 9 teaspoons in an average can). These inevitably end up adding to your body fat stores, while the combination of the sugar and the acidity of these drinks wrecks your teeth.

Diet versions are not much better. There is some evidence that these drinks negatively affect the balance of good and bad bacteria in the gut, and while they have no sugar they are still acidic and highly erosive to tooth enamel. Plus, they fire up the sweet drivers in your brain, making you crave sweet tastes more. Give them a miss.

SPORTS DRINKS

Being dehydrated by as little as 1–2 per cent affects athletic performance. For this reason, maintaining good hydration is absolutely key for professional athletes, but also for the weekend warriors and amateur sports people among us. In all of these instances, a scientifically formulated sports drink can be beneficial.

A word of warning, however. Sports drinks contain varying levels of sugar and kilojoules. If you're heading to the gym to help lose body fat and gain some muscle, but then down bottles of sports drinks along the way, you are hindering your progress. As a general rule, exercise of 90 minutes or less needs only water for hydration—you don't need a sports drink.

ALCOHOL

The relationship between alcohol, weight control and health is complicated. A little alcohol, such as the glass or two of wine with dinner as per the Mediterranean diet, seems to be beneficial for heart health. But when it comes to cancer, alcohol increases risk, while chronic drinking can irreparably damage the liver. So if you don't currently drink, don't start thinking it will be good for your heart!

When it comes to *Get Lean, Stay Lean*, there is no doubt alcohol can be a hindrance. It's not just the kilojoules found in booze, it's the situation drinking creates. Your resolve to eat well might go out the window, you sleep badly, you're tired and dusty the next day so you skip your exercise and find yourself turning to fatty or sugary foods to pick up your energy levels.

You may also find yourself reaching for your drink of choice after a particularly stressful day. If you stop at one or two that might well help you to wind down, but drink any more and the aforementioned cycle continues.

Fat and alcohol is a particularly bad combination. When alcohol is in your system, you can't store it and so you burn it for energy ahead of fat or carbohydrate. Meanwhile, it opens up your fat cells, priming them to take in any fat consumed in the meantime. So if you have a few drinks and then devour a pizza, there's definitely no 'get lean' happening.

My advice is to think along the lines of the Mediterranean diet where people enjoy wine with amazing fresh food. This is a far cry from the much more destructive habit of weekend binge drinking.

While actively trying to get lean, give yourself at least three alcohol-free days—and if you can do more, so much the better—and stick to only one or two drinks on the other days. Once in the stay lean phase, use government health guidelines for alcohol—these are typically two drinks a day with no more than four on a single occasion.

If you do drink more at a party or social gathering, get straight back on track the next morning. Fit in an extra long walk or other exercise and eat super well that day. Skip a snack or two, and hit the Dr Joanna Plate spot on for all meals. Drink lots of water to rehydrate and take a vitamin B complex supplement as alcohol depletes these, especially thiamin.

STEP 3: EXERCISE

Exercise really is an essential part of any healthy lifestyle and the benefits go way beyond any effect on weight control. The type of exercise you do, the intensity and time you spend doing it may change during your life and between people, but we all need to move if we want our bodies to work optimally.

The amount of energy you burn during exercise depends on several factors, including your size, your gender, the type of exercise and how hard you work. Essentially, the bigger and heavier you are, the more energy it will take you to perform any exercise. But on average most people will burn at least 1000 kJ (240 Cal) in an hour of gentle exercise, such as golf or a leisurely walk with the dog, while a more intense activity, such as a circuit workout or a run can burn 2000 kJ (480 Cal) or more.

For weight loss you're aiming for an energy deficit of around 2000 kJ (480 Cal) a day. So if you changed nothing about your eating and added in one hour of intense exercise, you'd meet that target and you would start to burn up fat stores to make up the deficit in energy.

It is certainly true that we can eat 2000 kJ (480 Cal) in just a few minutes. A slice of banana bread at the café as you leave the gym will do it. So exercise is not a licence to eat what you like. But this is the mistake many people make. I call it Gym Reward Syndrome. Mentally, you tell yourself, well I've done my exercise I deserve to have a little treat. That's fine once you are happy that you have achieved your weight and body fat goals, but while in an active get lean stage, it's important you don't fall into this trap.

The other point is that exercising three times a week, but otherwise sitting on your bum for most of the day, every day, is really not enough for a weight loss effect. But your health will benefit in other ways. Something is always better than nothing in the exercise game—if you only manage to fit in a ten-minute walk in your day, that's still better than nothing at all.

All that said, to weigh up the impact of exercise based on the kilojoules burned alone undermines the true benefits. The real role of exercise in weight control is over the long term. When you exercise you build muscle and muscle burns more energy, even at rest, than fat. It's also key in controlling blood glucose. Over time your body gets better at burning fat while preserving precious glycogen stores. The bottom line is that long term, exercise is a non-negotiable for both weight control and overall health. Plus, being fit is arguably more important than losing weight, so even in the absence of weight loss it is still crucial that you exercise regularly for optimal health and wellbeing.

What is it about exercise that makes it so hard?

Many people find it extremely difficult to find the motivation to fit exercise into their day. I'm not one of these people—I get frustrated when my day gets so busy that I can't make time for exercise. But that's because I know how good I feel after a workout. I hate missing it. Even though I don't always feel like doing it, I always feel good as a consequence and am glad I made the effort.

Our lives have become largely sedentary and raising a sweat is not something most of us can achieve during our working day. But it's something we need to find time for.

People often say, 'I don't like exercise for exercise's sake', meaning the idea of planned activities to give your body a workout is alien to them. Well, the thing is it's actually alien to all of us. We evolved moving and exercising as part of our daily routine to eat, live and survive—but would then rest when we could. We are designed to be active and do not function at all well if we remain sedentary. So in today's far more sedentary world we must create opportunities to exercise.

FITT principles

These are the four basic variables of exercise that combine together to depict how much energy and fat you burn and ultimately how fit you become. These are the four things you need to plan, and can manipulate, for an effective exercise program.

F = Frequency—the number of times in the week that you work out

I = Intensity—how hard you work out

T = Time—how long you work out

T = Type—what sort of exercise you choose for the workout

Using FITT principles helps you to work out the answer to questions such as 'Should I walk or run?'

Running raises the intensity of the exercise. This means you can burn more energy and improve your cardiovascular fitness in less time than walking. However, you can walk further than you can run, which increases the time of the workout. This makes walking a terrific fat burning workout when you have more time. In other words, when you have less time to work out, increase the intensity (within your own limits). On days you have more time, try going for a longer, but less intense session.

Of course, other factors come into account here. If you're carrying way too much weight, running will only put an enormous load through your joints. Similarly, if you have arthritis or other physical limitations, these things will need to be taken into account in deciding your best exercise plan.

4 steps to start exercising

1. Analyse your routine and find time in your day during which you can almost always fit in some exercise.

2. Once you've settled on the time of day, think about what kind of exercise you'll do and how you'll fit it in.

3. So you've settled on when and what. Now, you need to find your motivation: that's the WHY!

4. Now you know what you'll be doing, when and why! That's a great start. But let's be honest, there are always reasons you miss a workout—you might get sick, be too tired, or just don't feel like it. It's okay to miss a workout every now and then, but try not to miss more than one in a row unless you truly have good reason to (being sick is of course a valid one). If you skip more than a couple of days, don't let it become a habit, or it will be hard to get back on the bandwagon.

Making exercise part of your lifestyle isn't easy—it does take work and commitment. But once you're used to exercising regularly, you'll find it hard to live without because those health benefits we have talked about actually happen—and they feel great.

A guide to exercise choices

There are numerous ways to exercise and if you remember the foundation of JOY on *Get Lean, Stay Lean*, it's essential you find the right exercise for you. If you hate it, you're never going to keep it up. That said, I have to be honest and confess that it's human to not always feel like going for your exercise session, regardless of what it is. What I can guarantee is that you will (almost) always feel good afterwards and be glad you did it. So let's take a look at some of the options available to see what appeals.

EXERCISE CLASSES

If you think the exercise classes are all about the old-style aerobics, this couldn't be further from the truth. Today group exercise covers an enormous array of classes, catering for men and women, all ages, all levels of fitness, all levels of coordination and almost every exercise style you can think of.

Natural protein berry smoothie (see page 222)

All classes have several components in common; they are instructor-led (meaning you have someone guiding you as to what to do, how to do it, correcting your technique and inspiring you to work harder), they are at a set time (you can't put it off until later—get to the class and you're halfway there), and they last a set time (so you are less likely to skive off early if you lose motivation).

The group atmosphere is inspiring for most people and almost all classes use music to motivate and encourage you. In essence, all you need to do is find the right class for you and group fitness is a powerful means of helping you to achieve your *Get Lean, Stay Lean* goals.

There are three main types of exercise:

- Cardiovascular (or aerobic) training to get your heart and lungs fit.
- Resistance or strength training to work the muscular system.
- Flexibility training to improve the range of movement through joints, lengthen muscles and improve posture.

Often a group fitness class will include aspects of two or all of the above. For example, you might attend a combat-style class that incorporates a cardio workout as well as push-ups and other strength-training exercises. However, for the most part classes focus on one of these, although all will incorporate the other two to some degree.

YOGA

Yoga is increasingly popular, but can it help you to reach your *Get Lean, Stay Lean* goals?

The answer is most certainly yes, but don't expect the fat to be melting away just because you get yourself to a yoga class a couple of times a week. Yoga will only help as part of your total lifestyle change and it can help you to make those other changes too.

Those who doubt yoga's usefulness for weight loss are usually only looking at it from a kilojoule burning perspective. They argue that a typical yoga class burns far fewer kilojoules than a more intense aerobic-style workout. However, this is a very narrow view of exercise and ignores the bigger picture.

As we have learned, the benefits of exercise go far beyond the kilojoules burned through the session and yoga brings many of those benefits. Yoga has been shown to reduce weight gain over the years, to help with weight loss, to reduce blood pressure, blood cholesterol and blood glucose levels.

Yoga is also a fantastic stress release. When you spend an hour or longer focused on your breathing and your postures, work and life worries are pushed aside. Personally, I can say that without fail, I always feel more balanced and calm after a yoga class. And when you're less stressed you tend to eat better, you sleep better and your mood is improved.

PILATES

Pilates is another great option to add to your weekly routine. The key benefits are:

- You'll develop a strong core—these are the deep postural muscles that support your back, your pelvic floor and give you a narrower waist.
- You'll improve your flexibility—essential as we age, but also to maintain good joint health.
- You'll encourage strong lean muscles.
- Anyone can do it and so it's ideal for those rehabilitating from injury and for those who struggle with other forms of exercise. It can be challenging to a professional dancer, yet be adapted to suit an older person with sore knees and a bad back. Just be sure to speak with your instructor to ensure they can guide you safely and effectively.

GET WALKING

Walking is one of the easiest, most accessible ways to exercise. Unless you have a physical disability, pretty much everyone can head out the door for a walk, with very little dent on your wallet as all you need is a comfortable pair of shoes. Walking is a brilliant low-impact exercise, so it's good for all ages.

I strongly encourage you to have a daily walk, whether or not you also go to the gym or do some other form of exercise. A pedometer or activity tracker is a really useful tool that I highly recommend. Your goal is to reach 10,000 steps on most days. However, you may find you are falling far short of this. In that case, start by measuring your typical daily steps for a week. For the next week set yourself a goal 1000 steps higher than your typical day. When you're ready, increase again by another 1000 steps and so on until you are hitting the magic 10,000 steps known to be good for your health.

5 steps to an effective walking program

1. Keep up the pace.
2. Go for a long walk when you have more time.
3. Walk with friends.
4. Add stairs or hills to increase intensity.
5. Use a fitness App, pedometer or activity tracker to log your walks.

Most of all, enjoy your walks and take the time to notice your surroundings. Breathe deeply and cherish the time you've created away from life's demands.

Group fitness is a powerful means of helping you to achieve your *Get Lean, Stay Lean* goals.

STRENGTH TRAINING

A fit, young, athletic male is the stereotypical image that comes to mind when you think about exercise involving strength training. The problem is that this is the last person who really needs this type of exercise. The people we should see in the weights section of the gym are women generally because they tend to have less muscle naturally, and everyone over the age of 35.

In fact, your need for strength training increases substantially the older you get. That's because most men and women lose close to 50 per cent of their muscle mass between the ages of 20 and 90. This muscle wastage is called sarcopenia and is at the core of many age-related health concerns.

First and foremost, muscles are there to move limbs. Without sufficient strength we would be unable to perform everyday activities. This is exactly what so often happens in old age—reduced muscle size and strength make even relatively simple movements a challenge, such as lifting your own body weight out of a chair or opening a tin of soup. This might seem a long way off, but if you are not already strength training, the muscle wastage process is already under way.

Secondly if you have accepted middle-age spread as par for the ageing course, then think again. While it's true that our metabolism slows as we age, this can be almost entirely accounted for by the loss in muscle mass.

Muscle is active tissue and burns a lot more energy than fat every minute of the day and night. In other words, of two women, or men, with the same weight but different body fat percentages, the one with more muscle and less fat burns more energy every day than her, or his, fatter colleague. Over time this makes the person with more muscle more likely to stay lean.

If you have been on the dieting merry-go-round for years, losing and regaining weight, this situation is likely to be more pronounced. Losing weight quickly inevitably leads to both muscle and fat loss, but the weight you regain is almost entirely fat. Incorporating strength training into your weekly exercise routine can help break this cycle.

If you remain unconvinced perhaps the aesthetic aspect will win you over. Strength training is arguably the best means we have of really changing the shape of our bodies and it keeps us looking younger by maintaining a strong posture and frame.

How to start strength training

Lifting weights is undoubtedly one of the best ways to strength train, so it's well worth considering joining a gym where a qualified instructor can design you an individualised program. However, if you hate the idea of the gym or for whatever reason cannot get to a gym, the good news is you can strength train at home using hand weights, resistance bands or bags, your own body weight or even with makeshift weights such as bags of rice. You can purchase resistance bands, hand weights and other home fitness equipment at sports shops or online.

SETTING GOALS

Goal setting is all about deciding where you want to be and how you are going to get there.

Record your goals and you stand a much better chance of achieving them. They force you to be honest and, when used alongside a progress log, you get a real picture of how far you have come and where you want to get to.

To help you be effective in your goal setting, try using SMART goal principles:

Specific
Measurable
Attainable
Relevant
Time Bound

Then write your goals down. Having them in your head is not good enough. You need more definitive and careful planning. Start with your Ultimate Goal so that you have your eye on the big picture. Then break it down: choose three short-term goals that you will work on this coming week, medium-term goals for the coming month.

Let's take a closer look at the SMART goal principles.

SPECIFIC

Goals that are vague, such as 'I want to lose weight' are just not going to happen. You need to get specific in order to be able to focus your efforts and clearly define what you want to achieve and how you are going to achieve it. 'I want to be fitter' becomes 'I want to be able to run continuously for 20 minutes'.

Then decide on how you are going to achieve the change. Never have weight loss as your only goal. *Get Lean, Stay Lean* is about so much more than that. Step back and view your wellbeing holistically. Losing some body fat and getting leaner can certainly be your major goal, but add to it a fitness goal, a goal to improve your sleeping, give up smoking, manage your stress better or cut back on alcohol. Prioritise the changes so that you are not changing too many things at once.

MEASURABLE

A goal can't be reached unless you can measure it. This will also help you to work towards longer-term goals as you can measure your progress along the way. If you have a lot of weight to lose, break it down into smaller steps of centimetres lost from your waist and/or kilos lost each month. This will help to spur you on to the final goal.

ATTAINABLE

You want to set goals that you will realistically be able to achieve. If you don't, all you do is set yourself up for failure and disappointment. We might all want a body like our favourite celebrity, but this is a dream not a goal—at least for most of us. Goals should motivate you, not serve to discourage you when you don't get anywhere near them. Set attainable goals that stretch you, but are within your reach.

RELEVANT

Make your goals relevant to the big picture. If ultimately getting lean is your aim, then goals designed to address the six steps of *Get Lean, Stay Lean* are relevant.

TIME BOUND

Most of us need deadlines to commit to a project and make it happen. It's just the same for our own life projects. If you are to truly change the way you eat, move and live, you need to set time limits for when you will have accomplished each goal. Otherwise, everything will start tomorrow, and tomorrow will never come. Start now, this minute, and decide on the time goal. I will lose 2 cm (¾ inch) from my waist, becomes I will lose 2 cm from my waist by X date next month. You need an endpoint to the goal or you will just never get around to it.

Monitoring your progress

We need to be able to measure our progress in a tangible way. Listening to your body and feelings of wellbeing are terrific, but they are also subject to our emotions and mood. You may feel fatter the day after an indulgent meal, but in reality there would be no measureable difference in such a short space of time. Here are the pros, cons and recommendations for how to measure your progress.

BODY FAT

You may have heard over the last few years that weighing yourself is passé, and what is really important is body fat percentage. I couldn't agree more. The trouble is, getting an accurate body fat reading is not easy.

The most accurate and easily accessible way to have your body fat and muscle levels measured is to go and have a DEXA scan. There are a number of companies that offer this. The equipment is expensive and so of course there is a cost involved, however the results are fascinating. Having a repeat scan every six months or so can be highly motivating as you see your body change.

DEXA

DEXA stands for dual energy x-ray absorptiometry. The scan involves a kind of x-ray of the body, but uses a far lower level of radiation than a standard x-ray—less than two days worth of the natural background radiation we are all exposed to—so it is very safe for most people. (It is not however recommended for pregnant women.) It provides a very accurate measurement of your bone density and is therefore used in the diagnosis of osteoporosis, as well as telling you your total body fat, where that fat is stored and how much muscle you have.

What is a healthy body fat percentage?

Women usually start out with less muscle and more fat than men—healthy body fat percentages for women over 40 are in the range of 25–38 per cent and under 40, 20–35 per cent, whereas for men the healthy rates are 10–25 per cent and 8–22 per cent respectively.

For home use, you can purchase a special scale that estimates body fat percentage and lean mass (mostly muscle). These are available in department and sports stores. If you have one terrific, use it. But the trouble with these machines is that you get a fair amount of variability in the measurement, mostly due to changes in hydration, and unlike weight, it takes a relatively long time for the figure to change.

My advice is to use one of these machines if you have one, but record the changes alongside weight and tape measurements, so that you get an overall picture of your progress. Don't worry if you don't have one. It's amazing how much information a simple waist measurement gives you. If it's going down you're losing body fat and from exactly the right place to improve your health. It's that simple!

WAIST MEASUREMENT

The latest scientific research clearly shows that the fat most detrimental to health is that around your middle. That's why, despite its simplicity, this is such a powerful measurement to take.

The ideal range for women is under 80 cm (31½ inches)—with greatly increased risk over

88 cm (35 inches). For men these cut-offs are 94 cm (37 inches) and 102 cm (40 inches) respectively. Your ethnicity can move these cut-offs up or down, but this serves as a general rule of thumb.

You might like to take extra measurements, such as your mid upper arm, mid thigh, chest and so on. Feel free to do this and add them to your monitoring chart.

WEIGHT

Recording your weight has its pros and cons. It's entirely up to you as to whether you hop on the scales or not, and your decision should be based on what is motivating to you.

Firstly, understand what weight tells you. It's not just a measure of body fat changes. Weight is affected by fluid changes, such as dehydration or fluid retention, when you last ate, when you went to the bathroom, and change to your muscle mass. In fact, muscle weighs more than fat, yet takes up less space. So if you have a decent strength-training program as part of your *Get Lean, Stay Lean* plan, you may well find that your weight doesn't change or even goes up a little despite getting leaner.

Having said that if you are very overweight, there is no doubt that you want to see those figures go down on the scale, even if you are also strength training. So don't fool yourself into thinking you have always gained muscle!

I have monitored hundreds of people losing weight and no one has ever lost weight in a linear fashion. No one. There are always bumps in the road. So when you inevitably get those times when your weight has popped up, don't despair. Look back at the previous week or month, be honest with yourself on whether you have stuck to your menu plan and your Dr Joanna Plate, whether you have achieved your exercise goals, or if there is anything else that could explain the weight change. Then make those changes for the coming week, setting your goal for the month accordingly. Move on and accept that this is just part of the process of getting leaner.

How to take a waist measurement

- For men, measure directly around your navel, keeping the tape snug but not tight.
- For women, you should measure around the mid point between the top of your hip bone and the bottom rib

It's amazing how much information a simple waist measurement gives you. If it's going down you're losing body fat and from exactly the right place.

STEP 4: ACTIVITY

10 steps to break the sitting habit

1. Invest in a standing desk. I now have one in my office so that I can alternate between sitting and standing throughout the day. There are several clever options for these on the market, including one that fits on top of your existing desk.

2. When you don't need slides or paperwork in front of you, suggest a walking meeting. I have these frequently and it's a great way to brainstorm. In fact, your brain fires up with activity and you might just find yourself being more creative.

3. Leave your office to get a coffee or lunch from a café at least a block away or down a flight of stairs or two.

4. Take the time to walk to a colleague when you need a question answered, rather than email.

5. Stand when you commute via public transport.

6. Make a rule that every time you're on the phone, you have to stand. You can even pace up and down the corridor while you talk.

7. Limit your couch-time. Go for a walk after dinner or do a few chores around the house before sitting down at the TV.

8. When you meet friends for drinks or dinner, if it's within a 20-minute walk, get there and back on foot.

9. When watching TV, get up during the ads and do some squats, push-ups or stretches. Or how about doing the ironing or some other chore at the same time?

10. When working at your desk for prolonged periods, set your phone to alert you every hour or so to get up and move. There are several Apps designed to help you with this. Get up and stretch, walk to make a cup of tea or engage in some other activity for a few minutes.

I separate exercise from activity as, aside from your formal exercise sessions, how active or sedentary you are for the rest of time plays a crucial role in your health and wellbeing.

Sitting is the new smoking

It may sound dramatic, but studies show that our sedentary lifestyles are so bad for us that they are being put on par with smoking. And considering many of us sit for the majority of the day (at our desk, in our car, watching TV), it's a huge concern.

Researchers at the Mayo Clinic in the United States have been studying the effects of too much sitting for more than 15 years. And the results are grim. One study compared adults who spent less than two hours a day in front of the TV (or other screen-based entertainment), with those that logged more than four hours of recreational screen time. Those who used screens more had a nearly 50 per cent increase of death from any cause than those who used screens less! And the longer users also had a whopping 125 per cent increased risk of chest pain (angina) or heart attack.

But it's not just sitting in front of the TV for entertainment that's of concern. It's any sitting. Add up how many hours you spend a day sitting at your desk, in the car, at a restaurant, watching a movie or the TV ... on it goes.

You may be thinking—well, I'm fine because I work out for 30 minutes each day. Unfortunately, research shows that a few hours engaging in moderate exercise each week does not counterbalance the negative effects of sitting for hours every day. It's better than nothing, so don't stop. But it's not enough. Even if you exercise, sitting for more than eight hours a day has been shown to be an independent risk factor.

STEP 5: STRESS

A little bit of stress can actually be quite a good thing for us, even though the mere mention of the word conjures up negative connotations. The scientific community uses the term 'eustress' (or good stress), a term coined fifty-something years ago to describe the response to stress which gives a person a sense of fulfilment or other positive feelings. Science shows us that some stress actually boosts our brainpower, makes us more resilient and motivates us to be successful. But what if your stress is more prolonged or at such a level as to be detrimental to your health and wellbeing?

The classic 'fight or flight' stress response triggered by our bodies is an evolutionary mechanism to prepare us to either confront danger or run like crazy from it. You'll experience it acutely when you get a fright—your heart races, adrenaline courses through your veins, your blood glucose levels rise, all in preparation for you to literally fight or flee. However, in today's fast-paced world we are more likely to suffer from a lower level of this stress reaction, but have it go on for a much longer period of time. This is chronic stress.

But can the stress that inevitably accompanies such pressures of a busy life, be contributing to your weight problems?

The answer is a very definite yes. And the nature of that stress doesn't matter, only your perception of stress. The first point is that when you're stressed, a really common coping mechanism is to eat, and to eat certain foods. This is what I call swallowing your emotions with food. Perhaps from associations of certain foods with childhood or with other experiences, we gain comfort and an elevation of mood from eating those foods. Unfortunately, this doesn't really help us to deal with the stress and in the long-term it affects health instead.

Veggie san choy bau (see page 197)

There is also a physiological effect of stress. A number of hormones are involved, but the principal one of interest with relation to weight is cortisol. When you're stressed, cortisol rises and this has three negative effects on weight control:

1. It increases your appetite, making it more likely you'll overeat. If you are also an emotional eater this gives you a double whammy where you are likely to overeat comfort foods.

2. It's a catabolic hormone meaning it encourages fuels to be released into the blood and potentially for muscle to be broken down (to supply glucose for energy). This is appropriate if the stress is caused by a dangerous situation you're getting ready to run away from, but entirely deleterious if you're sedentary at your desk tearing your hair out over meeting a deadline.

3. Cortisol drives more fat storage around the abdominal area, or more correctly increases visceral fat. That's the fat around the internal organs rather than subcutaneous fat under the skin. This is the worst type of fat as it is associated with rises in blood pressure and risk of heart disease and type 2 diabetes.

So what can we do to try to lower cortisol levels? We can't live entirely stress-free lives and neither would most of us want to; the right amount of stress can be motivating. There is nothing like a looming deadline to focus your mind and get you completing tasks.

The trick is to keep that level of stress manageable and to recognise when the balance is tipping in the wrong direction. If you're snapping at your partner or your kids, feeling as if you can't cope, turning to food or alcohol as a coping mechanism or finding it hard to slow your mind and enjoy the moment, it's time to think about how you are managing stress.

10 stress busters

1. **Exercise**: When you're really stressed nothing beats going for a run to clear your head or punching a boxing bag to let out your anger and frustration.

2. **Go for a walk**: When we're stressed it can be hard to see that the most effective thing to do is to take a break. Going for a walk just might give you clarity.

3. **Yoga**: You can choose between more meditative forms that centre on breathing and flexibility, or stronger styles that are truly a full on workout.

4. **Meditation**: There are a number of excellent studies in support of meditation to bring down blood pressure and manage stress.

5. **Fish oils**: Fish oils have been shown to blunt the rise in adrenaline and cortisol, as well as the release of fats into the blood, in response to mental stress. Taking a daily fish oil supplement and consuming oily fish at least twice a week just might help manage your stress.

6. **Sleep**: For good health and well being you must address sleep issues and aim for 7–8 hours on most nights. Meditation and/or breathing techniques can help you to clear your mind and relax sufficiently to get a good night's sleep.

7. **Tea**: Tea contains an amino acid called L-theanine that has several effects on the brain that induce relaxation and relieves feelings of anxiety.

8. **Laugh**: Laughing is good for us physiologically and psychologically. Your brain chemistry shifts, your blood pressure comes down and stress is well and truly busted.

9. **Breathing**: One particularly effective technique during an acute feeling of stress is to focus on slow, deep breathing. Look for a nice quiet spot to do it and give yourself 5–10 minutes.

10. **Company**: We are at our roots pack animals that need others around us at least some of the time. Spending time with friends, family or loved ones is essential for keeping life's worries in perspective and for sharing problems and finding solutions. There is much truth to the old adage about a problem shared.

STEP 6: SLEEP

Sleep is one of the most neglected areas of lifestyle change, and is almost always forgotten about when it comes to weight loss. But yes, it really is true—a lack of good quality sleep really can lead to weight gain.

That might seem nonsensical. Surely if you're up more hours in the day, you're burning more energy right?

Well, the trouble is our bodies don't work in that way. Many of our hormones work in what's called a diurnal pattern, rising and falling through the day and night. That includes the hormones, such as leptin and ghrelin, involved in controlling metabolism, body composition (particularly body fat stores) and appetite. A lack of good quality sleep reduces leptin and increases ghrelin—in turn making you feel hungrier.

Additionally, while we are sleeping the body is repairing and building lean muscle (particularly after strenuous exercise) and without enough sleep this process is impaired. Exercise may then only lead to us feeling more tired instead of energised.

Scientific studies have repeatedly shown that those who sleep less are at greater risk of overweight, obesity, type 2 diabetes, cardiovascular disease and high blood pressure. Seriously it's true. In the modern world where we tend to think of spending time in bed as being a bit indulgent or lazy, the facts are that sleep is infinitely more important than most realise. Far from time wasted, those who sleep well and for long enough are more alert, creative, productive and healthier than those who reckon they can survive with far less sleep.

But here's the clincher, as far as *Get Lean, Stay Lean* is concerned; a meta-analysis in the *American Journal of Clinical Nutrition*, pulling together data from nine cohort studies, found that sleep duration is associated with a lower BMI—that means those who sleep longer weigh less for their height. Further, they found that in adults those who got more sleep also ate less saturated fat.

Now these kinds of associations do not show cause and effect, but they do allow us to question why they might occur. Are people who sleep less reaching out for less healthy snacks in an attempt to bolster their energy and get through the day? Previous research has certainly shown that less sleep equates to a higher kilojoule intake—you sleep less and eat more basically.

This is why I include sleep as a key step in achieving the lifestyle you need to *Get Lean* and *Stay Lean*.

How much sleep is enough?

While many people say they can survive on four or five hours sleep a night, when reflexes and brain performance are tested, this doesn't stand up to scrutiny. Most of us need a minimum of six hours and we function much better when we hit eight hours on a regular basis.

Put some concerted effort for the next week or two on getting to bed at roughly the same time and getting up at roughly the same time, allowing for that magical seven to eight hours. Then note how you feel and how it affects both your exercise and eating habits. The result just might surprise you and take you leaps and bounds towards your *Get Lean, Stay Lean* goals.

Those who sleep less are at greater risk of overweight, obesity, type 2 diabetes, cardiovascular disease and high blood pressure.

8 steps to a better night's sleep

1. Try to go to bed at the same time and, most importantly, get up at more or less the same time every day.

2. Have no caffeine after lunchtime in caffeine sensitive people, and not after 4 pm for most others. Remember caffeine can affect both your ability to fall asleep and the quality of your sleep.

3. Have at least an hour without looking at a screen before bed. That includes TV, computers, smartphones, tablets and other mobile devices.

4. Use that hour as wind-down time. Read a novel in bed, have a bath or listen to relaxing music.

5. Ensure your bedroom is not too hot or cold and use layers of bedclothes rather than one big, thick quilt so that you can get the temperature just right.

6. Keep the TV out of your bedroom. Sleep specialists say the bedroom should be for reading, sleep and sex only!

7. If you must have your phone on your bedside table, turn it to flight mode so your notifications don't disturb you in the night.

8. If you are tossing and turning in the night, give it roughly 15 minutes (but don't time this!), and if you're not back to sleep, turn on a low light and read—go to another room if you have a sleeping partner you don't want to disturb. Whatever happens, don't start working or watch TV—these things will stimulate your brain and make it harder to get back to sleep.

If you have tried all of these things and are still struggling, ask your doctor to refer you to a sleep clinic. Don't underestimate the importance of sleep for your overall health and the role it plays in you getting and staying lean.

Avoid caffeine in the evening and try drinking a cup of chamomile tea instead. It really can help you to sleep.

Your Get Lean, Stay Lean eating guide

Now we've looked at the six steps in detail, let's return to what's undoubtedly the step that has the biggest impact on getting and staying lean … food.

It's not just what we eat that's important, but how we eat. The habits you have around how often to eat, where to eat, what you eat and who you eat with, can all have implications on your long-term success in getting and staying lean.

A key strength of *Get Lean, Stay Lean* is that you can make this personal to what works for and suits your lifestyle. In Part 2 you'll find 106 recipes to give you delicious inspiration for every eating occasion from breakfast to dinner to snacks and treats, as well as catering for special diets such as vegetarian, vegan and gluten free. But first let's take a look at how to develop good eating habits and build a clear template of how and what to eat.

5 steps to eating mindfully

To become truly in tune with your body's cues to eat you need to eat mindfully. This will help you to both enjoy food more, but also eat less. Here are some tips as to how to do it:

1. Always eat at the table so that you can give full attention to the meal. Ban yourself from eating on the run, in the car, in the street, at the movies and so on, unless it truly is necessary or is an occasional treat, such as an ice cream at the beach.

2. Make mealtimes pleasurable—it's not the time to have an argument with your partner or your kids. Give mealtimes priority, even if only for 10 minutes.

3. Eat slowly, putting your cutlery down between mouthfuls.

4. Eat with others when you can to make the meal enjoyable and sociable.

5. Avoid other distractions (speaking with dining companions excepted) while eating, such as watching TV or working at your computer.

How often should I eat?

I find that three meals a day works for most people. Using the Dr Joanna Plate will ensure you get the perfect balance of nutrients at each meal. Try to take time out of the day to sit down and eat mindfully, enjoying the food, and ensure you are truly hungry by mealtimes.

It also allows enough time between meals for your body to move from a state of storing food energy to using up those stores. For most people adding one or two snacks a day can be helpful, but these are optional and you may find you don't need them. I recommend you have a snack only when you are truly hungry and there is still more than two hours to go until mealtime.

The Japanese, one of the healthiest nations in the world with a low level of overweight and obesity, have a wonderful cultural practice they call 'hara hachi bu'. This means 'eat until you are 80 per cent full'. Even my kids will announce they are 'hara hachi bu' at the table and I reckon this is a much more important lesson for them than the old-fashioned 'finish what's on your plate'.

Have a snack only when you are truly hungry and there is still more than two hours to go until mealtime.

Your Get Lean, Stay Lean kitchen

I've tried to include in the following list all of the pantry ingredients I use regularly throughout the recipes in Part 2. Plus, the beauty of a well-stocked pantry is that even on nights that you have failed to get in a few fresh ingredients, you can throw together a healthy meal. Here's my guide.

PANTRY

Tinned: tomatoes, beetroot (beets), corn, a variety of different types of beans e.g. kidney, borlotti, black and/or cannellini beans, chickpeas, lentils, tuna, salmon, sardines

Jars: passata (puréed tomatoes), marinated veggies, olives, anchovies, pure nut butters without additives, coconut oil (for occasional use)

Bottles: extra virgin olive oils (useful to have a light flavoured as well as a more robust flavoured oil), cold pressed nut oils, cold pressed sesame oil, selection of vinegars, soy sauce, tamari, mirin, Shaoxing rice wine (Chinese cooking wine), pomegranate molasses, maple syrup, honey

Packets: selection of different whole nuts and seeds, rolled (porridge) or steel-cut oats, barley, freekeh, wholegrain pasta, wholegrain couscous, soba (buckwheat) noodles, quinoa, amaranth, millet, brown rice, muesli (or make your own), wholegrain cereals

Dried herbs and spices

Iodised salt and salt flakes (although I encourage you to limit your salt intake, most of the salt in Western diets comes from highly processed food. When most of your food is home cooked a little is sometimes called for without pushing up your intake excessively. I like to use iodised salt when adding to a soup or stock, to help boost iodine intake and a pinch of salt flakes where I want the taste of fancier salts)

Selection of teas, coffee, pure cocoa powder

Fresh wholegrain bread and wholegrain wraps

FRIDGE

Lots of different fresh veggies, including plenty of leafy greens

Your choice of in-season fruit

Free-range or organic eggs

The lean meats, poultry or seafood you need for the week's menu plan

Natural yoghurt, cheese and milk—or a dairy-free alternative such as soy milk

Tofu or tempeh—invaluable for vegans and vegetarians

Tahini

Mustard, horseradish and any other condiments

Hummus, tzatziki and salsa—these are most delicious when made yourself, otherwise look for quality brands (always read the ingredients list)

FREEZER

Frozen berries

Frozen ripe bananas—when your bananas are getting too ripe in the fruit bowl, peel them and freeze in sealable plastic bags. These are ideal for using in smoothies and frozen desserts.

Selection of frozen veggies

Selection of frozen meat, poultry and seafood

Selection of best option flours (in cooler countries you can keep these in the pantry, while in hotter climates keeping them in the freezer prevents the growth of weevils and other bugs)—my favourites including a basic wholegrain wheat flour (look for stoneground) or wholegrain spelt flour (an ancient wheat variety), besan (chickpea) flour, lupin flour, quinoa flour, amaranth flour, buckwheat flour and coconut flour

Putting the Get Lean, Stay Lean theory into practice in the kitchen

If your lifestyle ambitions are only ever in your head with vague promises of 'I'll start on Monday' you are unlikely to ever make much progress. During the *Get Lean* phase when you are actively working on reducing your body fat, while maintaining or gaining lean mass, the FOOD step is critical. So set yourself up for success by making it easier to eat well.

Start by going through your kitchen cupboards, fridge and freezer, throwing out everything out of date or that you know is not good for you. You might think that's a waste, but really isn't it more of a waste when it ends up padding out your body fat stores?

Your next step is to shop and stock your kitchen with your new *Get Lean, Stay Lean* recommended foods. Clearly you needn't buy everything on the list opposite, and foods may vary from week to week depending on your menu, but this will give you a good start.

With your kitchen stocked accordingly you'll find it easy to get started with the recipes in Part 2. You'll just have to ensure you have the appropriate fresh ingredients to hand for your chosen dish. Once you are in the *Stay Lean* phase, ensuring your kitchen stays stocked in this way will help to keep you on track.

Develop kilojoule awareness

Despite the number of different diets and theories about what is best to eat for weight loss, there remains an inescapable fact that to lose weight you need to consume fewer kilojoules than you expend. Research studies have clearly shown that no matter the make-up of the three macronutrients (carbohydrate, fat

Kilojoules counting

If you still think in Calories, remember that kilojoules are measuring the same thing—energy. Kilojoules are the correct scientific unit of measurement. It's just like when we moved from inches to centimetres and the new unit is now accepted. In the US, Calories (Cal) are still used on food packaging, but in Australia we now use kilojoules (kJ) and the EU displays both. Don't get confused over it. 1 Calorie = 4.184 kilojoules. So long as you have a rough idea of your total for the day, the amount on the pack will make sense.

and protein), it is ultimately the kilojoule count that equates to weight loss when food intake is strictly controlled.

However, the picture is in reality more complicated than this. Our food intake is not strictly controlled and the macronutrient mix and types of foods we eat have an influence on appetite and therefore how much we eat. For example, eating more protein helps you to feel satisfied and therefore eat less. Similarly, fibre and low GI carbs play a role in this appetite regulation by keeping you fuller for longer so that you eat less later.

We also know that there are changes in the way the body processes and metabolises different foods. Digesting and metabolising protein takes far more energy than either carbohydrate or fat—another reason why a high protein diet has proven to be helpful for weight control. So where the kilojoules come from does matter and can influence whether they end up in body fat stores or burned for energy.

Nevertheless, the fact remains we need to eat fewer kilojoules to ensure our body has to dip into body fat stores to make up the deficit.

So does all this mean that a return to counting kilojoules is the way to go? I think not and this is backed up by the research. From my

Should I try fasting?

Intermittent fasting has become popular recently. One of the good things I have noticed about fasting is that those who have done it often say it's made them realise being a little hungry is okay!

There are various versions of the approach. One is that for two non-consecutive days of the week you dramatically reduce your kilojoule intake to only ~2000 kJ (480 Cal) and then eat pretty much what you like on the other days. This means you only have to 'diet' for want of a better word, on two or two days and that appeals to many people. Most of us can call on willpower to see us through one or two days, while slightly reducing kilojoules every day consistently might be more difficult.

Another increasingly popular approach is to fast for 16 hours a day and condense your eating to only 8 hours. Typically, this involves eating only between 11am and 7pm, or 12pm to 8pm. In essence you lengthen the overnight fast.

So does it work and is it worthy of trying? Truthfully we don't really know yet until further research gives us a clearer picture. But if it appeals and you want to give it a shot my advice is to continue with your Dr Joanna Plate template for all meals on normal eating days or times to ensure a good nutrient intake. Restrain from intense exercise on fast days and ensure you don't go short on your blocks of low GI carbs on the other days to top up glycogen levels – these will easily be used up on the fast day.

years of experience, I have seen so many women become completely obsessed with food and kilojoules, while I have never known a man to be remotely interested in counting his kilojoules! Either way it does not work.

There is also the practicality of the approach. How can we possibly always know how many kilojoules are in the foods we eat? Furthermore, we all get slightly different amounts of energy from foods—in part due to the bacterial populations living in our guts—and foods themselves vary between varieties, seasons and all sorts of other factors.

Finally, the kilojoules don't tell you how nutritious the food is. All up, counting kilojoules is only ever an estimate at best.

What I do recommend is developing a kilojoule awareness. Know roughly how many kilojoules you are aiming for in the day, so that when kilojoules are displayed in a food outlet or on a packet you understand what the figures mean.

Just don't become obsessed. Trust that if you feed your body natural, minimally processed, wholesome food, it will be more difficult to overeat, you'll feel more satisfied and your hunger levels will let you know if you are getting the energy level right. Embrace being a little hungry between meals—it means you are burning fat—and during a meal aim to be satisfied, not full. Combine this with kilojoule awareness and long-term weight control is yours.

The recipes in Part 2 have all been developed to fit with the Dr Joanna Plate. To help you see how it fits, the ingredients are listed and coded in the plate sections: Plants; Protein, Carbs and Fat. I also then give you the blocks per serve. This allows you to see at a glance whether it is a complete meal, or whether you need to add additional veggies, a smart carb and so on.

There is also a nutrition analysis displayed on the thumbnails at the foot of each recipe for those who want more detailed information. All meals are around the 2000 kJ (480 Cal) mark or less per serve. Those with bigger energy demands can simply increase their serving size.

All recipes are labelled for the following special diets: vegetarian, vegan, gluten free, dairy free and nut free. I have often given an ingredient substitute or suggestion to make the recipe suitable for a special diet so be sure to read the notes where applicable.

The recipes are intended to be a bank of inspiration to get you cooking more delicious meals at home. When we eat our own home-prepared meals we are in control of the quality of ingredients, how the food is cooked and how much is served on the plate. Studies show that we tend to eat smaller portions and fewer kilojoules when we eat at home. For this reason, I highly recommend you prepare most of your meals, particularly while in the *Get Lean* phase.

Eating out is, however, a regular part of most of our lives, and an immensely enjoyable part, and there is no need to cut it out completely. Just get savvy about ordering from the menu to match the Dr Joanna Plate as closely as possible—it can almost always be done! Order an extra veggie side, a salad or veggie soup for entrée, a lean meat or seafood for main and where possible seek out the smart carbs. If there are none available, skip the carb food and have extra veggies instead. It's a no-brainer to keep desserts to a minimum, but if you truly feel like having one, share with a dining companion, take your time to eat and savour and enjoy every mouthful. Finally, if you drink, slow yourself down with a big glass of water and be mindful about how alcohol affects how much and what you eat.

Use your Daily Blocks to help guide your portions

You've now learned how to start using more of your own body cues to help you to know when to eat and how much to eat. But this can take a little time to master. By the time you are on the *Stay Lean* phase, understanding your Daily Blocks will help you with portion control forever more. With practice this will become second nature and you won't have to think so much about the amount of food on the plate and will be able to resist external cues to eat far more easily.

However, when you are at the beginning of this journey and undoing old habits, you may need more guidance.

The thing is that our system is set up to ensure we survive famines. There are, therefore, strong internal cues driving us to seek food and fill our glycogen and fat stores. However, the cues that tell us fat stores are full, or are expanding and impacting on our health, are far less strong. They are easily over-ridden by the lure of a favourite delicious food.

The bottom line is that although almost every diet book I have read tells you their diet will never leave you hungry, if you want to lose weight, you need to feel a little hungry. Accept this and change your perception of what hunger is. Few of us have ever experienced true famine-type hunger and so we are a little fearful of being hungry.

So to help guide you towards the right amount of food for you to reach your goals you can use my Daily Block system.

Diet Codes

Each recipe contains a list of diet codes as a quick reference for people following special diets:

GF – gluten free
DF – dairy free

NF – nut free (no tree nuts or peanuts, may contain coconut)
V – vegetarian (no meat or seafood, may contain eggs or dairy)
VE – vegan (no animal food of any kind)

WHAT IS A BLOCK?

I use the term 'block' because the idea is that you build your blocks together to create the serve or portion that is right for you. So for each section of the Dr Joanna Plate, the foods are broken down into blocks.

You'll notice in many recipes there is a plus sign with a few additional ingredients. These are items that do not fit into any particular section of the Dr Joanna Plate such as salt, stock or a sauce or relish, and do not need to be counted as a block.

HOW MANY DAILY BLOCKS?

For women looking to *Get Lean* I recommend a Daily Block guide of 5 blocks of veggies (but more if you like), 2 of fruit, 4 of protein, 3 of carbs and 3 of fat. For men looking to *Get Lean* I recommend a Daily Block guide of 6 blocks of veggies (more if you like), 2 of fruit, and 4 each of protein, carbs and fat.

For women looking to *Stay Lean* I recommend a Daily Block guide of 7 blocks of veggies (but more if you like), 2–3 of fruit, 5 each of protein and carbs, and 4 of fat.

For men looking to *Stay Lean*, I recommend a Daily Block guide of 8 blocks of veggies (again more if you like, but I'm guessing I might be pushing it!), 3 of fruit, 6 each of protein and carbs, and 5 of fat.

You'll see that not just the protein, carbs and fat sections of the plate get bigger, but when you need more energy your plant food intake should also be bigger! The standard 5-a-day for veggies (this varies from country to country) is not in fact enough for many people—it's simply used as a national target thought to be realistic (and the fact is very few of us are meeting it).

If you think about it, the bigger you are, the bigger your energy needs, and the more you need of everything from vitamins, minerals, fat, protein and carbs, to phytochemicals and fibre. In essence your plate is bigger at each meal.

For each recipe you'll see that I have given you the block counts per serve. This will help guide you towards the appropriate block count for the day. You may need to increase your portion size, or add another food to match your needs. For example, add an extra block of a smart carb, or boost the serving of meat or fish in the recipe to suit.

Here's how the blocks are presented in recipes:

NUTRITION BLOCKS PER SERVE

 **1** PLANT   **1** PROTEIN   **1** CARB   **1** FAT

Most importantly, remember that the blocks are only a guide. I never expect you to weigh and measure everything to a tee. It is simply a starting point to help you control your food intake while you work on the six steps of *Get Lean, Stay Lean*. Ultimately, the goal once in the *Stay Lean* phase is to be able to trust and listen to your own body cues to know how much to eat. Once you're eating the right foods in the right balance, this is far easier to achieve.

Moroccan carrot and parsnip dip (see page 86)

1 PLANT

Veggies:

½ cup raw or cooked veggies, including cooked greens

1 cup raw leafy greens

Fruit:

1 medium-sized piece, such as apple, banana or pear

2 smaller pieces, such as apricots, plums, figs or kiwi fruit

1 cup diced fruit

1½ tablespoons small dried fruit, such as sultanas (golden raisins)

4 dried apricot halves

2 prunes

1 PROTEIN

Red meat:

90 g (3¼ oz) raw weight, 65 g (2¼ oz) cooked— 2 slices roast meat or 2 small chops, 2 lean sausages

Poultry:

100 g (3½ oz) raw weight, 80 g (2¾ oz) cooked

Fish:

115 g (4 oz) raw weight, 100 g (3½ oz) cooked

2 large eggs

250 ml (9 fl oz/1 cup) light milk or 185 ml (6 fl oz/¾ cup) full cream milk

250 ml (9 fl oz/1 cup) soy milk

2 slices (40 g/1½ oz) cheese

120 g (4¼ oz) full fat ricotta or cottage cheese

200 g (7 oz/¾ cup) low fat natural yoghurt or 130 g (4½ oz/½ cup) natural yoghurt

170 g (6 oz) tofu or tempeh

170 g (6 oz/1 cup) cooked lentils, beans or chickpeas (note these can also count as your smart carb)

If you are vegan you can also count 30 g (1 oz) of nuts or seeds as a Protein Block. These deliver less protein than the above sources, but are invaluable in a vegan diet.

1 CARB

1 slice wholegrain bread

1 medium-sized wholegrain tortilla or wrap

1 wholemeal English muffin

½ wholemeal thicker flat bread, such as pitta

½ cup cooked, ¼ cup uncooked wholegrains, such as brown rice, wholegrain pasta, soba (buckwheat) noodles, barley, oats and freekeh

150 g (5½ oz) raw weight (or 1 cup diced) starchy veg, such as sweet potato, small potatoes in their skins

1 corn on the cob or ½ cup corn kernels

½ cup cooked (¼ cup uncooked) pseudo-grains, e.g. quinoa, amaranth, buckwheat

35 g (1¼ oz/¼ cup) muesli

20 g (¾ oz/⅔ cup) wholegrain cereal

3 wholegrain crispbreads

35 g (1¼ oz/¼ cup) wholegrain, pseudo-grain or legume flour

100 g (3½ oz/½ cup) cooked lentils, beans or chickpeas (note these can also count as a Protein Block in a vegetarian meal in which case the serve is bigger to supply the necessary protein)

1 FAT

Small handful of nuts (30 g/1 oz)

2 tablespoons seeds

1 tablespoon nut butter or tahini

¼ avocado

2 tablespoons hummus

2 teaspoons extra virgin olive oil, cold pressed nut oil, cold pressed sesame, chia or flaxseed oil

2 teaspoons butter, coconut oil, duck fat (these are fine for occasional use but lack the proven health benefits of extra virgin olive oil)

The following two pages include an example of what a *Get Lean, Stay Lean* eating week could look like. Please treat it as a guide only. The plant serves include both veggies and fruit. Remember the quota for veggies is a minimum, so if you go over that's a gold star!

SAMPLE WEEKLY MENU PLAN DURING THE GET LEAN PHASE*

	SUNDAY	MONDAY	TUESDAY
BREAKFAST	Spanish baked eggs with ham and spinach (page 74) + Slice wholegrain toast BLOCKS PER SERVE 2 PLANT 1 PROTEIN 1 CARB 1 FAT	Muesli (see 3 options pages 67, 68 and 69) with milk/yoghurt/dairy alternative and fresh fruit OR wholegrain cereal with sprinkle of nuts/seeds fruit and yoghurt BLOCKS PER SERVE 1 PLANT 1 PROTEIN 1 CARB 1 FAT	Boiled/poached/scrambled eggs with 1 slice wholegrain toast, wilted spinach and grilled tomato BLOCKS PER SERVE 2 PLANT 1 PROTEIN 1 CARB 0 FAT
LUNCH	Soto ayam (Balinese chicken soup) (page 124) BLOCKS PER SERVE 1 PLANT 1 PROTEIN 1 CARB 0 FAT	Supergreens soup (page 117) with slice of wholegrain bread and cheese BLOCKS PER SERVE 3 PLANT 1 PROTEIN 1 CARB 0 FAT	Adzuki bean and tuna salad (page 96) BLOCKS PER SERVE 3 PLANT 1 PROTEIN 1 CARB 1 FAT
SNACK/DRINK	15 almonds and ½ cup pineapple chunks BLOCKS PER SERVE 1 PLANT 0 PROTEIN 0 CARB ½ FAT	Hummus two ways (page 85) with carrot and celery batons BLOCKS PER SERVE 1 PLANT 0 PROTEIN 0 CARB 1 FAT	Handful of nuts BLOCKS PER SERVE 0 PLANT 0 PROTEIN 0 CARB 1 FAT
DINNER	Lean and mean beef burritos (page 153) BLOCKS PER SERVE 2 PLANT 1 PROTEIN 1 CARB 1 FAT	MEATLESS MONDAY Mediterranean chickpea stuffed sweet potatoes (page 192) BLOCKS PER SERVE 3 PLANT 1 PROTEIN 1 CARB 1 FAT	Ricotta and basil meatballs in capsicum-tomato sauce (page 159) served with ½ cup steamed brown rice and green salad drizzled with extra virgin olive oil and lemon BLOCKS PER SERVE 2 PLANT 1 PROTEIN 1 CARB 1 FAT
SWEET TREATS	Drunken strawberries with citrus yoghurt and dark chocolate (page 217) BLOCKS PER SERVE 1 PLANT 0 PROTEIN 0 CARB ½ FAT	Hot spiced cocoa (page 231) BLOCKS PER SERVE 0 PLANT 1 PROTEIN 0 CARB 0 FAT	½ cup of mixed berries with Greek natural yoghurt BLOCKS PER SERVE 1 PLANT 1 PROTEIN 0 CARB 0 FAT
TOTAL DAILY BLOCKS	7 PLANT 3 PROTEIN 3 CARB 3 FAT	8 PLANT 4 PROTEIN 3 CARB 3 FAT	8 PLANT 4 PROTEIN 3 CARB 3 FAT

* For women staying lean and men either getting lean or staying lean, then simply increase the portion sizes accordingly to utilise your extra blocks. For example, a man could have a larger steak with Thursday's dinner suggestion to utilise one more Protein Block and so on. See 'How Many Daily Blocks' (page 56) for more information.

WEDNESDAY	THURSDAY	FRIDAY	SATURDAY
Muesli (see 3 options pages 67, 68 and 69) with milk/yoghurt/dairy alternative and fresh fruit OR wholegrain cereal with sprinkle of nuts/seeds fruit and yoghurt BLOCKS PER SERVE 1 PLANT 1 PROTEIN 1 CARB 1 FAT	Super veggie bowl (page 76) BLOCKS PER SERVE 4 PLANT 1 PROTEIN 1 CARB 1 FAT	Muesli (see 3 options pages 67, 68 and 69) with milk/yoghurt/dairy alternative and fresh fruit OR wholegrain cereal with sprinkle of nuts/seeds fruit and yoghurt BLOCKS PER SERVE 1 PLANT 1 PROTEIN 1 CARB 1 FAT	Spelt and lupin blueberry hotcakes (page 79) with ricotta and fresh strawberries BLOCKS PER SERVE 1 PLANT 1 PROTEIN 1 CARB 1 FAT
Black barley, kale and poached chicken salad (page 106) BLOCKS PER SERVE 3 PLANT 1 PROTEIN 1 CARB 1 FAT	Hearty chicken and barley soup (page 119) BLOCKS PER SERVE 2 PLANT 1 PROTEIN 1 CARB 0 FAT	Superfood salad with tahini dressing (page 108) + 65 g (2¼ oz) cold meat or small can of tuna BLOCKS PER SERVE 3 PLANT 1 PROTEIN 1 CARB 1 FAT	Thai beef salad (page 102) BLOCKS PER SERVE 3 PLANT 1 PROTEIN 0 CARB 0 FAT
My go-to green smoothie (page 224) BLOCKS PER SERVE 3 PLANT 0 PROTEIN 0 CARB 0 FAT	Handful of nuts BLOCKS PER SERVE 0 PLANT 0 PROTEIN 0 CARB 1 FAT	Natural protein berry smoothie (page 222) BLOCKS PER SERVE 1 PLANT 1 PROTEIN 0 CARB 0 FAT	Green smoothie with kale, pineapple and coconut (page 223) BLOCKS PER SERVE 2 PLANT 0 PROTEIN 0 CARB 0 FAT
Coconut fish fingers, sweet potato chips and broccolini (page 135) BLOCKS PER SERVE 1 PLANT 1 PROTEIN 1 CARB 1 FAT	Roast veggie salad with pomegranate dressing (page 95) and a grilled lean steak BLOCKS PER SERVE 3 PLANT 1 PROTEIN 1 CARB 1 FAT	Soba noodle soup with teriyaki pork and greens (page 120) BLOCKS PER SERVE 1 PLANT 1 PROTEIN 1 CARB ½ FAT	Spanish seafood stew (page 129) served with a green salad dressed with vinaigrette and a slice of wholegrain sourdough BLOCKS PER SERVE 2 PLANT 2 PROTEIN 1 CARB 2 FAT
Hot spiced cocoa (page 231) BLOCKS PER SERVE 0 PLANT 1 PROTEIN 0 CARB 0 FAT	½ cup of mixed berries with natural yoghurt BLOCKS PER SERVE 1 PLANT 1 PROTEIN 0 CARB 0 FAT	2 squares (20 g/¾ oz) dark chocolate BLOCKS PER SERVE 0 PLANT 0 PROTEIN 0 CARB ½ FAT	Custard filo tart with caramelised figs (page 201) BLOCKS PER SERVE 1 PLANT 0 PROTEIN ½ CARB 0 FAT
8 PLANT **4 PROTEIN** **3 CARB** **3 FAT**	**10 PLANT** **4 PROTEIN** **3 CARB** **3 FAT**	**6 PLANT** **4 PROTEIN** **3 CARB** **3 FAT**	**9 PLANT** **4 PROTEIN** **2½ CARB** **3 FAT**

Part 2

Get Lean, Stay Lean

Recipes

Breakfast

Quinoa porridge with rhubarb, pear and toasted coconut

This takes a little time to cook from scratch, but on a morning where you don't need to rush out the door, give it a go. You can make quinoa porridge far more quickly using quinoa flakes. However, I much prefer the texture of using the intact grain. You can, of course, cook both the quinoa and the rhubarb ahead of time and keep them in the fridge ready to reheat in the microwave for a speedier breakfast.

Serves 2 Time 35 minutes GF NF V

Wash the quinoa twice in fresh water and rinse in a sieve under the tap. Heat the milk and cinnamon stick in a saucepan over medium heat and once hot add the quinoa. Bring to a gentle simmer, cover with the lid, and cook for about 30 minutes, stirring every so often. Once almost all of the milk has been absorbed turn off the heat, leaving the lid on.

Put all the stewed rhubarb ingredients into a small saucepan over medium heat. Bring to the boil, then reduce the heat so that it just simmers. Cook for about 10 minutes until the fruit is softened. If it looks too thick add a tablespoon or two of water. Once ready turn off the heat.

Heat a small frying pan over medium heat. Add the coconut and toast, stirring frequently, until aromatic and browning slightly. Be careful not to burn the coconut.

Divide the quinoa into bowls and discard the cinnamon stick. Top with the yoghurt (you can mix this through if you prefer), a spoonful of the rhubarb, the diced pear and the honey, and sprinkle with the toasted coconut and sesame seeds. Serve.

1 cinnamon stick
½ pear (or apple), cored and diced

500 ml (17 fl oz/2 cups) light milk
100 g (3½ oz) natural yoghurt

100 g (3½ oz/½ cup) quinoa
1 tablespoon honey

20 g (¾ oz/¼ cup) shredded coconut
1 teaspoon black sesame seeds

Stewed Rhubarb

500 g (1 lb 2 oz) rhubarb, trimmed, washed and sliced (see note)
1 teaspoon grated ginger
Juice of ½ orange

See recipe photo on page 25.

Note Since rhubarb is usually sold in bunches of about 500 g (1 lb 2 oz), this recipe caters for that amount and will provide leftovers. You can store the remaining stewed rhubarb in an airtight container in the fridge for up to a week. You can also freeze it for a few months.

Per serve

energy	protein	tot. fat	sat	poly	mono	carb	sugars	fibre
1770 kJ 420 Cal	20 g	15 g	10 g	2 g	3 g	48 g	24 g*	7 g

NUTRITION BLOCKS PER SERVE

 PLANT  PROTEIN   CARB   FAT

1 PLANT 1 PROTEIN 1 CARB 1 FAT

*Only 2 g from added sugar in the honey, the remainder is naturally present.

Chia oats with stewed apple and prunes

Growing up in Scotland, oats were a winter breakfast staple. My mother made traditional Scottish porridge every morning using only four ingredients—oatmeal, water, salt and pepper. We then ate it with a cup of milk on the side, dipping a spoonful of hot porridge into the cold milk. It was surprisingly tasty, but having had 16 years of Sydney influence with its strong breakfast culture, this is my non-traditional version.

Serves 4   Time 15 minutes   V

Combine the oats, chia, cinnamon and milk in a saucepan. Place the pan over medium heat and bring to a simmer. Cook for about 10 minutes, stirring regularly until you have a nice thick porridge.

Meanwhile, combine the prunes and apple in a second saucepan with a splash of water. Bring to the boil, then lower the heat and simmer for about 5 minutes, stirring occasionally. Make sure the mixture doesn't dry out—add a little more water if you need to.

Spoon the porridge into bowls, top with the stewed apple and prunes, the yoghurt and scatter over the chopped almonds. Serve.

¼ teaspoon ground cinnamon
8 pitted prunes, diced
1 green apple, cored and diced

750 ml (26 fl oz/3 cups) light milk
190 g (6¾ oz/⅔ cup) natural yoghurt

95 g (3¼ oz/1 cup) rolled (porridge) oats (see note)

1 tablespoon chia seeds (see note)
60 g (2¼ oz) almonds, roughly chopped

Notes Contrary to what you might think, this is not a high carb, low fat meal. In fact, oats are about 11 per cent protein and when combined with the milk, yoghurt, almonds and chia, 18 per cent of the overall energy comes from protein. Fat contributes 37 per cent of the energy and carbohydrates 41 per cent ... plus there is no added sugar, the fruit is sweet enough. So you can see that it is in fact a very balanced meal.

Chia seeds are rich in plant omega-3 fats, antioxidants and protein, and contain both soluble and insoluble fibre. Chia is also one of the few foods that is truly wholegrain—you buy and eat them completely intact.

Per serve

energy	protein	tot. fat	sat	poly	mono	carb	sugars	fibre
1570 kJ 375 Cal	16 g	16 g	4 g	4 g	7 g	40 g	24 g	8 g

NUTRITION BLOCKS PER SERVE

 1 PLANT   1 PROTEIN   1 CARB   1 FAT

Fruit and nut toasted muesli

Toasted muesli is utterly delicious, but the bought varieties are often so loaded with added oil and sugar that you'd need to be running a marathon every day to work them off. So I experimented in my kitchen with the goal of creating a crunchy, lightly toasted muesli that satisfies the tastebuds without being so energy dense you could only have a spoonful. The result is delicious and far tastier than most supermarket shelf varieties.

Serves 8   Time 25 minutes   DF V Ve

Preheat the oven to fan-forced 165°C (320°F/Gas 2–3). Mix the oats, maple syrup, pepitas, hazelnuts, macadamias and extra virgin olive oil together in a large bowl.

Line a baking tray with baking paper and spread out the muesli mix on top. Place the tray in the oven and bake for 15–20 minutes, giving the mixture a good stir once or twice while toasting. When the muesli is golden and aromatic remove from the oven and set aside to cool.

Add the dried apricots and prunes to the toasted muesli. Mix together well and store in an airtight container in the fridge or cool pantry for up to a month.

Serve with milk, natural yoghurt or a dairy alternative and top with fresh berries or other fruit.

- 60 g (2¼ oz/⅓ cup) dried apricots, sliced
- 75 g (2½ oz/⅓ cup) pitted prunes, sliced (see note)

- 190 g (6¾ oz/2 cups) rolled (porridge) oats
- 1 tablespoon pure maple syrup

- 55 g (2 oz/⅓ cup) pepitas (pumpkin seeds) (see note)
- 50 g (1¾ oz/⅓ cup) hazelnuts, roughly chopped (see note)
- 45 g (1½ oz/⅓ cup) raw macadamia nuts, roughly chopped (see note)
- 1 tablespoon extra virgin olive oil

Notes Prunes are a good source of vitamin K, essential for healthy blood clotting; and potassium, important for blood pressure control. They're more energy dense than the fresh fruit, but have a very low GI, making them an ideal snack or addition to a meal. Just be sure to watch your portion.

You can basically use any nuts and seeds you like. I vary it from batch to batch. Just fill a cup—two-thirds nuts and one-third seeds—with whatever combination you like, and add to the mix.

Per serve

energy	protein	tot. fat	sat	poly	mono	carb	sugars	fibre
900 kJ 215 Cal	5 g	12 g	2 g	2 g	7 g	22 g	6 g	4 g

NUTRITION BLOCKS PER SERVE

0 PLANT   **0** PROTEIN   **1** CARB   **1** FAT

* The nutrition analysis does not include serving suggestions.

Bircher muesli with apple and blueberries

Soaking grains helps them to be more easily digested, so many people find bircher muesli a lighter eat than other muesli options. It's well worth taking five minutes the night before to put this together, and then popping it into the fridge for the next morning—then it's just another five minutes to add the final ingredients. If you make more than you need, it'll keep for a few days, just be sure to add the fresh fruit only at the time of serving.

Serves 4   Time 10 minutes (+ overnight soaking)   V

Roughly crush the hazelnuts and almonds using a mortar and pestle (or roughly chop with a large knife). Mix the crushed nuts, oats, cinnamon, orange juice, yoghurt and milk together in a bowl. Cover with plastic wrap and store in the fridge overnight.

Serve the bircher muesli in breakfast bowls topped with the sunflower seeds, pepitas, chia seeds, blueberries, grated apple and an extra dollop of yoghurt.

½ teaspoon ground cinnamon
Juice of 1 orange
125 g (4½ oz) blueberries
1 green apple, cored and grated

260 g (9¼ oz/1 cup) natural yoghurt, plus extra to serve
250 ml (9 fl oz/1 cup) light milk

95 g (3¼ oz/1 cup) rolled (porridge) oats

30 g (1 oz) hazelnuts
30 g (1 oz) almonds
1 tablespoon sunflower seeds
2 tablespoons pepitas (pumpkin seeds) (see note)
2 tablespoons chia seeds

Notes This is a fantastically fibre-rich breakfast with 9 g per serve. Your goal is to get to at least 25 g a day for women and 30 g a day for men, so this puts you pretty much a third of the way there in one meal. Not bad!

Around 70 per cent of the energy in pepitas comes from fat, but it's primarily healthy mono- and polyunsaturated fats. Including these fats in your diet is important for heart and brain health, and can help you to stay lean.

Per serve

energy	protein	tot. fat	sat	poly	mono	carb	sugars	fibre
1600 kJ 380 Cal	19 g	19 g	2 g	6 g	9 g	34 g	19 g*	9 g

*All sugars naturally present.

NUTRITION BLOCKS PER SERVE

 1 PLANT 1 PROTEIN 1 CARB 1 FAT

Crunchy gluten-free muesli

Although there are a few good gluten-free muesli options on the market, they're rare and often expensive. So why not create a homemade one? Whether you eat gluten or not, this muesli is yum and makes a perfect start to the morning.

Serves 10 Time 40 minutes DF GF V Ve

Preheat the oven to fan-forced 180°C (350°F/Gas 4).

Line a baking tray with baking paper. Mix the extra virgin olive oil and maple syrup together in a bowl. Pour in the quinoa flakes and stir to coat. Spread the quinoa evenly on the baking tray and place in the oven. Bake for about 25 minutes, stirring occasionally, until crunchy and golden. Remove from the oven and set aside to cool completely.

Mix all the other ingredients together in a large bowl. Add the roasted quinoa and mix well to combine.

Pour the muesli into a clean, dry glass jar and store in a cool pantry. This muesli will last for up to a month.

Serve with soy, almond or oat milk—or dairy milk if not dairy-free—and top with fresh berries or other fruit.

- 40 g (1½ oz/¼ cup) goji berries

- 90 g (3¼ oz/¼ cup) pure maple syrup
- 150 g (5½ oz/1½ cups) quinoa flakes
- 30 g (1 oz/1 cup) cornflakes

- 60 ml (2 fl oz/¼ cup) extra virgin olive oil
- 40 g (1½ oz/¼ cup) hazelnuts, roughly chopped
- 40 g (1½ oz/¼ cup) sunflower seeds (see note)
- 40 g (1½ oz/¼ cup) pepitas (pumpkin seeds)
- 20 g (1 oz/¼ cup) shredded coconut
- 70 g (2½ oz/½ cup) LSA (ground linseed/flaxseed, sunflower seeds and almonds—you can make this yourself or buy it ready made)

See recipe photo on page 28.

Note Sunflower seeds are one of the richest sources of vitamin E, with 1 tablespoon of seeds providing 22 per cent of the daily requirement for women and 16 per cent for men. It's important to eat the seeds in their intact form. This will give you high concentrated doses of omega-6 fats, as well as all the nutrients, fibre and protein the whole seeds contain.

A 30 g (1 oz) serve of sunflower seeds will also give you significant doses of iron, magnesium, thiamin, vitamin B6, phosphorus, copper, manganese and selenium. They really are a real food multivitamin and mineral!

Per serve

energy	protein	tot. fat	sat	poly	mono	carb	sugars	fibre
1100 kJ 260 Cal	6 g	16 g	3 g	5 g	7 g	20 g	8 g	5 g

NUTRITION BLOCKS PER SERVE

 **0** PLANT **0** PROTEIN **1** CARB **1** FAT

* The nutrition analysis does not include serving suggestions.

Slow-roasted tomato and scrambled egg breakfast wrap

I have to admit to being a creature of habit with my weekday breakfasts, but on the weekend I love to do something different. These wraps filled with scrambled eggs and veggies are so delicious, they fit the bill for a leisurely Sunday morning meal. I've used a sandwich press to toast the wraps, but if you don't have one you can do this in a large non-stick frying pan instead.

Serves 4 Time 40 minutes NF V

Preheat the oven to fan-forced 160°C (315°F/Gas 2–3). Line a baking tray with baking paper.

Put the tomatoes on the tray, drizzle with 2 teaspoons of the extra virgin olive oil and the balsamic vinegar, and season with salt and pepper. Roast for 30 minutes or until the tomatoes are soft and slightly caramelised. Remove from the oven and set aside to cool.

Preheat a sandwich press, if using.

Heat a teaspoon of the olive oil in a frying pan over medium heat. Add the garlic and mushrooms and sauté for 3–4 minutes or until browned.

Meanwhile, break the eggs into a bowl and whisk together with the milk.

Remove the mushrooms from the pan and set aside.

Wipe the pan with paper towel and place over medium heat. Drizzle the pan with the remaining teaspoon of olive oil and pour in the egg mixture. Cook gently, moving the eggs with a wooden spoon until just set (they should still be slightly wet as the mixture will continue to cook off the heat). Remove from the heat and set aside.

Lay out the wraps on your work surface. Divide the rocket between the wraps and place in the centre of each one, then top with the sautéed mushrooms, slow-roasted tomatoes and the scrambled eggs. Fold the bottom of the wrap up into the centre, then fold each side over the other to enclose the filling and form a parcel, open only at the top.

Place in the preheated sandwich press or in a frying pan over medium heat and cook for 1–2 minutes until sealed and heated through. If cooking in a frying pan, turn over after 1 minute to toast the other side.

Serve immediately.

12 cherry tomatoes, halved
Freshly ground black pepper
½ garlic clove, crushed
8 button mushrooms, sliced (see note)
70 g (2½ oz) rocket (arugula) leaves

8 free-range or organic eggs
125 ml (4 fl oz/½ cup) light milk

4 thin wholegrain wraps

1 tablespoon extra virgin olive oil

+
1 teaspoon balsamic vinegar
Pinch of salt flakes

Note I've just used button mushrooms here, but you could also try chestnut, shiitake or any other type of small mushroom. All mushrooms have an impressive nutrition profile and are a worthy addition to your diet.

Per serve

energy 1270 kJ 300 Cal | protein 18 g | tot. fat 14 g | sat 4 g | poly 2 g | mono 6 g | carb 24 g | sugars 5 g | fibre 5 g

NUTRITION BLOCKS PER SERVE

2 PLANT **1** PROTEIN **1** CARB **½** FAT

Ricotta, bacon and asparagus frittata

This is one of those dishes that looks pretty impressive but is deceptively simple to make. I don't recommend you eat bacon every day—it is a processed meat—but it does add a lot of flavour, and a little goes a long way. Serve this dish for a weekend breakfast, or a light meal any time with salad, tomato relish and wholegrain toast for your smart carbs.

Serves 4 Time 30 minutes GF NF

Preheat the oven to fan-forced 160°C (315°F/Gas 2–3).

Heat a frying pan over medium–high heat. Add the bacon and dry-fry for 2 minutes on each side until lightly browned (be careful not to overcook or the bacon will be dry). (Alternatively, preheat the grill to high. Grill the bacon for 2 minutes on each side.) Slice the bacon rashers in half and set aside.

Meanwhile, bring a saucepan of water to the boil. Place the asparagus in a steamer and place over the boiling water. Steam for 2 minutes until just softened but still *al dente*. (Alternatively you can microwave in a bowl with a splash of water on High for 2 minutes.) Set aside.

Whisk the eggs, ricotta, chia seeds, basil and black pepper together in a mixing bowl until well combined. Add the spinach and mix again.

Pour the egg mixture into a 36 x 12 cm (14¼ x 4½ inch) tart tin and arrange the cooked bacon rashers, tomatoes and asparagus evenly over the top. Place in the oven and cook for about 20 minutes, or until the egg is set and firm.

(If you don't have a tart tin you can use an ovenproof frying pan, but heat the bottom of the frittata over the stovetop first, until the outside edges start to cook, and then finish cooking in the oven for 10 minutes or until the egg is set and firm.)

Serve hot or cold.

6 asparagus spears

5 basil leaves, torn

Freshly ground black pepper

45 g (1½ oz/1 cup) baby English spinach, leaves washed

10 cherry tomatoes (or 1 tomato, cut into 8 wedges)

4 lean short bacon slices (about 140 g/5 oz total, see note)

6 free-range or organic eggs

130 g (4½ oz) full fat ricotta cheese

1 teaspoon chia seeds

Note Curing, smoking and salting meat are traditional ways to extend the shelf life of fresh meat, however, today nitrite preservatives are often added and these may be converted to carcinogens in the gut. A recent scientific review also concluded that processed meat can cause cancer, especially bowel cancer.

This doesn't mean you can never enjoy these foods. My advice is to try not to have processed meats more than once or twice a week. Portion size matters, so a little bacon to give flavour is totally different from loading your plate with processed meat.

Per serve

energy	protein	tot. fat	sat	poly	mono	carb	sugars	fibre
790 kJ 190 Cal	20 g	10 g	4 g	1 g	4 g	3 g	3 g	2 g

NUTRITION BLOCKS PER SERVE

 1 PLANT  **1** PROTEIN **0** CARB **0** FAT

Spanish baked eggs with ham and spinach

This is one of my favourite weekend breakfasts. It looks very fancy, but it honestly doesn't take long to make and is well worth the effort. I sometimes add cannellini beans and/or red capsicum (peppers) to the tomato mix before baking for boosted flavour and nutrition. Just be sure not to overcook the eggs. Serve with toasted grainy sourdough as your smart carb for a perfectly balanced *Get Lean, Stay Lean* meal.

Serves 2   Time 30 minutes   DF GF NF

Preheat the oven to fan-forced 180°C (350°F/Gas 4).

Heat 2 teaspoons of the extra virgin olive oil in a frying pan over medium heat. Add the onion and garlic and sauté for 3–4 minutes until the onion is translucent. Add the tomatoes, paprika and parsley. Cook, stirring occasionally, for 10 minutes, or until the mixture becomes a chunky sauce.

Divide the sauce between two individual ramekins or baking dishes. Spread the ham evenly throughout the sauce. Crack 2 eggs on the top of each dish. Bake for 10 minutes, or until the eggs are set to your liking.

When the eggs are nearly ready, bring a saucepan of water to the boil over high heat. Put the spinach in a steamer, cover with the lid and place on top of the pan. Cook for 1 minute or until wilted. (Alternatively, place the spinach in a microwave-proof bowl, cover and microwave on High for 1 minute.)

Pile the spinach on top of the baked eggs, drizzle with the remaining olive oil and scatter with the red chilli slices. Serve immediately.

- ½ red onion, diced
- 1 garlic clove, chopped
- 4 tomatoes, diced (or 400 g/14 oz tinned whole tomatoes)
- ¼ teaspoon sweet paprika
- 1 tablespoon chopped flat-leaf (Italian) parsley
- 150 g (5½ oz) baby English spinach, leaves washed and roughly chopped
- 1 red chilli, sliced (deseed for less spice)
- 100 g (3½ oz) sliced ham off the bone, chopped
- 4 free-range or organic eggs (see note)
- 1 tablespoon extra virgin olive oil

Note Eggs are a terrific breakfast choice. Studies have shown that people who eat eggs for breakfast are less hungry later and correspondingly eat less at lunch. They provide very high quality protein, with a near perfect balance of the amino acids that the human body needs. There's a reason why eggs have been a body-builders' staple for many years!

Pregnant women, young children and those with compromised immune systems should play safe and avoid raw or very runny eggs—cook them thoroughly.

Per serve

energy	protein	tot. fat	sat	poly	mono	carb	sugars	fibre
1240 kJ 300 Cal	24 g	19 g	5 g	2 g	10 g	5 g	5 g	4 g

NUTRITION BLOCKS PER SERVE

2 PLANT   **1** PROTEIN   **0** CARB   **1** FAT

Poached eggs on spiced sweet potato cakes

There's always great debate over whether or not to add vinegar to the poaching water for eggs. I'm on the vinegar side. But you have to use white vinegar or you'll colour the egg whites. I find the vinegar helps to keep the whites from spreading and firms them up nicely—although undoubtedly having fresh eggs is also key. In this recipe the eggs are paired with a lightly spiced sweet potato cake. It adds something different to plain old toast.

Serves 2   Time 20 minutes   DF GF NF V

Heat a frying pan over medium heat. Add the mustard, cumin and coriander seeds to the pan and dry-fry for about 1 minute, shaking the pan frequently, until lightly fragrant. Remove from the pan and crush using a mortar and pestle.

Combine the crushed spices in a large bowl with the sweet potato, coriander, chilli flakes, salt and 1 of the eggs. Mix well until combined.

Heat 2 teaspoons of the extra virgin olive oil in a frying pan over medium heat, then add tablespoonfuls of the sweet potato mixture to the pan to form patties no thicker than 1.5 cm (⅝ inch). Fry for 3–4 minutes on each side until golden. Cover lightly with foil and set aside.

Half fill a saucepan with water and place over high heat. Bring to the boil, add the white vinegar and carefully crack the remaining eggs into the pan. Poach for 4–5 minutes (depending on how runny you like your yolk) or until the egg whites are set.

Meanwhile, make the salad by combining the spinach, tomatoes and onion in a bowl. Shake the remaining olive oil with the extra vinegar in a small jar, drizzle over the salad and toss to coat the leaves.

Arrange 2 potato cakes on each plate, pile on the salad and top with the eggs. Season with black pepper and serve.

Note Sweet potato is a root vegetable and, despite its name, is only very distantly related to regular potatoes. The wonderful orange colour comes from the presence of beta-carotene. This carotenoid is an antioxidant in its own right, but can also be converted to vitamin A in the body. Vitamin A, among many roles, is essential for healthy eyes and good vision throughout life. A 100 g (3½ oz) serve of baked sweet potato provides more than three times your daily need for vitamin A.

The glycaemic index of sweet potatoes varies according to the variety and how it is cooked, however, given the nutritional value of this root vegetable, and the fact that, provided you exercise portion control, the glycaemic load is relatively low—it's counted as a smart carb.

½ teaspoon black mustard seeds

1 teaspoon cumin seeds

½ teaspoon coriander seeds

2 tablespoons finely chopped coriander (cilantro)

½ teaspoon dried chilli flakes

Freshly ground black pepper

90 g (3¼ oz) baby English spinach leaves, washed

6 cherry tomatoes, halved

½ small red onion, thinly sliced

5 free-range or organic eggs

1 sweet potato (about 300 g/10½ oz), unpeeled, scrubbed and grated (see note)

1 tablespoon extra virgin olive oil

+

Pinch of salt flakes

2 tablespoons white vinegar, to cook the eggs, plus 1 teaspoon, for the dressing

Per serve

energy	protein	tot. fat	sat	poly	mono	carb	sugars	fibre
1500 kJ 360 Cal	19 g	19 g	5 g	2 g	10 g	25 g	11 g	5 g

NUTRITION BLOCKS PER SERVE

 2 PLANT 1 PROTEIN  1 CARB 1 FAT

Super veggie bowl

Most people think of a bowl of cereal, or eggs on toast when they think about breakfast, but this meal is also a great opportunity to add some superfood veggies to help kickstart the day. They work really well in creating a perfect Dr Joanna Plate meal, getting you well on the way to meeting your Plant Blocks for the day. If you are a vegan, simply omit the eggs and double your portion of chickpeas, and substitute maple syrup for the honey.

Serves 2   Time 25 minutes   DF GF NF V

Bring a saucepan of water to the boil. Add the eggs, reduce the heat to a simmer, and cook for 7–8 minutes. Remove from the heat, drain and set aside to cool.

While the eggs are cooling, bring a large saucepan of water to the boil. Break the broccoli and cauliflower into florets, top and tail the snow peas, scrub the sweet potato, then cut it into rounds. Place a steamer over the boiling pan of water. Since the veggies will take different times to cook, add them separately to the steamer in the following order: Add the sweet potato first to cook for 10–12 minutes; after 4 minutes add the cauliflower; after a further 3 minutes add the broccoli; and for the last minute of cooking add the snow peas. The veggies should be just tender—be careful not to overcook. Carefully remove the veggies from the steamer and set aside. (Alternatively you can steam the vegetables in a microwave. Place the veggies, one at a time, in a microwave-proof bowl with a little water, cover and cook on High for 8 minutes for the sweet potato, 3 minutes for the cauliflower, 2 minutes for the broccoli and 1 minute for the snow peas.)

Combine the tahini, lemon juice, honey and 1 tablespoon of water in a small bowl and whisk well. Add in extra water, 1 teaspoon at a time, if you like a thinner dressing.

Peel the hard-boiled eggs and cut into quarters.

Divide the baby English spinach into serving bowls, top with the steamed veggies, sauerkraut, chickpeas, hard-boiled egg, pepitas and nori. Drizzle with the dressing to serve.

Note Tahini is just sesame seed paste and it makes a delicious base for a dressing, adding your good fats at the same time. If you're dairy free it's a good idea to use tahini often, as it's terrific for calcium. This recipe will give you in total 240 mg of calcium—that's 24 per cent of the recommended daily intake for most adults.

You can buy hulled or unhulled tahini. The hulled variety is where the outer seed coat of the sesame seeds are removed before toasting and grinding, whereas the seed is kept intact with the unhulled variety. The latter has a slightly stronger taste and the fibre level is a little higher. The nutritional differences are comparatively small so use whichever one you prefer.

150 g (5½ oz) broccoli
200 g (7 oz) cauliflower
100 g (3½ oz) snow peas (mangetout)
45 g (1½ oz) baby English spinach leaves
75 g (2½ oz/½ cup) store-bought sauerkraut
1 sheet nori, shredded

2 free-range or organic eggs
90 g (3¼ oz/½ cup) tinned chickpeas

1 small sweet potato (about 150 g/5½ oz)

2 tablespoons toasted pepitas
(pumpkin seeds)

Tahini dressing

Juice of ½ lemon

½ teaspoon honey

2 tablespoons tahini (see note)

Per serve

energy	protein	tot. fat	sat	poly	mono	carb	sugars	fibre
1930 kJ 460 Cal	26 g	25 g	5 g	9 g	8 g	27 g	12 g*	15 g

NUTRITION BLOCKS PER SERVE

 4 PLANT   **1** PROTEIN   **1** CARB   **2** FAT

*Only 3 g from added sugar in the honey, the remainder is naturally present.

Spelt and lupin blueberry hotcakes

I'm always looking for ways of improving the nutritional profile of recipes made with flour, while keeping the end result delicious. Lupin flour is well worth looking for with this in mind. Lupin is a legume, but it's unusual in that it has a low carbohydrate content (less than 10 per cent dry weight) and is higher in protein than almost all other plant foods. It works really well when used to substitute some of the flour in a baking recipe or, as I have done here, to make hotcakes.

Serves 6   Time 30 minutes   NF V

Whisk together the eggs, extra virgin olive oil, buttermilk, orange juice and zest, vanilla seeds and maple syrup in a bowl.

In a separate bowl, sift in the flours and add the baking powder and salt.

Pour the wet ingredient mixture into the dry, and gently combine, taking care not to over-mix. Fold through the blueberries and set aside to rest for a few minutes.

Preheat the oven to fan-forced 140°C (275°F/Gas 1).

Heat a pancake pan or hotplate over medium heat and spray or brush with olive oil. Pour 60 ml (2 fl oz/¼ cup) of the batter into the pan to form a circle. Depending on the size of your pan, you will be able to cook more than one hotcake at a time. Just ensure you leave enough room between hotcakes so they don't stick together. Cook for 1–2 minutes until beginning to bubble and then flip. Cook for a further 1–2 minutes until a nice golden colour. Place on an ovenproof plate lined with paper towel and transfer into the oven to keep warm while you cook the remaining hotcakes. Repeat, until all the batter is used—this quantity makes 12 hotcakes. Be sure to place a sheet of paper towel between each layer.

Serve the hotcakes topped with light cream cheese or ricotta and, if you like, a teaspoon of pure fruit spread or raspberry purée.

Juice and grated zest of ½ orange

1 vanilla bean, split lengthways and seeds scraped (or 1 teaspoon vanilla paste)

125 g (4½ oz) blueberries, plus extra to serve

2 free-range or organic eggs

375 ml (13 fl oz/1½ cups) buttermilk (or mix half and half milk and natural yoghurt if you don't have buttermilk)

140 g (5 oz/1 cup) lupin flour

1 tablespoon pure maple syrup

140 g (5 oz/1 cup) spelt wholegrain flour (see note)

2 teaspoons baking powder

2 tablespoons extra virgin olive oil, plus extra for frying

+

¼ teaspoon iodised salt

Note Spelt is an ancient variety of wheat that is making a comeback, largely due to anecdotal accounts of people claiming they have problems digesting regular modern wheat, yet are fine with spelt. Any differences have not yet been conclusively confirmed in research, but I'm all for diversifying the grain types in our diets and if you do have trouble with wheat, why not try it? For those without any intolerances you can happily substitute a regular whole-wheat flour here—they're certainly cheaper.

Per serve (of two pancakes)

energy	protein	tot. fat	sat	poly	mono	carb	sugars	fibre
1240 kJ 300 Cal	16 g	12 g	2 g	2 g	6 g	28 g	10 g	10 g

NUTRITION BLOCKS PER SERVE

 **0** PLANT **1** PROTEIN **1** CARB **1** FAT

* The nutrition analysis does not include serving suggestions.

Snacks

Smoked trout dip

Trout is often in the shadow of its more popular oily fish cousin, salmon. Yet it has a wonderful creamy taste and offers a nice variation in flavour. You need a robust-flavoured fish for this dip— an alternative would be smoked mackerel or hot-smoked salmon. The addition of horseradish gives it a little heat and lifts the whole flavour. Serve with wholegrain crackers, oatcakes or crudités (batons of raw veggies such as carrots, celery, capsicum/peppers and cucumber).

Serves 4   Time 5 minutes   GF NF

Flake the trout fillets into a mixing bowl. Add all the other ingredients and stir to combine. Season with black pepper and chill until you are ready to serve.

Juice and grated zest of ½ lemon
1 teaspoon horseradish cream
1 tablespoon fresh dill, finely chopped
1 tablespoon fresh mint, finely chopped
Freshly ground black pepper

100 g (3½ oz) smoked trout (see note)
2 tablespoons light cream cheese
1 tablespoon natural yoghurt

Note Smoking fish is a traditional means of food preservation, giving the fish a far longer shelf life. This does make it a convenient food and an easy way of getting more oily fish into your diet. However, do be aware that smoked fish has a high salt content. Be sure, therefore, not to add salt to recipes and meals that include smoked fish and those on a low fat diet (such as if you have high blood pressure) should avoid it.

Per serve

energy	protein	tot. fat	sat	poly	mono	carb	sugars	fibre
270 kJ 65 Cal	7 g	3 g	2 g	<1 g	1 g	1 g	1 g	0 g

NUTRITION BLOCKS PER SERVE

0 PLANT   **½** PROTEIN   **0** CARB   **0** FAT

Hot spiced nuts

I made these nuts for one of my morning TV show segments. The male hosts devoured them and renamed them 'Man Nuts'—so they're sure to be a hit with male guests! You can make these as spicy as you like, and if you don't have ras el hanout, you can use whatever spices you have in the pantry. I often use a homemade mix of cumin, coriander, chilli and a little sea salt.

Serves 6 Time 5 minutes DF GF V Ve

Heat the extra virgin olive oil in a frying pan over medium heat. Add the spice mix and chilli, if using, and stir for just a few seconds until fragrant. Add the nuts and cook, stirring for about 2 minutes, until well coated in the spice mix and starting to brown.

Remove from the heat as soon as you start to smell the nuts roasting (stand over them as they burn easily!). Remove from the pan, sprinkle with salt and serve.

1 teaspoon ras el hanout (Moroccan spice mix, see note)

Pinch of chilli flakes (optional, to taste)

2 teaspoons extra virgin olive oil

155 g (5½ oz/1 cup) mixed unsalted, raw nuts (see note)

+

Pinch of salt flakes

Notes You can buy ras el hanout in good grocers and delicatessens, but if you don't have any to hand the hot nuts are also delicious simply flavoured with chilli and salt.

Nuts are full of the good fats we want in our diet and that's why I specify them as a good choice for the fat slice of the Dr Joanna Plate. Most nuts are high in monounsaturated fats, just like extra virgin olive oil, and some are predominately polyunsaturated fats. They are fabulous sources of several vitamins and minerals including folate and magnesium, as well as many beneficial phytochemicals (like antioxidants), fibre and plant protein. Research shows a handful a day can reduce your risk of heart disease by as much as 50 per cent! Pretty incredible for such a delicious food.

Per serve

energy	protein	tot. fat	sat	poly	mono	carb	sugars	fibre
680 kJ 160 Cal	6 g	15 g	8 g	4 g	2 g	3 g	1 g	2 g

NUTRITION BLOCKS PER SERVE

0 PLANT 0 PROTEIN 0 CARB 1 FAT

Hummus two ways

Once you've made hummus at home, I guarantee you'll rarely, if ever, buy it again. Provided you have a food processor or a Vitamix, it's super easy and takes only a few minutes to make. It's especially delicious served straight away, slightly warm from the machine, but will keep in the fridge for about a week. From the basic hummus recipe you can create any number of flavour combinations. I've simply added beetroot as a variation here.

Serves 8   Time 5 minutes   DF GF NF V Ve

For the basic hummus recipe, put all the ingredients, except the paprika, and 60 ml (2 fl oz/¼ cup) of water into a food processor or Vitamix and turn the power up to maximum—it is much easier in a Vitamix, as you can use the tamper to push the ingredients down into the blades. If you're using a food processor you will need to stop a few times and scrape down the side. Blend for a couple of minutes until the hummus is completely smooth.

To make the beetroot hummus variation, simply add the beetroot along with the other ingredients before blending.

Scoop the hummus into a bowl and sprinkle with the paprika, if using, when ready to serve.

Juice of 1 lemon

½ garlic clove (see note)

½ teaspoon cumin seeds

¼ teaspoon smoked paprika, to serve (optional)

For beetroot hummus variation: 2 cooked beetroot (beets), peeled and halved

400 g (14 oz) tinned chickpeas, drained and rinsed

65 g (2¼ oz/¼ cup) unhulled tahini

2 tablespoons extra virgin olive oil, plus extra to serve

+

Pinch of salt flakes

Note Raw garlic can be really strong in a recipe, particularly when you use a powerful blender like a Vitamix. Hummus does need a little garlic, but you don't want it to be overpowering. I've used just half a garlic clove in this recipe, but for garlic lovers you could use the whole clove. For those who find raw garlic repeats on you, try cutting the garlic down the centre (lengthways) and discarding the middle stem.

Per serve (per 50 g/1¾ oz/2 tablespoons)

energy	protein	tot. fat	sat	poly	mono	carb	sugars	fibre
550 kJ 130 Cal	4 g	10 g	1 g	3 g	5 g	6 g	<1 g	3 g

Beetroot hummus variation per serve (per 50 g/1¾ oz/2 tablespoons)

energy	protein	tot. fat	sat	poly	mono	carb	sugars	fibre
600 kJ 140 Cal	4 g	10 g	1 g	3 g	5 g	7 g	1 g	3.5 g

NUTRITION BLOCKS PER SERVE

0 PLANT   **0** PROTEIN   **0** CARB   **1** FAT

Moroccan carrot and parsnip dip

Homemade dips usually taste infinitely better than bought ones, they save you money, and you know exactly what has gone into them without any of the added nasties that can be used in commercial varieties to preserve shelf life. This recipe combines roasted carrots and parsnips with spices, and is then blended with lentils and yoghurt. The end result is fibre rich, a good source of protein to help keep hunger pangs at bay, and has slow-release carbohydrates to fuel your body.

Serves 4 Time 40 minutes GF NF V

Preheat the oven to fan-forced 180°C (350°F/Gas 4). Line a baking tray with baking paper.

Heat a small frying pan over medium heat. Add the coriander and cumin seeds, and dry-fry for a minute or so until fragrant. Remove from the pan and crush using a mortar and pestle. (See note.)

Chop the carrot and parsnip into chunks and mix in a bowl with the extra virgin olive oil, the roasted spices and the garlic. Spread out on the prepared tray and roast in the oven for 30 minutes.

Meanwhile, put 500 ml (17 fl oz/2 cups) of water in a saucepan over high heat and bring to the boil. Add the lentils along with the thyme, then reduce the heat to a simmer. Cook for 15 minutes or until the lentils are tender. Drain.

Put the roast vegetables, the lentils, yoghurt, lemon peel and juice, mint, salt and pepper into a food processor or Vitamix. Roughly blend (if using a Vitamix, use level 5), but avoid over-processing so the dip retains some texture. Check the seasoning and serve.

Any unused dip will keep in your fridge for 4–5 days, or you can also freeze it for a few months.

2 teaspoons coriander seeds (see note)

2 teaspoons cumin seeds (see note)

1 carrot

1 parsnip

2 garlic cloves, smashed with the side of a large knife, then peeled

A few thyme sprigs

1 piece lemon peel and juice of 1/2 lemon

Handful mint, leaves picked

Freshly ground black pepper

130 g (4 1/2 oz/1/2 cup) Greek-style yoghurt

100 g (3 1/2 oz/1/2 cup) split red lentils

2 tablespoons extra virgin olive oil

+
Pinch of salt flakes

See recipe photo on page 56.

Note Spices add amazing flavours to your cooking without adding any kilojoules, but they are also a wealth of beneficial phytochemicals. In many countries they have been used medicinally for thousands of years and for good reason. We are only now understanding the science behind some of the chemicals they contain and how they benefit our health. They're also a great way to reduce your salt intake—with spice you don't need as much salt.

Per serve

energy	protein	tot. fat	sat	poly	mono	carb	sugars	fibre
820 kJ 195 Cal	8 g	12 g	3 g	1 g	7 g	16 g	6 g	5 g

NUTRITION BLOCKS PER SERVE

1 PLANT   0 PROTEIN   1 CARB   0 FAT

Corn fritters with smoked salmon and avocado salsa

This recipe is one of my favourites to serve as delicious, bite-sized canapés when you're entertaining. Following these quantities you can make 24 canapé-sized fritters. Alternatively, you can make the corn fritters bigger and serve this for weekend brunch for four. To do this simply use 2 tablespoons of mixture per fritter, to make 8 fritters in total to serve 2 per person. You can make the corn fritters ahead of time and pop them in the freezer until ready to use.

Makes 24 canapes or serves 4 for brunch   Time 30 minutes   GF NF

Preheat the oven to fan-forced 140°C (275°F/Gas 1).

To make the avocado salsa, gently mix the avocado, spring onion, coriander and cherry tomatoes together in a bowl. Squeeze over the lime juice and add plenty of black pepper to taste. Set aside.

For the corn fritters, slice the corn kernels from the cobs and mix in a bowl with the flours, spring onions, cumin and eggs. Season with salt and black pepper.

Heat the extra virgin olive oil in a frying pan over medium heat. Spoon a heaped teaspoon of mixture per fritter in the pan. Flatten the mixture slightly and cook for 2 minutes, or until golden, flip and cook the other side for a further 2 minutes. Place the cooked fritters on an ovenproof plate lined with paper towel and transfer to the oven to keep warm while you cook the remaining fritters.

To serve, place the corn fritters on a serving plate, top with a little avocado salsa, a crumble of goat's curd, a slice of smoked salmon and wedges of lemon on the side.

2 spring onions (scallions), thinly sliced
1/4 teaspoon ground cumin
Freshly ground black pepper
1 lemon, cut into quarters, to serve

2 free-range or organic eggs, whisked with a fork
1 tablespoon goat's curd (or feta)
200 g (7 oz) smoked salmon (see note)

2 corn cobs, husks and silks removed
60 g (2 1/4 oz/1/2 cup) chickpea flour (besan)
2 tablespoons amaranth flour

1 tablespoon extra virgin olive oil

+
1/4 teaspoon iodised salt

Avocado salsa

1 spring onion (scallion), thinly sliced
Handful coriander (cilantro), leaves picked
2 cherry tomatoes, diced
Juice of 1 lime
Freshly ground black pepper

1 avocado, diced into small pieces (see note)

Note This recipe is a wonderful balance of good fats, plenty of protein, low GI carbs and a plant food boost. Nutritionally, you'll benefit from the omega-3 fats in the salmon, and the monounsaturated fats in the avocado, not to mention the wealth of vitamins and minerals.

Canapé per serve (making 24, per canapé-sized fritter)

energy	protein	tot. fat	sat	poly	mono	carb	sugars	fibre
290 kJ 70 Cal	4 g	4 g	1 g	<1 g	2 g	3 g	<1 g	1 g

Brunch per serve (serving 4, per serve of 2 corn fritters)

energy	protein	tot. fat	sat	poly	mono	carb	sugars	fibre
1750 kJ 420 Cal	23 g	25 g	6 g	4 g	13 g	20 g	5 g	8 g

NUTRITION BLOCKS PER SERVE

 1 PLANT   1 PROTEIN   1 CARB   1 FAT

Lamb and cauliflower dolmades

Dolmades are usually filled with a rice-based mixture, but here I've lightened the load, boosted the nutrition and reduced the carbohydrate content by using cauliflower instead. The return is not just nutritional; I think they taste a whole lot better, too. Don't be put off, thinking this is fiddly. You honestly can't go wrong, and if they're not quite a perfect shape it really doesn't matter. In fact, it will just show that they are homemade.

Makes 20   Time 1 hour   DF GF

Preheat the oven to fan-forced 180°C (350°F/Gas 4).

Heat the extra virgin olive oil in a frying pan over medium heat. Add the onion and lightly fry for 3 minutes or until translucent. Add the lamb and continue to cook for about 5 minutes until browned.

Add the spices and oregano to the lamb and stir for a couple of minutes to combine. Add the raisins, chopped tomato, lemon zest, grated cauliflower and almonds. Stir for another 2–3 minutes to marry the flavours. Season with salt and black pepper. Set aside to cool.

Carefully unroll the grape leaves and lay them on a clean work surface. Spoon about a tablespoon of the lamb mixture at the base of each grape leaf near the stalk (the amount of mixture will vary with the varying sizes of the leaves). Fold the left and right sides of the leaf into the centre, then roll the bottom over the folded sides to form a parcel. Place into a baking dish, side by side.

Once you have finished rolling your dolmades and placed them into your baking dish, pour over 125 ml (4 fl oz/½ cup) of water. Roughly chop the 2 extra tomatoes and add them to the dish with the bay leaves and lemon slices. Cover with foil and bake for 30 minutes or until the leaves have turned a darker shade of olive.

Remove the dolmades from the poaching liquid. Discard the liquid. Serve as a snack with hummus (see page 85) or tahini mixed with natural yoghurt as finger food when you have guests over, or team with a chopped tomato salad and garlic yoghurt for a Greek-inspired meal.

If not using straight away, you can store the dolmades in the fridge for a few days, drizzled with a little extra virgin olive oil.

Notes Despite research to the contrary, cauliflower seems to be thought of as the poor cousin to broccoli. It's true that broccoli is higher in some nutrients, including riboflavin, magnesium and pre-vitamin A. But cauliflower has 26 per cent more folate, with 100 g (3½ oz) providing 16 per cent of your recommended daily intake. Cauliflower is also an excellent source of vitamin C; 100 g of raw cauliflower provides 1.5 times your daily requirement.

You'll find grape leaves (sometimes called vine leaves) packed in brine in a jar. Buy them in any good delicatessen or supermarket.

¼ red onion, finely diced

1 teaspoon freshly grated nutmeg

½ teaspoon ground cinnamon

1 teaspoon ground cumin

1 teaspoon dried oregano

1 tablespoon raisins

1 tinned peeled tomato, finely chopped, plus 2 whole, extra

Grated zest of ¼ lemon

100 g (3½ oz/½ head) cauliflower, grated or finely chopped (see note)

Freshly ground black pepper

20 grape leaves (see note)

2 dried bay leaves

1 lemon, sliced

300 g (10½ oz) minced (ground) lamb

1 tablespoon extra virgin olive oil

1 tablespoon raw almonds, chopped

+

Pinch of salt flakes

Per serve (per serve of 2 dolmades)

energy	protein	tot. fat	sat	poly	mono	carb	sugars	fibre
430 kJ / 100 Cal	7 g	7 g	2 g	1 g	4 g	2 g	2 g	2 g

NUTRITION BLOCKS PER SERVE

½ PLANT   ½ PROTEIN   0 CARB   ½ FAT

* The nutrition analysis does not include serving suggestions.

King prawn and avocado smash

Bored with the usual store-bought dips and chips for entertaining? While you can get some healthy ones, they're not all that inspiring, and the good ones can be expensive. This recipe is a little bit different and is utterly delicious. It's also packed with nutrition and light enough to serve as a pre-dinner nibble with drinks. The Mountain bread crackers are worth making as they are deliciously light and add just the right crunch.

Serves 6   Time 10 minutes   DF NF

Preheat the oven to fan-forced 160°C (315°F/Gas 2–3).

Lightly spray or brush the Mountain bread with extra virgin olive oil and bake for 5 minutes, or until golden brown and crispy. Remove from the oven and set aside to cool.

Meanwhile halve the avocado, remove the stone, scoop out the flesh and roughly chop. Place in a bowl and squeeze over the lime juice.

Roughly chop the tomatoes, coriander, mint and prawns, and place in a large bowl. Thinly slice the spring onions and add to the bowl. Season with salt and black pepper. Mix to combine and allow the flavours to infuse.

Break the crispy flatbreads into pieces, and serve with the king prawn and avocado smash.

Juice of ½ lime
6 cherry tomatoes, halved
2 handfuls coriander (cilantro), leaves picked
2 handfuls mint, leaves picked
2 spring onions (scallions), chopped
Freshly ground black pepper

6 cooked king prawns (shrimp) (about 100 g/3½ oz total), peeled and deveined, tails removed

4 wholegrain or rye Mountain breads (see note)

1 avocado (see note)
1 tablespoon extra virgin olive oil

+
Pinch of salt flakes

Notes If you can't find Mountain bread, any thin wholemeal flatbread will work, but the thinner the better.

Avocados are one of only two common fruits that are rich in fat—the other being olives—and both provide predominantly healthy monounsaturated fats. These fats can help you to achieve a healthier blood cholesterol profile, improve your insulin sensitivity, help you to control blood glucose levels, improve a fatty liver, and even reduce the amount of fat you store around your middle.

Per serve

energy	protein	tot. fat	sat	poly	mono	carb	sugars	fibre
635 kJ 150 Cal	6 g	9 g	2 g	1 g	6 g	9 g	1 g	2 g

NUTRITION BLOCKS PER SERVE

 **0** PLANT   **0** PROTEIN   **½** CARB   **½** FAT

Leek, thyme and goat's cheese tartlets

These tartlets are a fantastic finger food at a party, and also as a light meal with a generous mixed salad. They're most delicious when warm, so if you want to prepare them in advance, or use up leftovers, simply reheat in the oven for a few minutes to crisp up the pastry before serving.

Makes 24 tartlets   Time 40 minutes   NF

Preheat the oven to fan-forced 180°C (350°F/Gas 4). Line two 12-hole muffin tins with non-stick muffin cases.

Heat 1 tablespoon of the extra virgin olive oil in a frying pan over medium heat. Add the leek and thyme, and sauté for 2–3 minutes, until the leek is soft, but not browned (turn down the heat if you need to). Set aside to cool completely.

Whisk the eggs and milk in a pouring jug (pitcher) and season with a good grind of black pepper. Lay out all your filling ingredients—the sautéed leeks, shredded ham, goat's cheese and the whisked egg mixture—ready to assemble your tartlets.

Working quickly, lay out 1 sheet of filo and brush with a little of the olive oil. I like to drizzle a little oil over the length of the pastry in a zigzag pattern and then, using a pastry brush, brush the oil over the whole sheet (don't worry if it looks patchy). Place the second layer on top and repeat, then add the third layer. Cut the layered sheets into 4 even lengthways strips and then 6 crossways to make 24 squares. Push each square into your muffin tins with the sides extending up the sides of the holes.

Place a little leek mixture into the bottom of each tartlet case, then add the ham and goat's cheese. Pour the egg mixture into each tartlet and bake for 15 minutes or until the tartlets have risen and are slightly golden in colour. Remove from the oven and set aside to cool slightly in the tin. Remove after 4–5 minutes onto a wire rack to cool completely, or serve immediately.

Any leftover tartlets can be kept in the fridge for 3–4 days.

1 leek, white part and just a little of the green, thinly sliced

¼ teaspoon thyme leaves (or pinch of dried thyme)

freshly ground black pepper

3 free-range or organic eggs

125 ml (4 fl oz/½ cup) full fat milk (or you can use light milk if you prefer)

50 g (1¾ oz) ham off the bone, shredded

2 tablespoons soft goat's cheese (about 50 g/1¾ oz) (or feta)

3 sheets frozen filo pastry, thawed (see note)

60 ml (2 fl oz/¼ cup) extra virgin olive oil

Note Filo pastry needs to be used quickly, as it dries out fast. Only pull out the sheet you will be working with immediately, and have all of your ingredients ready to assemble the tartlets quickly.

Per serve (per serve of 4 tartlets)

energy	protein	tot. fat	sat	poly	mono	carb	sugars	fibre
760 kJ 180 Cal	7 g	14 g	4 g	1 g	8 g	6 g	2 g	<1 g

NUTRITION BLOCKS PER SERVE

 0 PLANT   **½** PROTEIN   **0** CARB   **½** FAT

Parmesan veggie muffins

Savoury muffins are delicious and make a fantastic alternative to sandwiches for lunch. Simply use them as your smart carb, team with a big salad as your plant food, add a little extra protein to the salad to match your blocks and dress with a drizzle of extra virgin olive oil and a squeeze of lemon. I also love them as my afternoon snack to boost my energy if I'm going to exercise after work. That helps to ensure I'm not so hungry come dinnertime that I overeat.

Serves 12   Time 45 minutes   NF V*

Preheat the oven to fan-forced 180°C (350°F/Gas 4). Line a 12-hole muffin tin with non-stick muffin cases.

Combine the flour, baking powder, oats, carrot, zucchini, sun-dried tomatoes and parmesan in a large bowl. Mix well so that the flour coats the veggies, preventing them from sticking together.

In a separate bowl, whisk the eggs, then add the extra virgin olive oil and yoghurt. Mix well and then add the wet ingredients to the dry. Finally, add the milk, a little at a time, as you may not need it all. Add just enough to give you a thick but moist dough. Do not over-mix or the muffins will be heavy.

Spoon the dough into the muffin cases and bake for 25–30 minutes, until brown on top and cooked through.

Remove from the oven and set aside to cool slightly in the tin. After 4–5 minutes remove from the tin onto a wire rack to cool completely, or serve immediately.

The cooled muffins can be stored in an airtight container for 2 days. If you're not likely to use them up in that time (or don't want to be tempted to eat too many!) pop the extras in individual freezer bags once cooled and freeze for up to 3 months. Let them defrost at room temperature and they are best warmed in the oven for a few minutes before eating.

1 carrot, grated
1 zucchini (courgette), grated
40 g (1½ oz/¼ cup) sun-dried tomatoes

60 g (2¼ oz/⅔ cup) grated parmesan cheese (vegetarians, see note)
2 free-range or organic eggs
200 g (7 oz/¾ cup) natural yoghurt
125 ml (4 fl oz/½ cup) light milk

300 g (10½ oz/2 cups) stoneground wholemeal flour
2 teaspoons baking powder
25 g (1 oz/¼ cup) rolled (porridge) oats

60 ml (2 fl oz/¼ cup) extra virgin olive oil

Note* In order to be called 'parmesan' this cheese has to be produced using traditional methods, which includes the use of animal rennet. To make this recipe suitable for vegetarians, you can purchase a similar style hard cheese made with rennet obtained from micro-organisms. These will clearly be labelled as vegetarian.

Per serve

energy	protein	tot. fat	sat	poly	mono	carb	sugars	fibre
795 kJ 190 Cal	8 g	8 g	2 g	1 g	4 g	20 g	3 g	4 g

NUTRITION BLOCKS PER SERVE

 **0** PLANT **½** PROTEIN **1** CARB **0** FAT

Salads

Roast veggie salad with pomegranate dressing

This is one of my favourite salads, ever. With the vibrant mix of colours, the depth of flavour from the roast veggies and the crunch from the pomegranate, it's a feast for the eyes as well as the tastebuds. The dressing is vital to inject the right flavours into the salad and the secret ingredient is pomegranate molasses (see note). If you can't get your hands on fresh pomegranate you can make this salad without it. You could just add some roasted red capsicum (pepper) instead.

Serves 4   Time 45 minutes   DF GF NF V Ve

Preheat the oven to fan-forced 180°C (350°F/Gas 4).

Cut the pumpkin into slices or chunks, cut the red onion into quarters, and toss together in a bowl with the extra virgin olive oil, the salt and plenty of black pepper. Spread out on a baking tray and roast for 30 minutes, turning over about halfway through the cooking process so they caramelise nicely all over. This can be done ahead of time and left at room temperature covered with foil. You can also use them straight away for a warm version of this salad.

Bring a saucepan of water to the boil over high heat. Put the broccolini in a steamer, cover with the lid and place on top of the pan. Cook for 1 minute, or until tender but take care not to overcook—the veggies should still have a little crunch. Remove from the steamer and rinse under cold running water to stop the cooking process. This will maintain bite and the vibrant green of the veggie. (Alternatively, place the broccolini in a microwave-proof bowl with a little water, cover and microwave on High for about 1 minute.)

To make the pomegranate dressing, put the garlic, pomegranate molasses, lemon juice, pomegranate arils, maple syrup, and olive oil into the small container of your Vitamix or use a hand-held blender—you will get a much smoother result with a Vitamix as it is much more powerful. Blend on the highest power level for about 30 seconds or until smooth.

Toss the rocket and broccolini in a bowl with half of the dressing, to coat, then place them in a serving bowl. Scatter over the roast veggies and the pomegranate arils. Drizzle with the remaining dressing and serve straight away.

Note Pomegranate molasses is the juice from tart pomegranates, reduced to form a thick, dark red liquid. It's commonly used in Turkish and Iranian cuisines. You'll find it in speciality grocers or those that stock Middle Eastern products.

A tablespoon adds 150 kJ (35 Cal) and 7 g of sugars to the total dish—so not significant when you divide that between four serves.

½ small kent pumpkin (winter squash), skin on

1 red onion

Freshly ground black pepper

100 g (3½ oz) broccolini

120 g (4¼ oz) rocket (arugula) leaves

120 g (4¼ oz) pomegranate arils (seeds) (the amount from about ½ pomegranate)

1 tablespoon extra virgin olive oil

+
Pinch of salt flakes

Pomegranate dressing

½ garlic clove

1 tablespoon pomegranate molasses (see note)

1 tablespoon lemon juice

1 tablespoon pomegranate arils (seeds)

1 teaspoon pure maple syrup

60 ml (2 fl oz/¼ cup) extra virgin olive oil

See recipe photo on page 2.

Per serve

energy	protein	tot. fat	sat	poly	mono	carb	sugars	fibre
1080 kJ 260 Cal	5 g	19 g	3 g	2 g	13 g	14 g	12 g	6 g

NUTRITION BLOCKS PER SERVE

3 PLANT **0** PROTEIN **0** CARB **1** FAT

Adzuki bean and tuna salad

I love a salad that I can throw together quickly using ingredients from my pantry and a few fresh veggies from the fridge. This one uses tinned tuna, tinned adzuki beans and quinoa—all ingredients you can stock in your pantry. I always have some sort of leafy greens and vary this recipe depending on what I have to hand. Spinach, watercress or a mixed lettuce pack all work equally well, although I do love the peppery taste of rocket.

Serves 4   Time 20 minutes   DF GF NF

Put the quinoa in a saucepan and cover with water. Drain in a sieve and repeat. This washes away the bitter compounds, called saponins, on the surface. Return to the pan and add 500 ml (17 fl oz/2 cups) of fresh water. Bring to the boil, then reduce the heat to a simmer and cook for about 15 minutes or until the water has been absorbed and the quinoa is cooked.

To make the dressing, mix the extra virgin olive oil, lemon juice and black pepper together in a small jar.

Mix the cooked quinoa, tuna, adzuki beans, rocket, spring onions, cucumber, lemon zest and avocado together in a large bowl. Toss through the dressing and serve on individual plates or in a serving bowl, sprinkled with sunflower seeds and a generous grind of black pepper.

120 g (4¼ oz) rocket (arugula) leaves
2 spring onions (scallions), sliced
1 Lebanese (short) cucumber, finely chopped
Grated zest of ½ lemon
Freshly ground black pepper

425 g (15 oz) tinned tuna in spring water, drained
420 g (15 oz) tinned adzuki beans, drained and rinsed (see note)

200 g (7 oz/1 cup) quinoa

½ avocado, chopped
1 tablespoon sunflower seeds

Lemon and pepper dressing
Juice of 1 lemon
Freshly ground black pepper

1 tablespoon extra virgin olive oil

Note Adzuki beans, as with other legumes, are particularly rich in folate. This B group vitamin is not just for those planning a pregnancy. A folate-rich diet is important for all of us as it protects against DNA damage. This makes beans terrific anti-ageing foods. This recipe provides 180 mg of folate—that gets you almost halfway there towards meeting your recommended intake for the day.

If you can't find them tinned, most health food stores stock dried adzuki beans. Just soak them for a few hours (or overnight), refresh the water and bring to the boil, reduce the heat to a simmer and cook until soft (about an hour). They're totally yum, so worth it!

Per serve

energy	protein	tot. fat	sat	poly	mono	carb	sugars	fibre
1840 kJ 440 Cal	32 g	14 g	3 g	4 g	7 g	39 g	4 g	10 g

NUTRITION BLOCKS PER SERVE

3 PLANT   1 PROTEIN   1 CARB   1 FAT

Chargrilled salmon, roast beetroot and quinoa salad

On a warm day, salad is just the ticket, but, I admit, it can get boring. This salad is anything but, with the addition of roast beetroot and baby carrots, a crunchy mix of red cabbage, quinoa, the slightly tart tang of blood orange and the fresh flavours of dill and mint. This complex flavour mix works wonderfully with the rich salmon. Although it takes half an hour to make this one from scratch, you can prepare it all in advance—just keep the dressing and the salmon separate.

Serves 4 Time 30 minutes DF GF NF

Preheat the oven to fan-forced 180°C (350°F/Gas 4). Line two small baking trays with baking paper.

Put the quinoa in a saucepan and cover with water. Drain in a sieve and repeat. This washes away the bitter compounds, called saponins, on the surface. Return to the pan and add 250 ml (9 fl oz/1 cup) of fresh water. Bring to the boil, then reduce the heat to a simmer and cook for about 15 minutes or until the water has been absorbed and the quinoa is cooked. Drain if any liquid remains and set aside to cool.

Place the carrots and beetroot onto one of the prepared trays. Lightly spray or brush with the extra virgin olive oil and season with plenty of black pepper. Roast for 15–20 minutes until tender and slightly deepened in colour. Remove from the oven and set aside to cool.

Meanwhile, place the salmon fillet on the second prepared tray, skin side down. Roast in the oven for 10 minutes. Remove the skin and break the flesh into large flakes.

Toss together the cooked quinoa, herbs, cabbage and spinach leaves and place on a serving plate. Assemble the roasted carrots, beetroot and blood orange segments around the quinoa and cabbage.

To make the dressing, shake the ingredients in a small jar to combine well and then pour over the salad. Top with the salmon and serve straight away. (See note.)

12 baby carrots, washed and trimmed

8 baby beetroot (beets), peeled and quartered

Freshly ground black pepper

2 tablespoons roughly chopped dill

2 tablespoons roughly chopped mint leaves

200 g (7 oz/¼ head) red cabbage, thinly sliced

90 g (3¼ oz/2 cups) baby English spinach, leaves washed

2 blood oranges, segmented

400 g (14 oz) salmon fillet, skin on

200 g (7 oz/1 cup) quinoa

2 teaspoons extra virgin olive oil

Orange and dijon mustard dressing (see note)

1 tablespoon blood orange juice (about ¼ juice from whole fruit)

Freshly ground black pepper

2 tablespoons extra virgin olive oil

+

1 teaspoon dijon mustard

Note If you're not ready to serve immediately, reserve the dressing and pop the salad in the fridge. Only add the dressing once you are ready to serve.

Per serve

energy	protein	tot. fat	sat	poly	mono	carb	sugars	fibre
1930 kJ 460 Cal	28 g	24 g	5 g	4 g	12 g	28 g	16 g	9 g

NUTRITION BLOCKS PER SERVE

3 PLANT   1 PROTEIN   1 CARB   1 FAT

Eggplant and tahini salad

Eggplant is a veggie I was never wild about, until I discovered I just hadn't eaten it prepared in the right way. That's so often the case. We think we don't like a food, but then try it in a different dish and suddenly it comes alive. This dish is responsible for my conversion to becoming an eggplant lover! The combination of grilled eggplant with the rich but tangy tahini dressing and the crunchy pomegranate and pistachios, is an absolute winner.

Serves 4 Time 15 minutes GF V

Slice the eggplant lengthways into 1 cm (½ inch) thick slices. Heat a barbecue plate, griddle pan or grill to high, brush the eggplant with the extra virgin olive oil and grill for 1–2 minutes on each side until lightly golden. Remove from the heat and set aside to cool.

Mix together the tahini, lemon juice, cumin and yoghurt in a small mixing bowl. Season with plenty of freshly ground black pepper.

Lay the eggplant on a serving dish, slightly overlapping one another. Drizzle with the tahini dressing. Scatter the mint, lemon zest and pomegranate arils over the top. Drizzle with the remaining extra virgin olive oil and top with the pistachios. Serve immediately.

1 large eggplant (aubergine) (see note)
Juice and grated zest of 1 lemon
¼ teaspoon ground cumin
Freshly ground black pepper
2 handfuls mint, leaves torn
½ pomegranate, arils (seeds) removed

1 tablespoon natural yoghurt

1 tablespoon unhulled tahini
1 tablespoon extra virgin olive oil
1 tablespoon pistachio nut kernels

Note Eggplant—or aubergine in Europe—is actually a fruit, but like tomatoes we think of them and eat them as vegetables. We don't often think of them as being particularly nutritious, but in fact they have much to offer us. Like most vegetables, eggplants are low in kilojoules, with 100 g (3½ oz) of eggplant containing only 100 kJ (24 Cal), while supplying 6 per cent of your folate and manganese for the day, and 8 per cent of your potassium for women and 6 per cent for men. You'll also get small amounts of vitamin C, vitamin K and B group vitamins.

Per serve

energy	protein	tot. fat	sat	poly	mono	carb	sugars	fibre
540 kJ 130 Cal	3 g	9 g	1 g	2 g	5 g	6 g	6 g	5 g

NUTRITION BLOCKS PER SERVE

1 PLANT 0 PROTEIN 0 CARB 1 FAT

Tofu, ginger and brown rice salad with sesame hoisin dressing

This is one of my favourite salads. It has a few different elements, but don't be daunted as there is nothing tricky and it's so worth making. The secret lies in the special dressing, using homemade hoisin sauce as the base. Alternatively, you can of course use a store-bought hoisin sauce, but do look for an authentic, good quality one.

Serves 2 as a main meal or 4 as part of a shared meal
Time 45 minutes or 15 minutes if using pre-cooked rice DF GF NF V Ve

Put the rice in a saucepan with 500 ml (17 fl oz/2 cups) of water. Place over high heat and bring to the boil. Reduce the heat to a simmer and cook with the lid on for about 30 minutes until the rice is tender. Drain if there is any liquid left (there shouldn't be much, if any) otherwise simply turn off the heat, fluff with a fork and allow to cool.

To make the dressing, whisk together the hoisin sauce, ginger, lime juice, sesame oil, extra virgin olive oil and sesame seeds in a small bowl.

Toss all of the salad ingredients together in a large bowl, then pour over the dressing and stir to coat. Divide between plates to serve or, if part of a meal, serve on a platter in the centre of the table to share.

Note Brown rice is nutritionally superior to white rice as only the outer husk of the grain is removed. This retains some fibre and many of the nutrients that are lost in making white rice. It has a nuttier taste that I for one prefer—it may take a little getting used to but I'm willing to bet you'll be a convert if you stick with it! It does take longer to cook than white rice, but you can also purchase ready-cooked brown rice in microwavable pouches. These are perfectly acceptable and make for quick easy meals.

Half a cup of cooked brown rice provides 23 per cent of your phosphorus for the day, 22 per cent of your niacin, 20 per cent of your magnesium, 16 per cent of your thiamin, 14 per cent of your zinc and 12 per cent of your vitamin E. You'll also get smaller but significant amounts of iodine and iron.

15 g (½ oz) snow pea (mangetout) sprouts

90 g (3¼ oz) baby English spinach leaves, washed

2 handfuls coriander (cilantro), leaves picked

½ red onion, sliced

115 g (4 oz/1 cup) bean sprouts (sometimes called mung bean sprouts)

1 celery stalk, thinly sliced

1 tablespoon thinly sliced pickled ginger

½ Lebanese (short) cucumber, sliced

4 handfuls mint, leaves shredded

150 g (5½ oz) firm tofu, diced

140 g (5 oz/⅔ cup) brown rice (see note)

Sesame hoisin dressing

1 teaspoon finely grated ginger

Juice of ½ lime

1 teaspoon sesame oil

1 tablespoon extra virgin olive oil

1 teaspoon sesame seeds

+

1 tablespoon hoisin sauce (preferably homemade, see page 155)

Per serve

energy	protein	tot. fat	sat	poly	mono	carb	sugars	fibre
1120 kJ 270 Cal	9 g	10 g	2 g	3 g	5 g	32 g	3 g	6 g

* The nutrition analysis is for serving 4. Simply double the figures if serving 2 as a main meal.

NUTRITION BLOCKS PER SERVE

 2 PLANT ½ PROTEIN 1 CARB ½ FAT

Thai beef salad

This is my take on a classic Thai beef salad. The amount of beef in this recipe is to give one Protein Block per serve. If you are on a higher energy level, simply make this recipe serve two instead so that you get 2 Protein Blocks. You can of course also just increase the amount of meat, but since those on higher energy levels also need more plant food I encourage you to be generous on that front, too!

Serves 4   Time 15 minutes   DF GF NF

Heat a grill plate or frying pan over high heat. Brush the meat with the extra virgin olive oil and add to the grill plate or pan. Cook for 3 minutes on each side, lowering the heat as necessary to prevent the meat from charring. Turn off the heat, cover with foil and allow to rest for 10 minutes.

Combine the salad leaves, capsicum, cucumber and herbs in a large bowl and toss well. Place on a large platter.

Combine the dressing ingredients in a small jar and shake well.

Once the meat has rested, slice and arrange on the salad and drizzle the dressing over the top. Scatter over the sliced spring onions, bean sprouts and chilli, if using. Serve.

230 g (8½ oz/4 cups) mixed Asian salad leaves

1 red capsicum (pepper), thinly sliced

2 Lebanese (short) cucumbers, thinly sliced

2 handfuls mint, leaves picked

2 handfuls Thai basil, leaves picked

Handful coriander (cilantro), leaves picked

6 spring onions (scallions), sliced

115 g (4 oz/1 cup) bean sprouts (sometimes called mung bean sprouts)

1 large red chilli, sliced, to serve (optional)

360 g (12¾ oz) lean beef (fillet or rump)

2 teaspoons extra virgin olive oil

Thai dressing

1 small red chilli

2 garlic cloves, crushed

1 tablespoon thinly sliced lemongrass

Juice of 1 lime

1 tablespoon rice malt syrup (see note)

1 teaspoon sesame oil

+

1 tablespoon fish sauce

Note Rice malt syrup (also sold as brown rice syrup) is produced by cooking brown rice flour with enzymes to break down the starch into the constituent sugars. The mixture is then filtered and the water removed to give a thick, sweet-tasting syrup. It is traditionally used in China and Japan as a sweetener in both sweet and savoury dishes, such as to create the glaze on Peking duck. It has become popular in health circles of late, but really it is no healthier than any other type of sugar. But just like other sugars, I see no problem in using it in small quantities. The bottom line is that a little sweetness in our lives is perfectly okay—the saying 'the poison is in the dose' is most apt when talking about sugar.

Per serve

energy	protein	tot. fat	sat	poly	mono	carb	sugars	fibre
870 kJ 210 Cal	23 g	8 g	3 g	1 g	4 g	8 g	7 g	4 g

NUTRITION BLOCKS PER SERVE

 3 PLANT  **1** PROTEIN   **0** CARB   **0** FAT

Vietnamese pork salad

I love the fresh flavours of Vietnamese food. In this recipe the Thai basil, chilli and fresh lime juice give a real zing to the salad. It's light, incredibly tasty and rich in protein to keep hunger pangs at bay. As is traditional in this dish, I've used vermicelli noodles. These are very thin noodles made from rice. Do look for those made with brown rice. They are a little harder to find but many supermarkets and health food stores now stock them. (See note.)

Serves 4   Time 20 minutes   DF GF

Put the noodles in a large bowl and cover with boiling water. Leave to soak for about 5 minutes until soft and tender. Strain off the water and rinse the noodles under cold water to stop the cooking process. Set aside.

Heat the extra virgin olive oil in a frying pan over medium heat. Add the pork and pan-fry for about 8 minutes, turning a few times to brown on all sides and cook through. Remove the meat from the pan and set aside to rest for 2–4 minutes.

Meanwhile, put the prepared veggies in a bowl and combine with the noodles. Make the dressing by mixing together the lime juice, fish sauce and brown sugar in a small bowl. Drizzle over the salad and toss to combine.

Slice the pork to the thickness of your liking, add to the bowl and toss. Serve sprinkled with the chopped peanuts and dried shallots.

2 long red chillies, sliced (optional)

4 spring onions (scallions), sliced

1 red capsicum (pepper), thinly sliced

2 carrots, julienned

4 handfuls Thai basil, leaves picked

100 g (3½ oz) snow peas (mangetout), trimmed and sliced

1 Lebanese (short) cucumber, thinly sliced

40 g (1½ oz/⅓ cup) bean sprouts (sometimes called mung bean sprouts)

2 tablespoons dried shallots, to serve (you'll find these in good grocers or Asian food stores—you can simply omit if you can't find them)

400 g (14 oz) pork fillet

160 g (5½ oz) rice vermicelli noodles (preferably brown, see note)

1 tablespoon extra virgin olive oil

50 g (1¾ oz/⅓ cup) chopped unsalted peanuts, to serve

Vietnamese dressing

Juice of 1 lime

+

60 ml (2 fl oz/¼ cup) fish sauce (check this is a gluten-free brand if coeliac)

1 tablespoon soft brown sugar

Note Because the portion size is small, and its combined with plenty of protein and good fats which slow digestion, even if you use regular vermicelli noodles the result is a well-balanced, nutritious meal. If you are coeliac do double check that the noodles are made from 100 per cent rice and therefore gluten free.

Per serve

energy	protein	tot. fat	sat	poly	mono	carb	sugars	fibre
1300 kJ 310 Cal	29 g	13 g	2 g	3 g	7 g	18 g	9 g	5 g

NUTRITION BLOCKS PER SERVE

 3 PLANT   **1** PROTEIN   **1** CARB   **½** FAT

Black barley, kale and poached chicken salad

I came across black barley at a café in Sydney one day and absolutely loved it. It has a nutty, wonderfully rich flavour, which works really well with more robust leaves, such as kale, and the succulent poached chicken.

Serves 4 Time 50 minutes DF NF

Preheat the oven to fan-forced 180°C (350°F/Gas 4).

Put the black barley in a saucepan and cover with plenty of water. Bring to the boil, then reduce the heat to a simmer. Cover with the lid and cook for about 45 minutes until soft but not mushy. Test a grain of barley to check that it is ready, then drain in a sieve and run under cold water to cool and keep the grains nicely separated.

While the barley is cooking, peel the beetroot, place on a baking tray and brush or spray with olive oil. Roast for 20–30 minutes until tender.

Meanwhile, put the chicken in a large saucepan and cover with water. Add the slice of lemon, the parsley stems, celery leaves and the peppercorns to the pan. (Alternatively you can poach the chicken in plain water—these additions just add a little more flavour.) Bring to a simmer and cook for about 10 minutes, until the chicken looks cooked and feels firm when pressed. Turn off the heat and leave the chicken in the hot liquid. It will continue cooking, but not dry out. Discard the poaching ingredients.

Brush or spray the zucchini and asparagus with extra virgin olive oil. Heat a non-stick frying pan over medium–high heat, add the zucchini and asparagus and chargrill for 2–3 minutes turning until nicely golden.

To make the honey and mustard dressing, combine all the ingredients in a jar. Shake to mix well.

Bring a saucepan of water to the boil over high heat. Put the kale in a steamer, cover with the lid and place on top of the pan. Cook for 2 minutes, or until just softened. Remove and rinse under cold running water to stop the cooking process. This will ensure it stays a lovely bright colour. (Alternatively, place the kale in a microwave-proof bowl with a little water, cover and microwave on High for about 2 minutes before running under cold water.)

Toss the black barley, kale, green peas, chopped parsley leaves and half the dressing together in a bowl. Divide between two plates. Arrange the roast beetroot and the chargrilled zucchini and asparagus around the sides. Finally, slice the poached chicken and layer on top. Drizzle with the remaining dressing and serve straight away.

Note If you can't find black barley, use regular pearl barley.

4 beetroot (beets)

1 lemon slice

Large handful flat-leaf (Italian) parsley, a few stems reserved, leaves roughly chopped

A handful leafy tops from a celery bunch

6 black peppercorns

2 zucchini (courgette), sliced lengthways

16 asparagus spears

200 g (7 oz) kale, stalks removed and leaves ripped into smaller pieces

80 g (2¾ oz /½ cup) shelled green peas (or frozen and thawed)

- 400 g (14 oz) skinless chicken breast fillet

- 90 g (3¼ oz/½ cup) black barley (see note)

- 2 teaspoons extra virgin olive oil

Honey and mustard dressing

Juice of ½ lemon

Freshly ground black pepper

1 teaspoon pure floral honey

2 tablespoons extra virgin olive oil

+

1 teaspoon dijon mustard

Per serve

energy	protein	tot. fat	sat	poly	mono	carb	sugars	fibre
1630 kJ 390 Cal	30 g	16 g	3 g	2 g	7 g	25 g	12 g	11 g

NUTRITION BLOCKS PER SERVE

 **3** PLANT   **1** PROTEIN   **1** CARB   **1** FAT

Greens and freekeh salad with pomegranate

Salads are a terrific way of boosting your plant food intake and I encourage you to get adventurous instead of using the same old ingredients every time. Smart carbs, such as cooked wholegrains, work really well in salads and that's what I've used here. The result is a deliciously robust salad that will fill you up and leave you feeling sated. For a vegan-friendly meal, simply substitute pure maple syrup for the honey.

Serves 4 Time 30 minutes DF NF V

Cook the freekeh for about 20 minutes or according to the packet instructions.

Heat the extra virgin olive oil in a frying pan over medium heat. Add the zucchini to the pan and cook for about a minute on each side until nicely charred.

Bring a saucepan of water to the boil. Place the broccolini and kale in a steamer and place over the boiling water. Steam for about 2 minutes or until just tender. Take care not to overcook—the veggies should retain their crunch. Remove from the pan and run under cold water to stop the cooking process and retain their bright green colour. Drain in a colander.

To make the pomegranate honey dressing, combine the extra virgin olive oil, pomegranate molasses, honey and lemon juice in a jar. Shake to mix well.

Mix the veggies in a serving bowl with the freekeh and drizzle over the dressing. Toss to combine, then scatter over the pomegranate arils. Serve.

2 zucchini (courgette), sliced

200 g (7 oz) broccolini, cut into bite-sized chunks

200 g (7 oz) kale, stalks removed and roughly chopped

120 g (4¼ oz) pomegranate arils (seeds) (the amount from about ½ pomegranate)

150 g (5½ oz/1 cup) cracked roasted freekeh (see note)

1 tablespoon extra virgin olive oil

Pomegranate honey dressing

Juice of ½ lemon

1 tablespoon pomegranate molasses

1 teaspoon honey

1 tablespoon extra virgin olive oil

Note Freekeh is an ancient Eastern Mediterranean grain food, made from roasted green wheat. Because the grain is harvested while young it has a far higher nutrient content, including more protein, than mature wheat. It's super-rich in fibre with four times that found in brown rice, has a low GI and is a good source of iron, magnesium, thiamin, copper and zinc. A good portion of the carbohydrate present is resistant starch, but also promotes the growth of good bacteria in your gut. This is important for gut health, but also boosts your immune system at the same time.

If you're coeliac, do note that freekeh is not gluten free.

If you can't find freekeh, you can use barley, burghul (bulgur) or, for gluten-free options, buckwheat or brown rice.

Per serve

energy	protein	tot. fat	sat	poly	mono	carb	sugars	fibre
1260 kJ 300 Cal	11 g	11 g	3 g	2 g	7 g	35 g	10 g	10 g

NUTRITION BLOCKS PER SERVE

 2 PLANT   0 PROTEIN  0 CARB   1 FAT

Superfood salad with tahini dressing

There are many everyday superfoods that are readily available to most of us in the supermarket. Here I've combined a selection of these to create the most stunning salad. The quinoa, almonds and tahini provide a significant amount of protein, making it a terrific vegan and vegetarian meal option. But, if you like, you can boost the protein further by adding a little chicken, red meat or fish using your Protein Blocks for the day.

Serves 4 Time 25 minutes DF GF V Ve

Put the quinoa in a saucepan and cover with water. Drain in a sieve and repeat. This washes away the bitter compounds, called saponins, on the surface. Return to the pan and add 375 ml (13 fl oz/1½ cups) of water. Bring to the boil, then reduce the heat to a simmer and cook for about 15 minutes or until the water has been absorbed and the quinoa is cooked.

Bring a separate saucepan of water to the boil over high heat. Put the kale, broccolini and asparagus in a steamer, cover with the lid and place on top of the pan. Cook for 2 minutes, or until just tender. Drain and rinse under cold running water to stop the cooking process. This will ensure they stay a lovely bright colour. (Alternatively, place the veggies in a microwave-proof bowl with a little water, cover and microwave on High for 2 minutes before running under the cold tap.)

Toss all the salad ingredients, except the micro herbs, if using, and the chia seeds in a serving bowl.

To make the dressing, whisk all the ingredients in a small bowl and add enough water to give a nice runny consistency. Drizzle over the salad.

Scatter over the micro herbs, if using, and the chia seeds. Serve.

- 200 g (7 oz) kale, stalks removed and leaves torn into pieces
- 125 g (4½ oz/1 bunch) broccolini, cut into bite-sized pieces
- 4 asparagus spears, sliced into bite-sized pieces (see note)
- 140 g (5 oz) mixed lettuce leaves
- ½ carrot, shredded using a mandolin or finely grated
- ½ red onion, thinly sliced
- Handful basil, leaves picked
- Handful flat-leaf (Italian) parsley, leaves picked
- 100 g (3½ oz) snow peas (mangetout), trimmed and thinly sliced diagonally
- 2 tablespoons micro herbs (such as micro rocket and radish, optional to serve, see note)

- 135 g (4¾ oz/⅔ cup) quinoa

- 40 g (1½ oz/¼ cup) almonds, roasted and roughly chopped
- 1 tablespoon pepitas (pumpkin seeds)
- 1 tablespoon sunflower seeds
- ½ avocado
- 1 tablespoon chia seeds, to serve

Tahini dressing

- Juice of ½ lemon
- 1 teaspoon pure maple syrup
- 2 tablespoons unhulled tahini

Notes Asparagus contains a pretty spectacular array of vitamins and minerals, including vitamin A, vitamin B6, vitamin C, vitamin K, thiamin, riboflavin, niacin, folate, iron, phosphorus, potassium, copper and manganese. Depending on where it is grown it can also be an excellent source of the antioxidant mineral selenium. If any vegetable gets to be called a 'superfood', asparagus should definitely qualify!

If you're making this salad for guests and want to add that extra touch, micro herbs add to the beauty of the dish, as well as adding another subtle dimension of flavour. For this dish, I suggest micro rocket and radish.

Per serve

energy	protein	tot. fat	sat	poly	mono	carb	sugars	fibre
1730 kJ 410 Cal	16 g	25 g	3 g	9 g	11 g	26 g	6 g	11 g

NUTRITION BLOCKS PER SERVE

3 PLANT **0** PROTEIN **1** CARB **1** FAT

Warm chicken and haloumi salad with tomato salsa

You'll be surprised how deliciously tasty this is with such simple ingredients. There are no smart carbs in this salad—so it's great for a light dinner if you have already used up all your blocks through the day, or have been sitting on your bum and just don't need them! If you need a more substantial meal, though, and have a Carb Block or more to use up, add some wholegrain sourdough to mop up the juices, or toss through some quinoa, tinned beans or lentils.

Serves 4 Time 1 hour 20 minutes GF NF

Put the chicken in a bowl and add the lemon juice, garlic and extra virgin olive oil. Cover with plastic wrap, place in the fridge and leave to marinate for at least an hour. (See note.)

To make the salsa, mix the tomato, onion, parsley, lemon juice and extra virgin olive oil in a bowl. Season with a pinch of salt and plenty of freshly ground black pepper. It's important to make the salsa early and set it aside as the longer you leave it the better; the salt draws out the juice from the tomato and creates the dressing for this dish.

When ready to cook and of course eat (as this really is a meal that you need to eat as soon as it's cooked), heat your barbecue to medium–high or a frying pan over medium heat. Add the chicken and cook for 4–5 minutes on each side until golden brown and cooked through (turn down the heat as needed to prevent the outside of the meat burning). When it's almost finished cooking, add the haloumi to the grill or pan and cook for 1 minute on each side or until golden in colour.

Pile the mixed lettuce or rocket onto each plate, top with the grilled haloumi and chicken, and spoon the tomato salsa dressing over the top, drizzling the juices over the leaves. Serve straight away.

Juice of ¹⁄₂ lemon

2 garlic cloves, crushed

200 g (7 oz) mixed lettuce or rocket (arugula)

360 g (12³⁄₄ oz) skinless chicken breast fillets (see note)

120 g (4¹⁄₄ oz) haloumi cheese, sliced

1 tablespoon extra virgin olive oil

Tomato salsa (see note)

4 tomatoes, finely diced

1 red onion, finely diced

4 tablespoons finely chopped flat-leaf (Italian) parsley

Freshly ground black pepper

Juice of ¹⁄₂ lemon

2 tablespoons extra virgin olive oil

+

Pinch of salt flakes

Note To save time for a mid-week dinner, pop the chicken in its marinade and make your salsa in the morning. That way when you get home in the evening, it'll only take you 20 minutes to cook and have it on the table.

Per serve

energy	protein	tot. fat	sat	poly	mono	carb	sugars	fibre
1420 kJ 340 Cal	30 g	21 g	6 g	2 g	11 g	6 g	6 g	4 g

NUTRITION BLOCKS PER SERVE

2 PLANT **1** PROTEIN **0** CARB **1** FAT

Soups

Chicken, quinoa and kale soup

I love soups that are the Dr Joanna Plate in a bowl. Pure veggie soups are great for snacks or an entrée to boost the plant content of your meal, but on their own they lack protein and the filling power of a low GI carb. Here I've teamed protein-rich chicken with low GI quinoa and the nutrient-packed, star food kale. This is one of my firm favourites, but do be sure to use a really good quality stock for flavour (see my recipe in the note below).

Serves 4   Time 40 minutes   DF GF NF

Heat the extra virgin olive oil in a soup pot over medium heat. Add the onion, garlic and celery and sauté for a few minutes until soft. Add the carrot and sauté for a couple of minutes more.

Add the stock to the pot, bring up to the boil, reduce the heat until just simmering and add the chicken breast. Cook for about 15 minutes or until the chicken is cooked through. Remove the chicken from the pot and shred.

Add the quinoa to the pot and simmer for 15 minutes or until the quinoa is cooked.

Add the kale and shredded chicken. Taste and, if it needs it, add a little salt and plenty of freshly ground black pepper. Simmer until the kale is wilted and serve immediately (otherwise the kale will lose its gorgeous bright green colour).

1 brown onion, finely chopped

1 garlic clove, finely chopped

2 celery stalks, finely chopped

2 carrots, finely diced

130 g (4½ oz) kale (or other robust greens such as silverbeet/Swiss chard or savoy cabbage), stalks removed and leaves shredded

Freshly ground black pepper

250 g (9 oz) skinless chicken breast fillet

100 g (3½ oz/½ cup) quinoa, rinsed

1 tablespoon extra virgin olive oil

+

1 litre (35 fl oz/4 cups) chicken stock (preferably homemade, see note, or good quality store-bought)

¼ teaspoon iodised salt

Note You can make your own chicken stock using either the leftover carcass of a roast chicken, a raw carcass or using a whole chicken where you can then shred the meat to use separately. Using raw bones results in a lighter stock, whereas using leftovers from a roast chicken gives you a richer flavour. Simply add the bones to a soup pot and add a quartered onion (skin on), a chopped carrot, 3–4 garlic cloves bashed with the back of a knife (skins on), a handful of celery leaves, 2 dried bay leaves, 6 black peppercorns and a handful of parsley stems. Cover with water, bring to the boil, reduce the heat and simmer gently for 3–4 hours. Turn off the heat and leave to cool. Strain into a bowl and discard the solids. Refrigerate overnight and then skim off the fat that will solidify on the surface. The stock will then keep in the fridge for 4–5 days or freeze for 4–6 months.

Per serve

energy	protein	tot. fat	sat	poly	mono	carb	sugars	fibre
1010 kJ 240 Cal	20 g	8 g	1 g	2 g	4 g	20 g	5 g	5 g

NUTRITION BLOCKS PER SERVE

2 PLANT   1 PROTEIN   1 CARB   0 FAT

White bean and root vegetable soup

Beans work really well in soups and are a great addition to vegetarian and vegan diets as a source of protein. But I encourage even the most dedicated meat-eaters to add beans into their weekly menu plan at least a couple of times. They add serious fibre and are among the lowest GI sources of carbohydrate, so are fantastic to boost your energy levels. A serve of this soup delivers an impressive 10 g of fibre, putting you well on your way towards your target of 25–30 g per day.

Serves 4   Time 30 minutes   DF GF NF V Ve

Heat the extra virgin olive oil in a soup pot over medium heat. Add the onion, carrots, celery, garlic and Italian herbs, and sauté for 3 minutes or until the veggies are softened. Add the turnip, sweet potato, parsnip, beans, stock and 375 ml (13 fl oz/1½ cups) of water, and bring to the boil. Reduce the heat to a simmer and cook, covered, for 20 minutes until the veggies are tender. Add the kale for the final 5 minutes of cooking. (See note.)

Taste and then adjust the seasoning, adding a pinch of salt if needed and plenty of black pepper. Spoon into four bowls, sprinkle with parsley and serve.

½ brown onion, diced

2 carrots, diced

2 celery stalks, diced

2 garlic cloves, diced

1 teaspoon dried Italian herbs (or a mix of dried oregano, basil, marjoram and thyme)

1 turnip, chopped

200 g (7 oz) kale, stalks removed and leaves shredded

Freshly ground black pepper

Handful flat-leaf (Italian) parsley, leaves roughly chopped

400 g (14 oz) tinned cannellini beans, drained and rinsed (see note)

1 small sweet potato (about 150 g/5½ oz), unpeeled, scrubbed and chopped

1 parsnip, chopped

1 tablespoon extra virgin olive oil

+

500 ml (17 fl oz/2 cups) vegetable stock (preferably homemade, or good quality store-bought)

Pinch of salt flakes

Notes Nutritionally, cannellini beans are pretty fabulous. They are high in protein and fibre, they have a very low GI of 31, and are low in fat. A half a cup of cooked beans provides 6 g of protein, 11 g of carbohydrate, 6 g of fibre and 0.5 g of fat, all for only 325 kJ (78 Cal). They are an excellent source of folate with that same half a cup providing 74 µg (19 per cent of an adult's recommended daily intake or RDI) and a good source of niacin (11 per cent RDI for women, 10 per cent for men) and iron (8 per cent RDI for women, 19 per cent for men). You'll also get a significant dose of magnesium, phosphorus and zinc.

For a thicker, creamier soup remove half the cooked veggies and beans, purée, then return to the pot before serving.

Per serve

energy	protein	tot. fat	sat	poly	mono	carb	sugars	fibre
780 kJ 190 Cal	8 g	6 g	1 g	1 g	3 g	21 g	10 g	10 g

NUTRITION BLOCKS PER SERVE

 3 PLANT   **½** PROTEIN   **1** CARB   **0** FAT

Supergreens soup

While green smoothies have gained all the accolades, what about a green soup for those days when something warm is what you need? I'm a massive fan of soups and this one is a terrific way of boosting your plant food intake in a totally delicious way. I make a big pot to keep in the fridge and then have it for lunch with wholegrain bread and cheese to complete my Dr Joanna Plate. I also have it on its own as a low kilojoule, tasty snack that delivers a serious nutrient boost.

Serves 6 Time 25 minutes DF GF NF V Ve*

Heat the extra virgin olive oil in a soup pot over medium heat. Add the onion, ginger, garlic and celeriac and sauté for a few minutes until the onion is translucent and the celeriac is starting to brown.

Add the stock and 500 ml (17 fl oz/2 cups) of water, and season with the salt and black pepper. Increase the heat to high and bring to the boil, then reduce the heat and simmer for 10 minutes with the lid on.

Add the broccoli and cook for a further 4–5 minutes until the broccoli is tender. Add the watercress and spinach, put the lid on and cook for 1–2 minutes until the leaves begin to wilt. Do not let the soup cook for too long at this point or you'll lose the lovely bright green colour.

Carefully transfer the soup into a food processor or Vitamix. Blend for a couple of minutes (on level 10 if using a Vitamix) until completely smooth and creamy. You will probably have to do this in two batches.

Divide the soup among six bowls and, provided you're not dairy-free, add a dollop of yoghurt or crumble over some feta. Sprinkle with parsley and serve.

1 brown onion, diced

1 tablespoon chopped or grated ginger

2 garlic cloves, crushed

1 whole (600 g/1 lb 5 oz) celeriac, peeled and diced (or the same weight of cauliflower)

Freshly ground black pepper

200 g (7 oz/1 head) broccoli, cut into florets

185 g (6½ oz) watercress, roughly chopped (see note)

200 g (7 oz) English spinach, leaves washed and roughly chopped

Handful flat-leaf (Italian) parsley, leaves chopped, to serve

150 g (5½ oz) natural yoghurt or feta cheese* (optional—omit if dairy free or vegan)

2 tablespoons extra virgin olive oil

+

500 ml (17 fl oz/2 cups) vegetable stock (preferably homemade, or good quality store-bought)

1 teaspoon iodised salt

Note Watercress has an exceptionally high vitamin K content—a cup provides your requirement for the day. It is also rich in the carotenoids lutein and zeaxanthin, essential for good eye health. If you don't eat dairy products, consider eating more watercress to boost your calcium intake—100 g (3½ oz) of this peppery leafy veg contains 120 mg of calcium, that's 12 per cent of the average adult's daily requirement.

Per serve

energy	protein	tot. fat	sat	poly	mono	carb	sugars	fibre
530 kJ 125 Cal	6 g	7 g	1 g	<1 g	4 g	8 g	5 g	8 g

NUTRITION BLOCKS PER SERVE

3 PLANT   **0** PROTEIN   **0** CARB   **0** FAT

* The nutrition analysis does not include the natural yoghurt or feta serving suggestions.

Protein-packed lamb and lentil soup

When you think of a high protein meal, I'm guessing soup wasn't front of mind. Yet this recipe ticks all the boxes for high protein, plus being low GI, high fibre and nutrient-packed (including a serious boost of iron and zinc). Soups like this are a terrific staple for your *Get Lean, Stay Lean* weekly menu plan. Make a big pot and freeze in single serve portions. That way you always have a homemade ready-prepared meal to hand for quick lunches or easy suppers. Delicious!

Serves 4   Time 1 hour 30 minutes   DF GF NF

Heat 2 teaspoons of the extra virgin olive oil in a large heavy-based saucepan over medium–high heat. Add the meat and cook for about 5 minutes, turning frequently to brown all over (you can do this in batches). Remove the meat from the pan and set aside.

Heat the remaining olive oil in the saucepan, add the onion, garlic, carrot and celery, and sauté for 3–4 minutes until softened. Return the lamb to the pan, add the stock, tomatoes, thyme and bay leaf, and season with black pepper. Simmer, covered, for 30–40 minutes.

Rinse the lentils under cold water to remove any impurities. Add the lentils to the soup and cook for a further 30 minutes or until the lentils are softened. Taste before adding a little salt and plenty of black pepper. Serve topped with the fresh parsley.

1 brown onion, finely chopped

2 garlic cloves, crushed

1 carrot, diced

1 celery stalk, diced

400 g (14 oz) tinned whole tomatoes, roughly chopped

1 teaspoon dried thyme

1 dried bay leaf

Freshly ground black pepper

1 tablespoon flat-leaf (Italian) parsley leaves, to serve

400 g (14 oz) lean boneless lamb, diced (see note)

100 g (3½ oz/½ cup) split red lentils

1 tablespoon extra virgin olive oil

+

1 litre (35 fl oz/4 cups) vegetable or chicken stock (preferably homemade, see note page 113 for chicken stock, or good quality store-bought)

¼ teaspoon iodised salt, or to taste

Note There are concerns that a high intake of red meat may increase your risk of bowel cancer. However, the evidence is not as strong as it is for processed meats. It may be that those who eat lots of red meat are not eating enough veggies alongside. Or it may be down to how the meat is cooked. For example, high heat searing of meat that chars the surface, as with a very hot barbecue, creates carcinogenic compounds. On the other hand, red meat is an excellent source of iron and zinc, minerals that are often low in our diets. If you enjoy your red meat, soups like this are an excellent way to gain the benefits while minimising any risk. The meat is cooked slowly and gently, a little goes a long way as the soup is filling, and the meat is accompanied with stacks of veggies. Win-win!

Per serve

energy	protein	tot. fat	sat	poly	mono	carb	sugars	fibre
1230 kJ / 295 Cal.	31 g	12 g	3 g	1 g	6 g	16 g	5 g	6 g

NUTRITION BLOCKS PER SERVE

2 PLANT   1 PROTEIN   1 CARB   0 FAT

Hearty chicken and barley soup

While in summer I'm happy to get my veggies in salads, wraps and smoothies, in winter soup is definitely the way to go. We should eat differently then, and we need hot meals to warm us up from the inside out. Soups fit the bill and the added bonus is that, made in the right way, they are low in energy density, but high in nutrient density. Exactly what we want to see on the Dr Joanna Plate. And just as importantly, they need to rank high on taste!

Serves 4   Time 1 hour 30 minutes   DF NF

Heat the extra virgin olive oil in a soup pot over medium heat. Add the onion and sauté for a few minutes until translucent. Add the carrot, celery and garlic, and sauté for a few minutes more until softened.

Add the stock, chicken and barley. Bring to the boil, then reduce the heat until the stock is simmering. Cover with the lid and simmer for 45–60 minutes until the barley is soft and slightly chewy.

Add the broccoli and continue to cook for 2–3 minutes until soft. Finally, add the parsley and stir through. Season to taste with salt and black pepper. Serve in warmed bowls. (See note.)

2 brown onions, finely chopped

2 carrots, finely diced

2 celery stalks, diced

2 garlic cloves, finely chopped

200 g (7 oz/1 head) broccoli, cut into small bite-sized pieces

Handful flat-leaf (Italian) parsley, leaves roughly chopped

Freshly ground black pepper

400 g (14 oz) skinless chicken breast fillet, cut into small strips

150 g (5½ oz/¾ cup) pearled barley

1 tablespoon extra virgin olive oil

+

2 litres (70 fl oz/8 cups) chicken stock (preferably homemade, see note page 113, or good quality store-bought)

¼ teaspoon iodised salt, or to taste

Note This soup includes everything you need for a balanced meal—it's the Dr Joanna Bowl! The plant food is plentiful with all the veggies, the protein levels are high thanks to the chicken, the smart carb is the barley (low GI and bountiful fibre—1 serve gets you a third of the way towards your daily target of 30 g) and a dash of healthy fat from the extra virgin olive oil.

Even if you're on your own, make the full batch and either keep the remainder in your fridge for other meals—it will last for 3–4 days— or pop into the freezer in individual serves.

Per serve

energy	protein	tot. fat	sat	poly	mono	carb	sugars	fibre
1400 kJ 310 Cal	32 g	10 g	2 g	2 g	5 g	30 g	5 g	10 g

NUTRITION BLOCKS PER SERVE

 2 PLANT   **1** PROTEIN   **1** CARB   **0** FAT

Soba noodle soup with teriyaki pork and greens

I absolutely love Asian-style soups. They really are a meal in a bowl and can easily be adjusted to match the Dr Joanna Plate. This version uses beautifully lean pork, marinated in a teriyaki-style sauce as the protein, soba noodles as the smart carb, a combination of sesame and extra virgin olive oils as the good fat, and a generous portion of greens as the veggies. You could even add additional veggies to the broth if you like.

Serves 4　Time 45 minutes　DF GF NF

Combine all the ingredients for the marinade in a bowl and whisk to combine. Add the pork fillet and coat well with the marinade. Marinate for 30 minutes or longer if you have time.

Heat the extra virgin olive oil in a frying pan over medium heat. Remove the pork from the marinade (reserving the marinade) and add to the pan. Fry on all sides for about 7–8 minutes until golden brown and cooked through, basting with the leftover marinade as you cook. Be careful not to overcook or the meat will be tough; pork can be slightly pink in the middle. Remove from the pan, cover with foil, and set aside to rest.

Heat the chicken stock in a large saucepan over medium heat and add the sesame oil, tamari and rice wine. Stir to combine and bring to a gentle boil, then reduce the heat to a simmer until you are ready to serve.

Bring a large saucepan of water to the boil and add the soba noodles. Boil rapidly for 4 minutes, drain into a colander and run the noodles under cold water. Strain off the water and portion among soup bowls.

Bring a saucepan of water to the boil over high heat. Put the bok choy in a steamer, cover with the lid and place on top of the pan. Cook for 2 minutes, or until softened. (Alternatively, place the bok choy in a microwave-proof bowl with a little water, cover and microwave on High for about 1 minute.) The bok choy should still have a little crunch and retain their bright green colour.

Slice the pork fillet and place on top of the prepared noodles along with the bok choy, then pour over the hot stock. Sprinkle the pork with sesame seeds and serve immediately.

Note If you're following a gluten-free diet, be sure to check the ingredients list of the soba noodle packet. Authentic soba noodles should be 100 per cent buckwheat, but some may have wheat flour mixed in. I like to buy the authentic ones, regardless, as they are delicious and work really well in soups and salads. They are a step above most other noodles as they are rich in fibre.

- 4 bok choy (pak choy)
- 360 g (12¾ oz) pork fillet
- 270 g (9½ oz) dried soba (buckwheat) noodles (see note)
- 1 tablespoon extra virgin olive oil
- 1 teaspoon sesame oil
- 1 teaspoon sesame seeds, to serve

+

- 1 litre (35 fl oz/4 cups) chicken stock (preferably homemade, see note page 113, or good quality store-bought)
- 2 teaspoons tamari
- 1 tablespoon Shaoxing rice wine (Chinese cooking wine, available at leading supermarkets and Asian food stores)

Teriyaki marinade

- 1 teaspoon finely grated ginger
- 2 tablespoons pure maple syrup
- ½ teaspoon sesame oil

+

- 2 tablespoons brown rice vinegar
- 1½ tablespoons tamari
- 2 tablespoons mirin

Per serve

energy	protein	tot. fat	sat	poly	mono	carb	sugars	fibre
1410 kJ 340 Cal	27 g	10 g	2 g	2 g	5 g	31 g	12 g	5 g

NUTRITION BLOCKS PER SERVE

1 PLANT　1 PROTEIN　1 CARB　½ FAT

Enoki mushroom dashi broth with salmon

Mushrooms have a wealth of beneficial compounds, particularly the more exotic ones such as the ones used here. In this recipe I've teamed this star food with another—omega-3-rich salmon—and low GI gluten-free soba noodles. It sounds exotic, but it's really quick and easy. You can buy instant dashi and miso in the Asian food section of the supermarket. To complete your Dr Joanna Plate for this meal I suggest serving it with a lovely Asian green salad or steamed Asian veggies.

Serves 4 Time 20 minutes *DF GF NF*

Bring 1 litre (35 fl oz/4 cups) of water to the boil in a large saucepan. Add the dashi, miso, tamari, mirin, rice wine and sesame oil. Stir to combine. Add the mushrooms and simmer for about 5 minutes until the mushrooms are softened and tender.

Heat a chargrill pan over medium–high heat and add the salmon fillets, skin side down. Cook for 2–3 minutes, or until the skin is nice and crispy. Turn and cook for about 2 minutes on the other side, or to your liking. If you prefer your salmon to be cooked through, turn the heat down, pop the lid on and cook for a further 1–2 minutes.

Bring a large saucepan of water to the boil and add the soba noodles. Boil rapidly for 4 minutes, drain into a colander and run the noodles under cold water. Divide the noodles among four bowls.

Pour over the broth. Place the salmon fillet, mushrooms, spring onion and coriander on top. Serve immediately.

- 250 g (9 oz) enoki mushrooms
- 8 shiitake mushrooms (see note)
- 1 spring onion (scallion), thinly sliced
- Small handful coriander (cilantro), leaves picked

- 4 x 100 g (3½ oz) salmon fillets, skin on

- 180 g (6½ oz) dried soba (buckwheat) noodles

- A few drops of sesame oil

+
- 10 g (¼ oz) instant dashi
- 1 tablespoon miso paste
- 60 ml (2 fl oz/¼ cup) tamari
- 2 tablespoons mirin
- 2 tablespoons Shaoxing rice wine (Chinese cooking wine, available at leading supermarkets and Asian food stores)

Note Shiitake mushrooms originated in Asia where they have been consumed and used medicinally for thousands of years. Some of the earliest books on Asian herbal medicine discuss the therapeutic value of the shiitake mushroom. Today scientific research is uncovering various phytochemicals in shiitakes, and other mushrooms, which may account for the legendary health benefits.

Per serve

energy	protein	tot. fat	sat	poly	mono	carb	sugars	fibre
2015 kJ 480 Cal	38 g	15 g	4 g	4 g	5 g	42 g	6 g	6 g

NUTRITION BLOCKS PER SERVE

 1 PLANT   1 PROTEIN  2 CARB   1 FAT

Soto ayam (Balinese chicken soup)

Street vendors in Bali sell this soup in the hot humid climate, not only to fill people's bellies with goodness, but also to keep them hydrated. It's refreshing, tasty and filling with a good balance of protein and low GI carbs. There aren't quite enough plant foods to complete your Dr Joanna Plate, so I'd add a handful of greens, such as bok choy (pak choy) or another Asian leafy green. Alternatively, you could serve this with an interesting mixed leaf salad with Asian dressing.

Serves 4 Time 25 minutes DF GF NF

Fill a saucepan with water, place over high heat and bring to the boil. Add the eggs and boil for 8 minutes. Remove from the heat, drain and run under cold water until cool enough to handle. Peel and quarter the hard-boiled eggs.

Meanwhile, bring the chicken stock to the boil in a soup pot over high heat. Add the chicken breast to the stock, reduce the heat to a simmer and poach for 15 minutes or until the chicken is cooked through. Remove the chicken from the stock and shred the meat.

Add the carrot to the stock and simmer for 5 minutes or until softened.

Bring a large saucepan of water to the boil and add the soba noodles. Boil rapidly for 4 minutes, drain into a colander and run the noodles under cold water.

Portion the noodles and shredded chicken into four bowls.

Pour over the hot stock, dividing the carrot between the bowls. Top with the boiled eggs, kaffir lime leaves, coriander, tomato and spring onion. Serve immediately.

2 carrots, diced

3 kaffir lime leaves, finely shredded

Handful coriander (cilantro), leaves picked

2 tomatoes, cut into small dice

1 spring onion (scallion), thinly sliced

4 free-range or organic eggs (see note)

250 g (9 oz) skinless chicken breast fillet (see note)

270 g (9½ oz) dried soba (buckwheat) noodles (see note)

+

1 litre (35 fl oz/4 cups) chicken stock (preferably homemade, see note page 113, or good quality store-bought)

Note From a nutritional perspective this recipe is protein-rich, coming from the chicken and egg, the soba noodles add just the right amount of carbohydrate. Traditionally, rice vermicelli noodles would be used, but I much prefer soba noodles as they are low GI, wholegrain and gluten free (for those who need no gluten).

Per serve

energy	protein	tot. fat	sat	poly	mono	carb	sugars	fibre
1080 kJ 260 Cal	25 g	7 g	2 g	1 g	2 g	21 g	4 g	6 g

NUTRITION BLOCKS PER SERVE

 1 PLANT 1 PROTEIN 1 CARB   0 FAT

Black bean soup

Black beans are the key ingredient in this satisfying soup recipe. I've cooked them from scratch here as I think it really adds to the flavour of the dish, but if you'd prefer to use tinned black beans to speed up the cooking time, they are available so go ahead. You'll need to simmer your veggies for about half an hour, add the rinsed, tinned beans and simmer for a further 15 minutes or so to let the flavours develop. This soup freezes well.

*Serves 3   Time 3 hours 15 minutes (+ overnight soaking)   GF NF V**

Put the yoghurt in a bowl and add 300 ml (10½ fl oz) of water. Add the beans, add more water to ensure they are well covered and soak for at least 6 hours, or overnight. Discard the soaking yoghurty water and rinse the beans.

Heat the extra virgin olive oil in a soup pot over medium heat. Add the onion and sauté gently for 3 minutes or until translucent—don't brown. Add the thyme, cumin, coriander and garlic and cook for another 3 minutes, stirring often.

Add the beans, sweet potato, corn, carrot, capsicum, tomato paste and stock to the pot and stir to combine. Cover with the lid and slowly cook for 3 hours, checking the liquid now and again, adding extra water if it gets low.

The soup should be a lovely thick, chunky texture. Test a black bean to ensure they are cooked through. Add the tamari and chipotle sauce to taste, balancing the flavours to your liking. You can either leave the soup chunky, or I like to blend half of the soup in a Vitamix, then return to the pot of unblended soup. This gives you a creamier soup while maintaining the chunky texture with some whole beans.

Serve the soup with a dollop of yoghurt, chopped coriander and a grating of parmesan and enjoy!

1 brown onion, diced

1 teaspoon chopped thyme leaves

1 teaspoon ground cumin

1 tablespoon chopped coriander (cilantro) leaves, plus extra to serve

1 garlic clove, finely chopped or crushed

2 carrots, finely diced

1 red capsicum (pepper), finely diced

1 tablespoon no added salt tomato paste (concentrated purée)

1½ tablespoons natural yoghurt, plus extra to serve

220 g (7¾ oz/1 cup) black beans (see note)

40 g (1½ oz) parmesan cheese*, grated (vegetarians, see note page 93)

400 g (14 oz) sweet potato, peeled and diced

1 corn cob, kernels sliced off with a small sharp knife

1 tablespoon extra virgin olive oil

+

3 litres (105 fl oz/12 cups) vegetable stock (preferably homemade, or good quality store-bought)

1 tablespoon tamari

chipotle sauce, to taste

Note Legumes, such as black beans, are an amazing group of plant foods. They provide protein, low GI carbohydrates, all three types of fibre and a whole host of vitamins, minerals and phytonutrients. They are a particularly good source of folate, essential throughout our lives to help prevent DNA damage that ultimately is at the root of ageing, and they're one of the best plant sources of iron. We should be eating them more often.

Per serve

energy	protein	tot. fat	sat	poly	mono	carb	sugars	fibre
1240 kJ 300 Cal	19 g	9 g	3 g	1 g	4 g	36 g	10 g	13 g

NUTRITION BLOCKS PER SERVE

 1 PLANT 1 PROTEIN 1 CARB 0 FAT

Thai-inspired beef broth with omelette ribbons

This is a high protein, low carb soup that packs in flavour for a truly satisfying lunch or light dinner. You can, of course, add a smart carb if you have Carb Blocks left for the day—or just use those carbs for one of your snacks or other meals. You can also vary the veggies in this and swap the beef for chicken or pork as you prefer. The trick to making this soup flavoursome is the stock (see my recipe in the note below).

Serves 4 Time 20 minutes DF GF NF

Whisk the eggs in a bowl with a good grind of black pepper.

Heat 2 teaspoons of the extra virgin olive oil in a frying pan over medium heat until the oil starts to glisten. Pour the whisked eggs into the pan and swirl around to make a thin round omelette. Leave on the heat for 10 seconds, or until the eggs just set, then remove the frying pan from the heat, gently roll the omelette up and slide onto a chopping board. Slice the rolled omelette into strips about 5 mm (¼ inch) wide.

Divide the omelette ribbons between four soup bowls. Put the beef stock in a large saucepan and bring to a simmer.

Heat the frying pan over medium–high heat. Drizzle the beef with the remaining oil and season with salt and black pepper. Pan fry the beef for 2 minutes on both sides, depending on the way you like your steak and the thickness of the meat. (I recommend you under-cook the meat as it will continue to cook in the hot stock.)

Slice the meat and place on top of the omelette ribbons. Add the shiitake mushrooms and the green veggies. Pour over the hot beef stock and scatter over the chopped spring onion and coriander. Serve immediately.

Freshly ground black pepper
8 shiitake mushrooms, cut in half
120 g (4¼ oz/2 cups) chopped greens (such as bok choy/pak choy, choy sum or spinach leaves)
2 spring onions (scallions), thinly sliced
Handful coriander (cilantro), leaves picked

6 free-range or organic eggs
400 g (14 oz) beef fillet

1 tablespoon extra virgin olive oil

+

1 litre (35 fl oz/4 cups) beef stock (preferably homemade, see note, or good quality store-bought)
Pinch of salt flakes

Note To make your own beef stock, preheat the oven to fan-forced 200°C (400°F/Gas 6). Place 1 kg (2 lb 4 oz) raw beef bones, 2 quartered onions, 2 chopped carrots and 2 celery stalks into a roasting tin. Roast in the oven for 1½ hours, turning the bones and veggies occasionally. Transfer the roasted mixture into a soup pot and add a large handful of celery leaves, 2 bay leaves, 6 black peppercorns and a handful of parsley stems. Add 4 litres (140 fl oz/16 cups) of water, bring to the boil, then reduce the heat until just simmering and cook for roughly 3 hours. Turn off the heat and leave to cool completely. Drain over a bowl to reserve the liquid and discard the solids. Refrigerate overnight, then remove any fat from the surface. This makes about 2 litres (70 fl oz/8 cups) of stock. The stock will then keep in the fridge for 4–5 days, or pop in 500 ml (17 fl oz/2 cup) amounts in zip-lock bags in the freezer where it will keep for 4–6 months.

Per serve

energy	protein	tot. fat	sat	poly	mono	carb	sugars	fibre
1190 kJ 280 Cal	34 g	15 g	5 g	1 g	6 g	4 g	2 g	2 g

NUTRITION BLOCKS PER SERVE

2 PLANT   **2** PROTEIN   **1** CARB   **0** FAT

Seafood

Spanish seafood stew

When my parents visited recently my mum declared this her favourite dish from everything I cooked, even making me cook it again on their last night as a farewell meal. Since my mum is a pretty awesome cook I took that as a resounding success for this recipe. The trick to this one lies with the sauce. Don't cut corners in how long you sauté the veggies, and be sure to use a good quality extra virgin olive oil. You can really use any seafood you like.

Serves 4 Time 1 hour DF GF NF

Heat 2 tablespoons of the extra virgin olive oil in a large saucepan over medium heat. Add the onion and sauté for 3–4 minutes until soft and translucent (do not allow it to burn). Add the garlic and capsicum to the pan and continue to sauté for a further 10 minutes, stirring regularly. Don't cut this time short as this is important to develop a rich flavour for the sauce.

Add the tomatoes, paprika and white wine, bring to the boil, then reduce the heat and simmer for about 30 minutes.

When the sauce is almost ready, heat the remaining oil in a frying pan over medium heat. Add the prawns and fry for just a few minutes until they turn pink and slightly browned on the outside. Remove from the pan and set aside. Once cool enough to handle, remove the heads, peel and devein but leave the tails intact. (You can use the heads and shells to make a fish stock for another meal.) Alternatively, leave the prawns intact for diners to peel themselves at the table. They do look gorgeous in the final dish when serving.

Put the salmon, skin side down, into the same pan. Cook for 2–3 minutes or until the skin is crispy. Turn and add the squid to the pan. Cook for 2 minutes or until the squid is slightly browned, tossing the squid rings frequently so that they cook evenly. Be careful not to overcook—the salmon should still be pink in the middle. Turn off the heat. Remove the salmon skin and cut into 4 pieces.

Cut the perch into 4 pieces and add directly to the sauce to poach gently. Add the prawns, salmon, squid and the pipis. Put the lid on the pan so that the steam helps to cook and opens the pipis. This will only take 2–3 minutes. Do not overcook as the pipi meat will toughen if cooked for too long. Drizzle over the brandy, if using, and set alight with a match to burn off the alcohol. Sprinkle with micro rocket sprouts and serve immediately.

Notes You can buy prawns ready peeled, but these generally do not have as much flavour as those in their shells. Although it's a little work to peel, it's well worth the effort for the extra flavour.

1 red onion, finely diced

3 garlic cloves, finely chopped

1 red capsicum (pepper), finely diced

400 g (14 oz) tinned whole roma (plum) tomatoes, mashed or roughly chopped (buying them whole they are more flavourful than ready chopped)

1 tablespoon smoked paprika

micro rocket (arugula) sprouts (or flat-leaf/ Italian parsley), to serve

8 large raw king prawns (shrimp), deveined (see note)

150 g (5½ oz) salmon fillet, skin on

100 g (3½ oz) squid, cut into rings

150 g (5½ oz) perch fillet (or any white fish)

150 g (5½ oz) pipis (or vongole or clams)

60 ml (2 fl oz/¼ cup) extra virgin olive oil

+

250 ml (9 fl oz/1 cup) dry white wine

2 tablespoons brandy (optional)

See recipe photo on page 31.

Per serve

energy 1590 kJ 380 Cal | protein 38 g | tot. fat 20 g | sat 4 g | poly 3 g | mono 11 g | carb 7 g | sugars 6 g | fibre 3 g

NUTRITION BLOCKS PER SERVE

 1 PLANT  **2** PROTEIN   **0** CARB   **1** FAT

Chilli crab with black bean spaghetti

I usually try to use ingredients that are widely available and familiar to most. However, sometimes there are special ingredients worth mentioning. Look in health food aisles or Asian food stores for pastas made from black beans, mung beans or soy beans. Made from the ground bean mixed with water, they have four times the protein of regular pasta, are low in carbohydrates and have stacks of fibre. They are also gluten free. Experiment with them all!

Serves 4 Time 20 minutes DF GF NF

Heat 1 tablespoon of the extra virgin olive oil in a frying pan over medium heat. Add the onion, garlic, chilli and coriander stems (reserve the leaves), and gently fry for about 3 minutes until the onion is soft. Add the wine and continue to cook for a few minutes. Add the stock and lemon zest and simmer for 10 minutes or until the liquid is reduced by about half.

Meanwhile bring a large saucepan of water to the boil. Add 1 tablespoon of the extra virgin olive oil and a pinch of salt. Add the black bean spaghetti and simmer gently for 5–6 minutes until *al dente*. Drain.

Add the crab to the sauce and just heat through. Season with black pepper and a little salt to taste. Add the spinach leaves and the cooked spaghetti. Toss to combine.

Divide the chilli crab spaghetti among four bowls. Drizzle with the remaining olive oil, scatter over the coriander leaves, squeeze over the lemon juice and serve immediately.

1 red onion, finely diced

1 garlic clove, crushed

1 small red chilli (remove the seeds out if you don't like it hot!)

Handful coriander (cilantro), separated into stems and leaves

Juice and grated zest of 1 lemon

Freshly ground black pepper

150 g (5½ oz) baby English spinach leaves, washed

200 g (7 oz) dried black bean spaghetti (or dried mung bean or soy bean pasta)

400 g (14 oz) picked white crabmeat (you can buy this tinned or in a tub in the refrigerator section at the supermarket, see note)

60 ml (2 fl oz/¼ cup) extra virgin olive oil

+

125 ml (4 fl oz/½ cup) dry white wine

250 ml (9 fl oz/1 cup) fish stock (preferably homemade, see page 142, or good quality store-bought)

Pinch of salt flakes

Note We don't often think of crab as a particularly healthy food, but in fact it has so much to offer us. The nutrition of crabmeat does vary depending on the variety, but in general it is an excellent source of protein, is very low in fat and has no carbohydrate. It contains more water than chicken or red meat, so compared weight for weight it has only about half the kilojoules. It's a rich source of vitamin B12 and several minerals including zinc, phosphorus, copper, magnesium and selenium. It's also an excellent source of iodine with 100 g (3½ oz) of tinned crabmeat providing half of an adult's recommended daily intake.

Per serve

energy	protein	tot. fat	sat	poly	mono	carb	sugars	fibre
1350 kJ 320 Cal	36 g	12 g	2 g	1 g	7 g	7 g	6 g	12 g

NUTRITION BLOCKS PER SERVE

 2 PLANT   **1** PROTEIN  **0** CARB   **1** FAT

Nori-crusted salmon

I'm a huge salmon lover, so I'm always looking for new ways to prepare and serve it. Here I've teamed it with nori, and its salty sea flavour works perfectly with the succulent rich fish. Then served on a fresh, ginger-flavoured bed of soba noodles as the smart carb and a gorgeous mix of veggies.

Serves 4 Time 25 minutes DF GF NF

Put the nori sheets, salt, black pepper, chilli flakes, paprika and half of both the sesame seeds in a food processor or Vitamix and pulse until grainy (be careful not to over-process).

Heat 2 teaspoons of the extra virgin olive oil in a frying pan over medium heat. Add the onion, garlic and ginger and gently sauté for a few minutes until the onion is soft but not browned. Add the nori sesame mix and stir to combine over the heat for 1 minute to marry the flavours. Transfer to a bowl and set aside.

Heat the remaining oil in the pan, add the salmon and gently fry for 2–3 minutes on each side. Place the fillets in a baking dish and top with the nori mixture. (At this stage you can place them in the fridge until you are ready to cook if you want to prepare them ahead of time.)

Preheat the oven to fan-forced 200°C (400°F/Gas 6). Bring a large saucepan of water to the boil. Place the broccolini in a steamer and place over the boiling water to cook for 1–2 minutes or until tender. Remove and run under cold water to stop the cooking process and maintain the gorgeous bright green colour.

Add the soba noodles to the boiling water. Boil rapidly for 4 minutes or until *al dente*, drain into a colander and run the noodles under cold water twice. Place into a mixing bowl and combine with the carrot, spring onion, snow peas, broccolini and the remaining sesame seeds.

Put all the dressing ingredients in a jar and shake to combine. Pour over the soba noodle salad and toss to combine.

Put the salmon in the oven and bake for 5 minutes to cook through and crisp the top. Divide the soba noodle salad among four plates and top with the baked salmon. Enjoy hot or cold.

Note Atlantic salmon ranks among the richest food sources of the long chain omega-3 fats, EPA and DHA. Salmon is especially rich in DHA, the most abundant omega-3 fat in the brain and in the retina of the eye. DHA is therefore considered to be particularly important for brain health and functioning.

The long chain omega-3 fats are anti-inflammatory and so can be useful in treating arthritis, and may help to control asthma by lowering inflammation in the lungs.

4 nori sheets, torn into pieces
1 teaspoon freshly ground black pepper
1 teaspoon chilli flakes
2 teaspoon sweet paprika
1 red onion, finely diced
2 garlic cloves, crushed or finely chopped
1 teaspoon finely grated ginger
200 g (7 oz) broccolini, cut into bite-sized pieces
2 carrots, grated or finely julienned
2 spring onions (scallions), thinly sliced
200 g (7 oz) snow peas (mangetout), trimmed and thinly sliced

4 x 100 g (3½ oz) skinless salmon fillets (see note)

180 g (6½ oz) soba (buckwheat) noodles

1 tablespoon sesame seeds
1 tablespoon black sesame seeds
1 tablespoon extra virgin olive oil

+
Pinch of salt flakes

Ginger and sesame dressing

2 teaspoons finely grated ginger

1 tablespoon extra virgin olive oil (preferably light flavour)
2 teaspoons sesame oil

+
2 tablespoons brown rice vinegar
1 tablespoon tamari

Per serve

energy	protein	tot. fat	sat	poly	mono	carb	sugars	fibre
2280 kJ 545 Cal	36 g	26 g	5 g	6 g	12 g	37 g	5 g	7 g

NUTRITION BLOCKS PER SERVE

2 PLANT **1** PROTEIN **1** CARB **1** FAT

Chimichurri barbecued prawns

Chimichurri sauce originally comes from Argentina, but is now popping up everywhere with other herb variations. It's really a type of salsa verde and it adds a vibrant flavour—and stacks of antioxidants and other phytochemicals—to a simple grilled meal. This is my version, teamed here with succulent king prawns. To complete your meal, serve with an interesting salad that includes a smart carb such as freekeh, quinoa or beans.

Serves 4 Time 25 minutes DF GF NF

Put 20 wooden skewers (you'll need one skewer per prawn) in a bowl of water and leave to soak for 15 minutes. This helps to prevent the skewers from burning on the barbecue. Preheat the barbecue to hot.

Put the garlic, parsley, oregano, coriander and basil in a food processor or Vitamix and blitz until roughly chopped—if using a Vitamix do this on level 5 so that you maintain a rough texture rather than a smooth paste. Add the lemon juice, chilli, if using, extra virgin olive oil and red wine vinegar. Pulse a couple of times to combine, but be careful not to over blend. Set aside to marry the flavours. (See note.)

Skewer the prawns, brush with a little extra virgin olive oil and season with black pepper. Put the skewers on the barbecue hotplate or grill and cook for a couple of minutes on each side, just until the prawn is nicely pink.

Serve the prawn skewers with the chimichurri sauce on the side or drizzle over the hot prawns.

500 g (1 lb 2 oz/about 20) raw king prawns (shrimp), peeled and deveined, tails left intact (see note)

Chimichurri sauce (see note)

2 garlic cloves, roughly chopped

4 handfuls flat-leaf (Italian) parsley, leaves picked

2 tablespoons oregano leaves

4 handfuls coriander (cilantro), leaves picked

2 small handfuls basil, leaves picked

Juice of 1 lemon

1 teaspoon chilli flakes or 1 fresh red chilli (remove the seeds if you don't want too much heat, or leave the chilli out completely)

Freshly ground black pepper

250 ml (9 fl oz/1 cup) extra virgin olive oil, plus extra for basting

+

2 tablespoons red wine vinegar

Notes This recipe makes 600 g (1 lb 5 oz) of Chimichurri sauce but you won't use it all. The remaining sauce will keep in a screw-top jar in the fridge for a couple of weeks. It will solidify slightly, so be sure to remove about half an hour before using to allow it to come up to room temperature when the oil will liquefy. It goes equally well with grilled meat as it does with seafood.

Prawns are protein rich, relatively low in kilojoules and provide several key nutrients. They're rich in selenium—an essential mineral with antioxidant properties—and are a good source of iron, vitamin B12, phosphorus, copper and niacin. Not bad for a delicious food we can throw on the barbie for a quick meal!

Per serve

energy	protein	tot. fat	sat	poly	mono	carb	sugars	fibre
1020 kJ / 240 Cal	26 g	15 g	3 g	2 g	10 g	0 g	0 g	<1 g

NUTRITION BLOCKS PER SERVE

 0 PLANT  **1** PROTEIN **0** CARB   **1** FAT

* 25 g (a generous tablespoon) of chimichurri sauce is included in the analysis per serve.

Coconut fish fingers, sweet potato chips and broccolini

I grew up in Scotland where on the odd occasion my mum would buy us all a newspaper-wrapped pack of fat greasy chips and battered fish for dinner. I've got fond memories of those meals, but they weren't the healthiest, so I set out to make a *Get Lean, Stay Lean* worthy version that tasted just as good, and felt even better. And here it is—coconut fish fingers and sweet potato chips, baked rather than deep-fried, and broccolini to give a powerful phytonutrient boost.

Serves 4 Time 40 minutes DF NF

Preheat the oven to fan-forced 180°C (350°F/Gas 4). Line two baking trays with baking paper. Cut the sweet potato into chip shapes and lay out on one of the prepared trays. Brush with extra virgin olive oil. Sprinkle with a little sea salt and bake in the oven for 30 minutes or until golden brown. Give them a shake a couple of times during cooking to ensure they crisp up on all sides.

Cut the fish into finger shapes. Whisk the egg with a fork in a bowl. In a separate bowl mix the coconut with the breadcrumbs. Dip the fish in the egg and then coat with the coconut mixture. Lay on the second baking tray. Add to the oven halfway through cooking the sweet potato chips—the fish will only take around 15 minutes. They should look slightly browned. Do not overcook or the fish will dry out.

Bring a saucepan of water to the boil. Place the broccolini in a steamer and place over the boiling water. Steam for 2 minutes or until tender. (Alternatively, place the broccolini in a microwave-proof bowl with a little water, cover and cook on High for 2 minutes, or until tender.) Take care not to overcook—the broccolini should be slightly crunchy and retain its bright green colour.

Mix the sweet potato chips with the broccolini spears and pile onto plates, top with the fish fingers and serve.

- 200 g (7 oz) broccolini
- 440 g (15½ oz) skinless snapper fillets
- 1 free-range or organic egg
- 2 sweet potatoes (about 600 g/1 lb 5 oz), unpeeled and scrubbed
- 2 slices day-old sourdough grainy bread, made into breadcrumbs (see note)
- 1 tablespoon extra virgin olive oil
- 35 g (1¼ oz/½ cup) shredded coconut

+

Pinch of salt flakes

Note If using fresh bread, crisp up slightly in the oven first. For those needing a gluten-free version, you can either omit the breadcrumbs and just coat with the coconut (it's just not quite so crispy this way), or mix with a gluten-free crumb mixture.

Per serve

energy	protein	tot. fat	sat	poly	mono	carb	sugars	fibre
1610 kJ 385 Cal	31 g	14 g	7 g	1 g	4 g	29 g	10 g	7 g

NUTRITION BLOCKS PER SERVE

1 PLANT   1 PROTEIN   1 CARB   1 FAT

Spanakopita fish pie

Who doesn't love a fish pie? But usually they are rich with butter and cream, and have a heavy fat-laden pastry topping. The *Get Lean, Stay Lean* version ticks so many nutritional boxes, yet you won't believe how delicious this is until you try it. The protein-rich fish, egg and cheese filling, combined with nutrient-rich silverbeet makes my nutritionist heart sing! Serve with steamed greens or a crunchy, mixed salad.

Serves 8 Time 1 hour 30 minutes NF

Trim the stems of the silverbeet and discard; wash the leaves and shred. Place in a large bowl and stir through the dill and spring onion.

In a separate bowl, lightly whisk the eggs. Crumble in the feta and ricotta, add the pecorino and fish and season with black pepper. (The feta is salty enough so you do not need extra salt.)

Combine the egg mix with the silverbeet using your hands—run your hands under cold water first to prevent the mixture sticking. Mix well. Set aside.

Preheat the oven to fan-forced 180°C (350°F/Gas 4).

Lightly brush or spray a 20 x 30 cm (8 x 12 inch) baking dish with extra virgin olive oil. Lay the filo out on your work surface, one sheet at a time, and lightly brush each sheet with the oil. Place the first three sheets on top of one another on the bottom of the dish.

Pour the silverbeet mixture on top of the 3 layers of filo, then top with the remaining 3 sheets of filo (ensuring they too have been lightly brushed with oil), layering one on top of another. Tuck in any overhanging filo into the sides of the baking dish. This seals your pie.

Using a sharp knife, score the pastry into diamond shapes and lightly sprinkle with water. Bake for 40–60 minutes or until well browned. Cover with foil if over browning.

Shake the dish to release the sides when you remove it from the oven. Serve.

320 g (11¼ oz) silverbeet (Swiss chard)
Handful dill, chopped
4 spring onions (scallions), chopped
Freshly ground black pepper

5 free-range or organic eggs
200 g (7 oz) feta cheese (see note)
100 g (3½ oz) fresh full fat ricotta cheese (see note)
50 g (1¾ oz/½ cup) finely grated pecorino or parmesan cheese (see note)
500 g (1 lb 2 oz) skinless blue eye fillets (or other firm white fish), chopped into small diced chunks

6 sheets frozen filo pastry, thawed

60 ml (2 fl oz/¼ cup) extra virgin olive oil

Note Although government dietary guidelines continue to recommend low fat dairy products, recent studies have questioned this. All dairy foods, including full fat, have been shown to be helpful for weight control when part of a balanced diet. Meanwhile, heart disease research has shown that when consumed as cheese, milk or yoghurt, dairy foods do not raise cholesterol levels. There are also beneficial nutrients in dairy fat including fat-soluble vitamins and specific fats that seem to be beneficial. Taking all this into account I much prefer to use full fat cheeses in my recipes and just watch overall portion size. Plus full fat cheese tastes infinitely better!

Per serve

energy	protein	tot. fat	sat	poly	mono	carb	sugars	fibre
1250 kJ 300 Cal	24 g	18 g	8 g	1 g	8 g	8 g	2 g	1 g

NUTRITION BLOCKS PER SERVE

1 PLANT 1 PROTEIN 0 CARB 1 FAT

* The nutrition analysis does not include serving suggestions.

Mussels in rich tomato sauce with chickpeas

Shellfish is a terrific choice with sustainability in mind (see note). Here I've teamed them with chickpeas for slow-release smart carbs and stacks of fibre, all in a velvety rich tomato sauce. Gentlemen, this is a particularly good dish for you, being rich in zinc and lycopene—both necessary for men's health. So tuck in! Team with a salad or whatever other veggies you like. If you have Carb Blocks left, add some grainy sourdough to mop up the sauce.

Serves 4   Time 25 minutes   DF GF NF

Heat the extra virgin olive oil in a large pot over medium heat. Add the onion and garlic and sauté for a few minutes until the onion has softened. Add the fennel and sauté for a few minutes more.

Add the tomatoes and white wine to the pan and simmer for about 10 minutes to allow the flavours to develop. Add the chickpeas and plenty of black pepper. Stir well.

Add the mussels and cover with the lid. Shake the pan every minute or so, leaving the lid on; the steam will cook the mussels. Within about 5 minutes all of the shells should be open. Scatter with basil leaves and chilli if using. Serve straight away.

2 red onions, finely diced

4 garlic cloves, finely chopped

1 fennel bulb, finely chopped

800 g (1 lb 12 oz) tinned whole roma (plum) tomatoes, chopped or mashed (buying them whole they are more flavourful than ready chopped)

Freshly ground black pepper

2 handfuls basil, leaves roughly torn

1 large red chilli, thinly sliced (optional)

2 kg (4 lb 8 oz) mussels, scrubbed and de-bearded (you can buy them this way, see note)

800 g (1 lb 12 oz) tinned chickpeas, drained and rinsed

2 tablespoons extra virgin olive oil

+

250 ml (9 fl oz/1 cup) dry white wine

Note From a nutritional and environmental perspective, mussels get 5 stars. Nutritionally, they are rich in several nutrients including iron, zinc and iodine, all commonly low in our diets. They are also protein-rich and have a good amount of omega-3 fats present.

Environmentally, they are a sustainable seafood option and they don't carry the risks of mercury contamination. We need to be eating fewer large fish nearer the top of the food chain, as well as those species that have been overfished and are at risk. Eating more shellfish helps to boost our levels of important nutrients, easing the strain on fish availability. Shellfish have also been a part of human diets for millennia, so for those interested in evolutionary diets, these should definitely be on your plate!

Per serve

energy	protein	tot. fat	sat	poly	mono	carb	sugars	fibre
1760 kJ 420 Cal	31 g	15 g	2 g	4 g	7 g	36 g	11 g	12 g

NUTRITION BLOCKS PER SERVE

1 PLANT   1 PROTEIN   1 CARB   1 FAT

Snapper en papillote

If you're worried about cooking fish, start with this recipe. You really can't go wrong. Wrapping fish in baking paper means no fish stuck to the pan or the barbecue and it cooks quickly without any fuss. Plus, you needn't worry about much cleaning up afterwards! I love this dish and make variations regularly (see note).

Serves 4 Time 30 minutes DF GF NF

Preheat the oven to fan-forced 180°C (350°F/Gas 4).

Cut four rectangles of baking paper, large enough to make an enclosed parcel for each fish fillet. Arrange half the lemon slices, and half the onion in the centre of each paper. Lay the snapper fillets on top and then top with the remaining lemon slices, onion and the bay leaves. Drizzle each one with a teaspoon of wine and a teaspoon of extra virgin olive oil, and season with a tiny pinch of salt and good grind of black pepper.

Bring together the two long sides of the baking paper to enclose each fish fillet, fold the top edge down three or four times and crease well. Twist the ends or fold in towards the centre and secure with skewers to create a pouch. Bake for 15–20 minutes then remove from the oven and rest for 5 minutes before opening.

Meanwhile, as soon as you put the fish in the oven, put the quinoa in a saucepan and cover with water. Drain in a sieve and repeat. This washes away the bitter compounds, called saponins, on the surface. Return to the pan and add 500 ml (17 fl oz/2 cups) of water. Bring to the boil, then reduce the heat to a simmer and cook for about 15 minutes or until the water has been absorbed and the quinoa is cooked. Fold the silverbeet through the hot quinoa to wilt.

While the quinoa is cooking, toss the broccolini and beans in the remaining tablespoon of oil. Place the broccolini on a baking tray and season with a pinch of salt and pepper. Bake for 7 minutes, then add the beans and bake for a further 3–4 minutes until the veggies are golden and tender-crisp.

Carefully open the fish parcel—hot steam will be released. Discard the bay leaves and garnish with parsley.

Serve the fish in the opened paper parcels with the roasted green veg and silverbeet quinoa on the side.

1 lemon, thinly sliced

1 red onion, thinly sliced

4 bay leaves (fresh or dried)

Freshly ground black pepper

4 silverbeet (Swiss chard) leaves, washed and chopped

200 g (7 oz) broccolini (see note)

180 g (6½ oz) green beans, trimmed (see note)

Handful flat-leaf (Italian) parsley, leaves torn

4 x 120 g (4¼ oz) snapper fillets, skin on (see note)

200 g (7 oz/1 cup) quinoa

2 tablespoons extra virgin olive oil

+

1 tablespoon dry white wine (or good-quality fish or vegetable stock or simply water)

Pinch of salt flakes

Note Rather than the roast veggies you could just serve a salad. I'll often then mix the cooked quinoa through the salad rather than serving separately. You can also vary the fish—this works equally well with salmon, trout or any white fish.

Per serve

energy	protein	tot. fat	sat	poly	mono	carb	sugars	fibre
1710 kJ 410 Cal	34 g	14 g	2 g	3 g	8 g	32 g	5 g	9 g

NUTRITION BLOCKS PER SERVE

 3 PLANT   1 PROTEIN 1 CARB 1 FAT

Citrus fish with pistachio quinoa tabouleh

This is such a refreshing, light, yet tasty dish that it's perfect for those nights when you're heading out and don't want to feel weighed down, or when you've had a bigger lunch and want a lighter dinner. Herbs are so often just thought of as flavourings, but in fact they are packed with nutrients and are among the highest antioxidant sources of all plants. Tabouleh is fantastically nutritious and fibre rich—this dish gives you roughly a third of your fibre target for the day.

Serves 4   Time 30 minutes   DF GF

Preheat the oven to fan-forced 180°C (350°F/Gas 4). Line a baking tray with baking paper.

Put the quinoa in a saucepan and cover with water. Drain in a sieve and repeat. This washes away the bitter compounds, called saponins, on the surface. Return to the pan and add 400 ml (14 fl oz) of water. Bring to the boil, then reduce the heat to a simmer and cook for about 15 minutes or until the water has been absorbed and the quinoa is cooked.

Combine the cooked quinoa, parsley, mint, spring onion, tomato and pistachios in a large bowl.

To make the dressing, pour 2 tablespoons of the extra virgin olive oil, half the lemon juice, the garlic, salt and pepper to taste into a jar and shake to combine. Pour over the tabouleh and toss to coat. Set aside.

Place the fish on the prepared tray, pour over the remaining lemon juice and drizzle with the remaining olive oil. Bake for 10 minutes or until cooked through. Serve the fish with the tabouleh salad and the lemon slices.

5 handfuls flat-leaf (Italian) parsley, leaves picked and chopped

4 handfuls mint, leaves picked and chopped

3 spring onions (scallions), thinly sliced

2 large tomatoes, finely chopped

Juice of 1 lemon

1 garlic clove, crushed

Freshly ground black pepper

1 lemon, sliced

4 x 120 g (4¼ oz) firm white fish fillets (such as blue eye, snapper or barramundi)

150 g (5½ oz/¾ cup) quinoa

70 g (2½ oz/½ cup) pistachio nut kernels (see note)

60 ml (2 fl oz/¼ cup) extra virgin olive oil

+

Pinch of salt flakes

Note Pistachios are relatively high in protein with a 30 g (1 oz) handful providing 6 g. You'll also get almost 3 g of fibre and a whole bunch of vitamins, minerals and antioxidants. They're also rich in healthy fats, with over half the fat present monounsaturated and almost a third polyunsaturated, while they contain low levels of saturated fats. By replacing less healthy fats and refined carb-rich foods with nuts, such as pistachios, you can significantly reduce your risk of heart disease, type 2 diabetes, and improve insulin sensitivity.

Pistachios are different from other nuts in that they contain the antioxidant carotenoids beta-carotene—that can be converted to vitamin A—and lutein. Both vitamin A and lutein are essential for good eye health.

Per serve

energy	protein	tot. fat	sat	poly	mono	carb	sugars	fibre
2020 kJ 480 Cal	33 g	25 g	4 g	6 g	15 g	27 g	6 g	7 g

NUTRITION BLOCKS PER SERVE

2 PLANT   1 PROTEIN   1 CARB   1 FAT

Seafood farro risotto

Farro is often used in traditional Italian cooking, but is less well known here in Australia. It's a type of wheat, but is in wholegrain form and has a delicious nutty, chewy taste. Here, it's teamed with a medley of seafood. I'm a huge fan of using more shellfish, as they are packed with nutrients, including iron, zinc and iodine, while the oily fish adds those essential omega-3 fats. Serve with a gorgeous, generous green salad to boost the plant food content.

Serves 4 Time 45 minutes DF NF

Put the farro, stock and 250 ml (9 fl oz/1 cup) of water into a saucepan. Bring to the boil, reduce the heat and simmer for 30 minutes or until the farro is cooked. If there is any liquid remaining, drain.

Heat the extra virgin olive oil in a large frying pan over medium heat. Add the onion and garlic and sauté for a few minutes until the onion is soft. Add the wine and simmer for a minute to cook off the alcohol.

Add the seafood to the pan and stir gently. Put the lid on and cook for 2–3 minutes until the shellfish shells have opened.

Add the cooked farro, corn and peas. Stir gently to ensure you don't break up the fish, adding a little water or stock if it looks too dry.

Add the basil, season with salt and black pepper to taste and serve immediately.

Notes Farro is the Italian name for emmer, which is an ancient variety of wheat. It's relatively high in protein for a grain with 14 g per 100 g (3½ oz) and is a terrific source of fibre. You'll find farro in better grocers and health food stores. If you can't find it, try using brown rice, freekeh or barley instead.

How to make your own fish stock: Soak 1 kg (2 lb 4 oz) of fish heads and bones (you could also include prawn shells) in water and a teaspoon of salt for an hour. Rinse well. Heat 1 tablespoon of extra virgin olive oil in a large saucepan and sauté for 3–4 minutes, add a diced onion, finely chopped garlic clove, diced fennel bulb and a sliced celery stalk. Add the fish bones and heads and cover with water. Add a teaspoon of black peppercorns, a slice of lemon and a handful of parsley stems. Bring to the boil, then reduce the heat and simmer gently for 20 minutes. Pass through a fine sieve and leave to cool for an hour before refrigerating. Fish stock will keep in the fridge for 3–4 days or pop it into freezer bags and store in the freezer for up to 3 months.

1 red onion, finely chopped
2 garlic cloves, finely chopped
140 g (5 oz/1 cup) frozen green peas
Handful basil, leaves picked
Freshly ground black pepper

100 g (3½ oz) skinless salmon fillet, cut into large cubes
100 g (3½ oz) raw prawns (shrimp) peeled, deveined and tails left intact
100 g (3½ oz) smoked mackerel, cut into bite-sized pieces
500 g (1 lb 2 oz) pipis (or vongole or clams), scrubbed
12 mussels, scrubbed and de-bearded

175 g (6 oz/1 cup) farro (see note)
1 corn cob, kernels sliced off with a small sharp knife

2 tablespoons extra virgin olive oil

+

500 ml (17 fl oz/2 cups) fish, crab or vegetable stock (preferably homemade, see note for fish stock, or good quality store-bought)
125 ml (4 fl oz/½ cup) dry white wine
Pinch of salt flakes

Per serve

energy	protein	tot. fat	sat	poly	mono	carb	sugars	fibre
1810 kJ 430 Cal	32 g	15 g	3 g	4 g	8 g	36 g	4 g	8 g

NUTRITION BLOCKS PER SERVE

 PLANT   PROTEIN  CARB   FAT

Prawn and spinach wholegrain spaghetti

Pasta has had a bad name in recent years when it comes to weight control, but really that's grossly unfair. All pasta has a low GI and the durum wheat used to make traditional pastas has a relatively high protein content. Choosing a wholegrain variety also delivers a good dose of cereal fibre, shown to be especially protective against colon cancer. Here I've combined it with prawns for protein, olive oil for good fat and a bunch of veggies as the plant food section of the plate.

Serves 4   Time 30 minutes   DF NF

Bring a large saucepan of salted water to the boil and cook the pasta until *al dente*. Wholegrain pasta does take a little longer so allow around 15–20 minutes depending on the brand.

Heat the extra virgin olive oil in a large frying pan or wok over medium heat. Add the onion, garlic and fennel, and sauté for a few minutes. Add the zucchini slices and fry for a few minutes until golden brown.

Add the chilli and the prawns and stir-fry for a few minutes until pink. Add the fish stock and the white wine. Bring to a simmer.

Add the spinach and basil, then pile the hot cooked pasta on the top. Gently toss and the heat of the pasta will wilt the spinach. Season with the salt and black pepper to taste and serve immediately.

1 onion, finely chopped
2 garlic cloves, thinly sliced
1/2 fennel bulb, thinly sliced
1 zucchini (courgette), sliced
1 large red chilli, sliced (remove the seeds if you like less heat)
150 g (5½ oz) baby English spinach leaves, washed
30 g (1 oz/1 cup) basil leaves
Freshly ground black pepper

400 g (14 oz) raw king prawns (shrimp), peeled, deveined and tails left intact (see note)

350 g (12 oz) dried wholegrain spaghetti

2 tablespoons extra virgin olive oil

+

125 ml (4 fl oz/½ cup) fish stock (preferably homemade, see page 142, or good quality store-bought)
60 ml (2 fl oz/¼ cup) dry white wine
Pinch of salt flakes

Note Prawns are protein rich, relatively low in kilojoules and provide several key nutrients. They're rich in selenium—an essential mineral with antioxidant properties—and a good source of iron, vitamin B12, phosphorus, copper and niacin.

You might think only of oily fish like salmon for your omega-3 fats, but in fact prawns provide a significant amount. These fats are crucially important in the brain and seem to play a role in cognitive function and brain health as we age. In children these fats are essential for optimal brain development. Omega-3 fats are anti-inflammatory and therefore can be helpful in relieving all sorts of inflammatory conditions, including arthritis, but may also help to reduce the low-grade inflammation that occurs alongside many chronic diseases and obesity.

Per serve

energy	protein	tot. fat	sat	poly	mono	carb	sugars	fibre
2080 kJ 500 Cal	34 g	12 g	2 g	2 g	7 g	56 g	3 g	11 g

NUTRITION BLOCKS PER SERVE

2 PLANT   1 PROTEIN   2 CARB   1 FAT

Pan-roasted blue eye with silverbeet and beans

This recipe is one of my absolute favourites and works equally well with chicken. The saltiness of the prosciutto, combined with garlic and lemon, is a perfect match with flavours of the robust greens. Here I've used blue eye fillet, but any firm fish will work well. The beans add the smart carb and the healthiest oil on the planet, extra virgin olive oil, adds our good fat. The result is a fantastically nutrient-rich, delicious mid-week dinner that's super rich in fibre too!

Serves 4 Time 15 minutes DF GF NF

Heat 1 tablespoon of the extra virgin olive oil in a frying pan over medium heat. Add the garlic and chilli, if using, and gently fry for 1 minute or until soft and fragrant. Add the prosciutto and cook for 2 minutes or until crispy.

Add the silverbeet, salt and black pepper to the pan and cook for 2–3 minutes until the silverbeet is slightly wilted. Stir in the beans and cook for a further 2 minutes until heated through and ready to serve.

Meanwhile, heat the remaining olive oil in a separate frying pan over medium heat. Add the fish and cook, skin side down, pressing firmly on the fish for the first 10 seconds to get an even heat on the skin to crisp. Turn the fish and cook for about 2 minutes until the flesh is cooked through and the fillet is opaque in colour.

Spoon the silverbeet and beans onto each serving plate and top with the blue eye fillet. Serve with a squeeze of lemon.

2 garlic cloves, crushed

2 long red chillies, finely chopped (optional)

300 g (10½ oz) silverbeet (Swiss chard) leaves, shredded (see note)

Freshly ground black pepper

Lemon wedges, to serve

4 prosciutto slices, diced (or lean bacon)

4 x 100 g (3½ oz) blue eye fillets (or other firm white fish fillets), skin on

800 g (11 lb 12 oz) tinned cannellini or borlotti beans, drained and rinsed

2 tablespoons extra virgin olive oil

+

Pinch of salt flakes

Note Silverbeet is fabulously nutrient-rich with 1 cup of raw leaves providing about a quarter of your recommended vitamin C for the day and 16 per cent of your vitamin A. The latter comes from the carotenoids present in silverbeet that can be converted to vitamin A in the body. Those carotenoids also have an antioxidant role in the body and so are important nutritional components in their own right.

Silverbeet is a good plant source of iron with a little over 1 g per cup. However be aware that this iron is very poorly absorbed, as with all dark leafy greens, due to the presence of phytates. You can improve the absorption of iron by consuming a vitamin C–rich food in the same meal, and avoiding drinking tea with or immediately after the meal. Like most leafy greens, silverbeet has a very low energy density with 1 cup providing only 25 kJ. This combination of low energy density and high nutrient density, makes it a winner for weight control.

Per serve

energy	protein	tot. fat	sat	poly	mono	carb	sugars	fibre
1420 kJ 340 Cal	33 g	14 g	3 g	2 g	8 g	17 g	4 g	11 g

NUTRITION BLOCKS PER SERVE

 1 PLANT   1 PROTEIN 1 CARB   1 FAT

Salmon and sweet potato red curry

You might not think of salmon and curry together, but the robustness of this fish works really well with the spices and rich flavour. Traditionally, curry is served with rice and usually not the most nutritious varieties. Here there is no need for rice as the sweet potato is your smart carb and is intrinsic to the dish. Simply serve in bowls with a spoon.

Serves 4   Time 25 minutes   DF GF

Heat the curry paste in a frying pan over medium–high heat then add the sweet potato—the paste will already contain some oil so there is no need to add any more. Fry for a few minutes.

Add about 250 ml (9 fl oz/1 cup) of water and allow to simmer for 10 minutes until the sweet potato is softened.

Add the coconut milk, beans and capsicum, and simmer for a further 5 minutes.

Add the salmon and frozen peas. Simmer for a few minutes until the fish is almost cooked through.

Finally, add the spinach and stir gently, taking care not to break up the salmon pieces, to just wilt the leaves and no more.

Serve immediately in bowls, topped with the coriander.

Handful green beans, sliced into bite-sized pieces

1 green capsicum (pepper), cut into bite-sized pieces

140 g (5 oz/1 cup) frozen green peas

45 g (1½ oz) baby English spinach, leaves washed

Handful coriander (cilantro), leaves picked

2 large skinless salmon fillets (320 g/11¼ oz total), cut into large dice (see note)

500 g (1 lb 2 oz) sweet potato, unpeeled, scrubbed and diced

250 ml (9 fl oz/1 cup) tinned coconut milk

+

70 g (2½ oz/¼ cup) red curry paste

Note Increasing levels of mercury in our waters has occurred through industrial pollution and this mercury then builds up in the flesh of certain fish. All fish contain some trace of mercury, but it is the larger fish at the top of the food chain, or those with a longer lifespan, which accumulate higher levels.

Women planning a pregnancy, those who are pregnant and young children should take care as to which fish to consume on a regular basis as it can affect the child's attention, memory and learning. (Very little mercury is transferred in breast milk.) In adults it takes a lot more mercury to cause any symptoms—tingling in the lips, fingers and toes is usually the first sign—but this is extremely unlikely to occur as a result of eating fish within health guidelines.

Per serve

energy	protein	tot. fat	sat	poly	mono	carb	sugars	fibre
1720 kJ 410 Cal	27 g	15 g	7 g	3 g	3 g	36 g	16 g	10 g

NUTRITION BLOCKS PER SERVE

 **2** PLANT   **1** PROTEIN   **1** CARB   **1** FAT

Meat

Sausage roll makeover

Store-bought sausage rolls are a potential source of the worst kind of fat—trans fat. Plus, they tend to include cheap, fattier meat and contain few or no veggies. So, since sausage rolls are a family favourite I decided a *Get Lean, Stay Lean* makeover was in order! I think you'll be most happy with the results. You can make them little bite-sized rolls to serve as finger food at your next party, or as large single rolls, as I've done here, served with a big salad or veggies for dinner.

Serves 6 Time 40 minutes DF NF

Preheat the oven to fan-forced 180°C (350°F/Gas 4). Line a baking tray with baking paper.

Mix the pork and veal mince together in a large bowl with all the grated vegetables and apple. Mix in the parsley and season with salt and black pepper.

On a clean work surface (and working quickly so as not to dry out the filo pastry), place 1 sheet of pastry. Lightly brush or spray a very thin layer of extra virgin olive oil. Place the second sheet of pastry over the first.

Divide the pork, veal and veggie mixture into 6 portions, moulding each portion into a long sausage shape. Place one portion of the sausage mix at one end of the filo and roll the pastry to enclose the mixture. Press the ends slightly to close. Place onto the lined baking tray.

Repeat until you have made all 6 sausage rolls.

Whisk the egg in a bowl and brush over the finished sausage rolls, then sprinkle with sesame seeds.

Bake in the oven for 10–15 minutes, watching carefully that you do not burn the pastry. You want them to be a nice golden colour without overcooking, particularly if you want to reheat them to eat at a later date. If need be, turn the tray around to get an even golden colour on all sides of your sausage rolls. Serve hot.

1 carrot, grated

1 small turnip, grated

1 small brown onion, grated

1 zucchini (courgette), grated

1 green apple, cored and grated

2 tablespoons finely chopped flat-leaf (Italian) parsley

Freshly ground black pepper

250 g (9 oz) lean minced (ground) pork (see note)

250 g (9 oz) lean minced (ground) veal (see note)

1 free-range or organic egg

12 sheets frozen filo pastry, thawed

2 tablespoons extra virgin olive oil

1 tablespoon sesame seeds (black look particularly good)

¼ teaspoon iodised salt

Note If you don't eat pork or veal, you can make these rolls with any other minced (ground) meat, including beef, lamb, chicken or turkey. Experiment and find your favourite combinations! You could even make a vegetarian version using corn.

Per serve

energy	protein	tot. fat	sat	poly	mono	carb	sugars	fibre
1280 kJ 300 Cal	24 g	13 g	3 g	2 g	7 g	22 g	5 g	2 g

NUTRITION BLOCKS PER SERVE

 1 PLANT 1 PROTEIN 1 CARB 1 FAT

Get lean cheeseburger

I love doing favourite meal makeovers in the *Get Lean, Stay Lean* kitchen, so here I've created a *Get Lean*–worthy cheeseburger. You might think this would be a tricky one to get right, but in fact by using good quality meat and teaming it with veggies and a wholegrain bun, the end result hits the mark. Don't be limited by the toppings here. If you're not a gherkin fan leave them out and add another veggie instead.

Serves 8   Time 1 hour   NF

Mix together the mince, onion, parsley, mint, chilli, mustards and worcestershire sauce in a bowl until well combined. Divide the mixture into 8 portions and then roll into burger shapes. Place on a plate, cover with plastic wrap, and refrigerate for 30 minutes. This helps firm the mixture before cooking.

Heat a frying pan or barbecue hotplate to medium. Place the burger patties in the pan and cook for about 5 minutes on each side until evenly brown. Place a slice of cheese on each patty, to slightly melt the cheese.

Meanwhile, toast the rolls on the inside, by placing in the hot pan and cooking until slightly crisp or toasted. (Do not turn over—this gives the burger a soft outside edge with a toasted inside edge.)

Place a lettuce leaf onto each burger base, followed by a cheese patty, then add the sliced tomato and gherkins. If you like, add a dollop of tomato relish and immediately enjoy!

Burgers

1 small white onion, finely chopped or grated

Handful flat-leaf (Italian) parsley, leaves picked and finely chopped

2 tablespoons finely chopped mint

1 long green chilli, finely chopped

500 g (1 lb 2 oz) lean minced (ground) lamb

+

1 teaspoon dijon mustard

1 teaspoon wholegrain mustard

1 tablespoon worcestershire sauce

Toppings

8 lettuce leaves

2 tomatoes, sliced

2–3 gherkins (pickles), sliced

8 gouda cheese slices (or any aged cheddar)

8 wholegrain or rye bread rolls (about 60 g/2¼ oz each, see note)

+

2 tablespoons tomato relish (optional)

Note I know in this era of carbophobia, people might think a bread roll is off the menu, but when this meal is put together it is in fact high in protein, providing almost 30 per cent of the kilojoules, with the remainder coming fairly equally from carbohydrate and fat. That bread roll also delivers most of the fibre and if you're careful with the bread type you choose you have a low GI meal.

Per serve

energy	protein	tot. fat	sat	poly	mono	carb	sugars	fibre
1630 kJ 390 Cal	28 g	15 g	8 g	1 g	5 g	34 g	7 g	5g

NUTRITION BLOCKS PER SERVE

2 PLANT   **1** PROTEIN   **1** CARB   **1** FAT

Lean and mean beef burritos

With three males in the house I'm always looking for inspiring dinners that satisfy all our tastes. Burritos are one of those meals. I can add extra salad, my partner likes extra meat and my boys fight over extra cheese. But making our own is all part of the fun. Put all the ingredients in the middle of the table and tuck in!

Serves 4 Time 1 hour 5 minutes NF

Heat a large frying pan over medium heat. Add the mince (you shouldn't need to add any oil as there is enough fat in the meat) and cook for 7–8 minutes, stirring often and using a wooden spoon to break up any clumps, until the meat is evenly browned.

Add the carrot, celery, shallots, capsicum, garlic, paprika and passata to the pan. Bring to the boil, then reduce the heat, cover and simmer for about 45 minutes.

Add the beans, tomato paste and red wine. Cook for a further 10 minutes to cook off the alcohol and heat the beans.

Meanwhile, preheat the oven to fan-forced 140°C (275°F/Gas 1). Wrap the tortillas in foil and warm in the oven for about 10 minutes.

Serve the burrito filling in the middle of the table with separate bowls of the mashed avocado, lettuce, salsa, grated cheese, yoghurt and warmed tortillas for everyone to make up their own burritos.

½ carrot, diced

½ celery stalk, diced

2 French shallots, finely chopped

¼ green capsicum (pepper), diced

2 garlic cloves, finely chopped

2 teaspoons smoked paprika

250 ml (9 fl oz/1 cup) tomato passata (puréed tomatoes)

2 tablespoons no added salt tomato paste (concentrated purée)

1 small cos (romaine) lettuce, washed and pulled apart into individual leaves

Tomato salsa (see page 111, or store-bought)

300 g (10½ oz) lean minced (ground) beef (or lamb, pork or veal mince, or a mixture of two meats works really well)

50 g (1¾ oz/½ cup) grated mature cheddar cheese

130 g (4½ oz/½ cup) natural yoghurt

400 g (14 oz) tinned black beans, drained and rinsed (you can use red kidney beans if you can't find black beans)

8 mini wholegrain tortillas (25 g/1 oz each)

½ avocado, mashed with the juice from a wedge of lemon and freshly ground black pepper (see note)

+

splash of red wine (or beef stock)

Note Avocados are an impressively good source of fibre; half an avocado contains 6–7 g of fibre. They also give you a good dose of folate and vitamin E, nutrients important for protecting body cells and DNA as we get older. You may also be surprised to know that avocados are a good source of vitamin C. This makes them a great addition to a vegetarian meal as they will help you to absorb more plant iron.

Per serve

energy	protein	tot. fat	sat	poly	mono	carb	sugars	fibre
2080 kJ 500 Cal	30 g	24 g	10 g	2 g	9 g	37 g	12 g	7 g

NUTRITION BLOCKS PER SERVE

 2 PLANT **1** PROTEIN **1** CARB **1** FAT

Tandoori lamb cutlets with spiked cucumber salad

This is a magic recipe for a balmy summer evening when you want a simple light meal that doesn't involve standing in front of a hot stove. Although it takes 45 minutes or so, half an hour of that time is simply to marinate the meat. Once that's done—and you could do that in the morning and leave the meat in the fridge during the day—the cooking only takes a few minutes and, bingo, a tasty meal is on the table in less time than it would take you to order takeaway.

Serves 4 Time 45 minutes GF NF

Mix the tandoori paste and yoghurt together in a large non-metallic bowl. Add the lamb cutlets and mix to coat, then cover with plastic wrap and set aside to marinate for at least 30 minutes (or longer in the fridge).

To make the cucumber salad, slice the cucumbers into rough chunks. Add the garlic, chilli and mint, and toss to combine.

Heat the barbecue grill or a chargrill pan to medium.

To make the dressing, whisk the ingredients in a small jug and pour half the dressing over the cucumber. Add more if not dressed all over. You want the cucumber to be lightly dressed, not soaked.

Put the cutlets on the grill and cook for 3 minutes on each side or until browned and cooked to your liking—lamb is best when still pink in the middle (see note). Serve the tandoori lamb with the cucumber salad, an extra dollop of yoghurt and a squeeze of lemon.

- 2 tablespoons store-bought tandoori paste
- 4 Lebanese (short) cucumbers
- 1 garlic clove, thinly sliced
- 1 red chilli, finely diced
- 2 tablespoons roughly chopped mint
- 1 lemon, cut into wedges, to serve

- 2 tablespoons natural yoghurt, and 4 tablespoons extra, to serve
- 12 lamb cutlets (about 370 g/13 oz total), fully trimmed (see note)

Rice wine vinegar dressing

- ½ teaspoon pure maple syrup
- 2 tablespoons extra virgin olive oil

+

2 tablespoons rice wine vinegar

Note Charring your meat on the barbie results in carcinogenic compounds being formed on the surface of the meat. Therefore, avoid very high heat when cooking meat. Turn down the burner to medium, use marinades (these protect the meat and reduce the production of carcinogens) and opt for slow cooking methods more often.

Per serve

energy	protein	tot. fat	sat	poly	mono	carb	sugars	fibre
1370 kJ 330 Cal	23 g	20 g	5 g	2 g	11 g	11 g	9 g	5 g

NUTRITION BLOCKS PER SERVE

1 PLANT 1 PROTEIN 0 CARB 1 FAT

Hoisin pork ribs

I'm guessing you weren't expecting ribs to appear in a health book, but here they are! I'm a fan of the trend towards nose-to-tail eating. If we are to breed animals for our food, then we should at the very least make sure we are making use of every part. Certainly, some cuts are fattier than others, but provided you cook them the right way and accompany them with the right ingredients and sides, you can create a truly delicious *Get Lean, Stay Lean*-worthy meal.

Serves 4   Time 2 hours 40 minutes   DF GF NF

To make the hoisin sauce, heat the extra virgin olive oil in a small saucepan over low heat. Add the garlic and five-spice and gently fry for about a minute until you can smell the aromas. Add the red miso paste, maple syrup and brown rice vinegar. Stir to combine over the heat for 4 minutes, then set aside to cool.

Mix all the marinade ingredients together in a large non-metallic bowl with 125 ml (4 fl oz/½ cup) of water. Add the ribs and mix to coat, then cover with plastic wrap and marinate for at least 30 minutes in the fridge (or up to 1 day).

Preheat the oven to fan-forced 150°C (300°F/Gas 2).

Put the marinated ribs in a roasting tin and cover with foil. Place the tray in the oven and bake for 1½ hours, basting the ribs at least once during this time.

Remove the foil, turn the oven up to 180°C (350°F/Gas 4) and bake for another 30 minutes to allow the outside of the ribs to caramelise nicely.

Remove the ribs from the oven and carefully slice. Serve—napkins essential!

585 g (1 lb 4½ oz) pork ribs, trimmed of excess fat

Hoisin sauce (see note)

1 garlic clove, crushed

½ teaspoon Chinese five-spice powder

145 g (5 oz/½ cup) red miso paste

2 tablespoons brown rice vinegar

170 g (6 oz/½ cup) pure maple syrup

1 tablespoon extra virgin olive oil (preferably light flavoured)

Marinade

2 garlic cloves, crushed

1 teaspoon finely grated ginger

90 g (3¼ oz/¼ cup) pure maple syrup

+

75 g (2½ oz/¼ cup) Hoisin sauce (see above)

100 ml (3½ fl oz) tamari

Note This homemade hoisin sauce is infinitely tastier and healthier than commercial varieties. But of course you can substitute with a bought one if need be. This recipe makes more hoisin sauce than is required for the dish. Pour any leftover hoisin sauce into a jar with a lid and store in the fridge for up to 2 weeks.

Per serve

energy	protein	tot. fat	sat	poly	mono	carb	sugars	fibre
1440 kJ 345 Cal	34 g	14 g	5 g	2 g	6 g	20 g	18 g	<1 g

NUTRITION BLOCKS PER SERVE

0 PLANT   **1** PROTEIN   **1** CARB   **1** FAT

Oyster beef noodles

This is so quick and easy to throw together that you'll never buy takeaway noodles again. Proper soba noodles are 100 per cent buckwheat (if you are coeliac, double check the ingredients list as wheat flour is sometimes added) and so are gluten free. I like them because they're low GI and add extra fibre to the dish. This is a mid-week favourite in our house.

Serves 4   Time 20 minutes   DF GF

Heat a wok over high heat. Coat the beef with 2 teaspoons of the extra virgin olive oil. Place the beef in the wok (working in three batches so as not to overcrowd the pan) and stir-fry for 3–4 minutes or until the meat is browned, stirring constantly. Reserve each batch to rest. Reheat the wok between each batch.

Bring a saucepan of water to the boil. Add the soba noodles to the boiling water. Boil rapidly for 4 minutes or until *al dente*, drain into a colander and run the noodles under cold water. Set aside.

Reheat the wok, add the remaining oil and, once the oil starts to glisten, add the carrots and capsicum and stir-fry for 1 minute. Add the corn and snow peas and stir-fry for a further 30 seconds.

Add the noodles to the wok and heat until they are hot.

Return the beef to the wok, add the oyster sauce, soy sauce, cashew nuts and stock, and toss to warm through. Serve immediately.

1 carrot, thinly sliced or julienned

1 red capsicum (pepper), sliced into strips

425 g (15 oz) tinned baby corn spears (or fresh)

250 g (9 oz) snow peas (mangetout), trimmed and halved

360 g (12¾ oz) lean beef (such as rump), thinly sliced

180 g (6½ oz) dried soba (buckwheat) noodles

1 tablespoon extra virgin olive oil

60 g (2¼ oz) raw or roasted cashew nuts (see note)

+

80 ml (2½ fl oz/⅓ cup) oyster sauce

2 tablespoons soy sauce

100 ml (3½ fl oz) beef stock (preferably homemade, see page 126, or good quality store-bought, or water)

Note Compared to other common nuts, cashews (along with pine nuts) top the charts for iron and zinc. They are also rich in magnesium with a handful delivering you about 20 per cent of your RDI, and protein, with a 30 g (1 oz) handful supplying about 5 g. Of the total energy in cashews, 75 per cent comes from fat, 12 per cent comes from protein and 12 per cent comes from carbohydrates. Although fat rich, cashews are full of exactly the good fats we want in our diets. Almost two-thirds of the fat present is monounsaturated, with the remaining a fairly even split between polyunsaturated and saturated fats. Monounsaturated fats are a cornerstone of the Mediterranean diet, and a high intake of these fats is associated with a lower risk of heart disease and less fat around the middle.

Per serve

energy	protein	tot. fat	sat	poly	mono	carb	sugars	fibre
1990 kJ 480 Cal	30 g	17 g	4 g	2 g	10 g	45 g	9 g	8 g

NUTRITION BLOCKS PER SERVE

 1 PLANT   1 PROTEIN   1 CARB   1 FAT

Ricotta and basil meatballs in capsicum-tomato sauce

Meatballs are one of my favourite meals and fortunately they can be superbly healthy when made in the right way. Here I've taken inspiration from the Mediterranean diet, using the classic flavours of the region with garlic, tomato and basil. Serve with a big green salad or steamed green veggies to boost the plant content. If you have Carb Blocks left for the day you can also add wholegrain fettuccine, or as a gluten free option, red, brown or black rice.

Serves 4   Time 50 minutes   GF NF

Heat 2 teaspoons of the extra virgin olive oil in a saucepan over medium heat. Add half the onion and sauté for a few minutes until softened.

Transfer the sautéed onion into a large bowl and combine with the beef mince, ricotta and basil. Season with salt and black pepper and mix together well using your hands. Form the mixture into balls—run your hands under cold water first to prevent the meat sticking—place them in a bowl, cover with plastic wrap and pop them into the fridge while you make the sauce.

In the same saucepan, heat the remaining olive oil over medium heat, add the remaining onion and the garlic and sauté for a few minutes until softened. Add the capsicum and sauté for a further 2–3 minutes until the capsicum is soft. Add the passata and bring to the boil. Reduce the heat, add the red wine and simmer for about 15–20 minutes until you have a richly flavoured sauce. Season to taste.

Drop the meatballs into the sauce and shake the pan to ensure they are completely covered. Simmer for another 20 minutes or until the meatballs are cooked through. Serve.

1 red onion, finely diced

2 handfuls basil, leaves picked and finely chopped

Freshly ground black pepper

2 garlic cloves, finely chopped (see note)

1 red capsicum (pepper), finely diced

400 ml (14 fl oz) tomato passata (puréed tomatoes)

500 g (1 lb 2 oz) lean minced (ground) beef

115 g (4 oz/½ cup) fresh full fat ricotta cheese

1 tablespoon extra virgin olive oil

+

¼ teaspoon iodised salt, plus extra to season

125 ml (4 fl oz/½ cup) red wine

Note Garlic stands out as having particularly potent anti-cancer effects. It has high levels of allicin and other sulphur compounds that are thought to be responsible. Garlic is also anti-bacterial, it can block the formation of carcinogenic substances, can enhance the repair of DNA in cells around the body and can assist in killing off rogue cells that may progress to cancer. Some compounds may be lost during cooking but since many people find raw garlic doesn't agree with them, rest assured that you are getting many of the benefits through cooking with garlic. Just be sure not to burn the garlic when sautéing—you'll notice I usually recommend a medium heat when cooking garlic and onion for that reason.

Per serve

energy	protein	tot. fat	sat	poly	mono	carb	sugars	fibre
1360 kJ 325 Cal	31 g	18 g	7 g	1 g	9 g	6 g	6 g	3 g

NUTRITION BLOCKS PER SERVE

1 PLANT   **1** PROTEIN   **0** CARB   **½** FAT

Lamb and quinoa stuffed capsicums

This is one of those 'looks fancier than it really is' recipes. It's equally perfect for a family dinner or to serve to dinner guests. Roasting the capsicums brings out their sweetness and the overall combination is a treat. As an alterative to quinoa you could use brown rice or wholegrain couscous. Serve with a generous green salad and an eggplant dip or perhaps some hummus (see page 85). Delicious!

Serves 4 Time 1 hour GF

Put the quinoa in a saucepan and cover with water. Drain in a sieve and repeat. This washes away the bitter compounds, called saponins, on the surface. Return to the pan and add 250 ml (9 fl oz/1 cup) of water. Bring to the boil, then reduce the heat to a simmer and cook for about 15 minutes or until the water has been absorbed and the quinoa is cooked. Turn off the heat and leave the lid on.

Heat the extra virgin olive oil in a frying pan over medium heat. Add the onion and sauté for a couple of minutes until translucent. Stir in the garlic and spices and continue to cook for a minute or so more. Add the lamb and cook for 4–5 minutes, stirring often, to brown all over.

Once the meat is cooked, remove from the heat and add to the pan of cooked quinoa, along with the parsley, goat's curd, pine nuts, raisins and lemon zest.

Prepare the capsicums by cutting the core out, then remove the inside seeds by tapping the whole capsicum upside down. Retain the top of the core so you can use it as a lid for the capsicums once filled, but do remove any seeds attached.

Preheat the oven to fan-forced 180°C (350°F/Gas 4).

Stuff the capsicums with the lamb mixture. Press the lids on top and place in a casserole dish or on a lined baking tray. Cook for 30 minutes or until the capsicums are softened on the outside. The skin should be slightly wrinkled. Serve immediately.

½ red onion, diced

2 garlic cloves, chopped

½ teaspoon ground cinnamon

1 teaspoon ground cumin

¼ teaspoon freshly grated nutmeg

3 tablespoons chopped flat-leaf (Italian) parsley

Grated zest of 1 lemon

2 tablespoons raisins or sultanas (golden raisins)

4 red capsicums (peppers) (see note)

360 g (12¾ oz) lean minced (ground) lamb

2 tablespoons goat's curd (or feta)

100 g (3½ oz/½ cup) quinoa

1 tablespoon extra virgin olive oil

2 tablespoons pine nuts

Note It's not only oranges that are fabulous for vitamin C, half a red capsicum gives you well over your entire daily requirement. Vitamin C is one of the major antioxidants and an essential player in supporting optimal immune function. Capsicums also provide an array of carotenoids, including beta-carotene, with antioxidant functions. Beta-carotene can also be converted to vitamin A in the body, a nutrient that is critical for good vision and healthy eyes. It is also necessary for new cell formation and is therefore essential for healthy skin and many organs including the heart, lungs, liver and kidneys.

Per serve

energy	protein	tot. fat	sat	poly	mono	carb	sugars	fibre
1870 kJ 450 Cal	28 g	26 g	7 g	5 g	11 g	24 g	10 g	5 g

NUTRITION BLOCKS PER SERVE

 1 PLANT 1 PROTEIN 1 CARB 1 FAT

Braised pork hock with homemade baked beans

Be warned, this dish will be devoured within minutes. The pork knuckle or hock needs long slow cooking, but it's well worth the wait. Here I've taken inspiration from American southern soul cooking and included with smoky, spicy flavours and beans. The result is serious comfort food and melt-in-the-mouth flavour. To complete your Dr Joanna Plate serve with steamed robust greens, such as broccolini, asparagus, kale and green beans as additional Plant Blocks.

Serves 4   Time 2 hours   DF GF NF

Preheat the oven to fan-forced 180°C (350°F/Gas 4).

Place the hock in a saucepan, cover with cold water and add the salt. Bring to the boil and cook for 3 minutes, removing any froth from the surface of the water. This removes any impurities from the hock. Drain the water and reserve the hock.

Heat 2 teaspoons of the extra virgin olive oil in a heavy-based flameproof casserole dish over medium heat. Add the leek, half the onion, half the garlic, the carrot, celery, rosemary and half the thyme, and gently fry for 4–5 minutes until the vegetables are tender.

Add the bay leaf, mushroom, red wine, stock and the reserved hock to the dish. Season with salt and black pepper then cover with the lid and place in the oven. Cook for 1 hour 30 minutes or until the pork is tender.

Meanwhile, heat the remaining olive oil in a frying pan over medium heat. Add the remaining onion, garlic and thyme and sauté for 3–4 minutes or until softened.

Add the tomatoes, cannellini beans, sauces and mustard, and simmer gently for 10 minutes or until the flavours infuse the beans.

Place the beans on each plate, top with the melt-in-the-mouth pork hock and serve.

Notes Pork hock has less meat on board than it looks, as when you pull it apart you'll find a lot of fat. But pork is different from most other meats in that the fat is very easily separable from the meat—it doesn't marble as beef and lamb do. Once you ease it all apart and shred the meat, it's deliciously lean.

In this meal I've counted the beans as the smart carbs since the pork meat delivers the Protein Blocks. For the analysis I have assumed 65 g (2¼ oz) of cooked meat per serve, equivalent to 1 Protein Block. You can of course adjust this to give you more Protein Blocks if you need them. Shred any leftover meat, discarding the fat, and store in the fridge for sandwiches and salads over the next few days.

1 leek, white part and a little of the green, thinly sliced

1 brown onion, finely diced

4 garlic cloves, crushed

1 carrot, finely diced

1 celery stalk, finely diced

1 teaspoon finely chopped rosemary

2 teaspoon thyme leaves

1 bay leaf (fresh or dried)

1 field mushroom, sliced

Freshly ground black pepper

425 g (15 oz) tinned whole roma (plum) tomatoes (buying them whole they are more flavourful than ready chopped)

1 kg (2 lb 4 oz) pork hock (see note)

425 (15 oz) tinned cannellini beans, drained and rinsed (see note)

1 tablespoon extra virgin olive oil

+

200 ml (7 fl oz) red wine

250 ml (9 fl oz/1 cup) chicken stock (preferably homemade, see page 113, or good quality store-bought)

1 tablespoon good quality barbecue sauce

1 tablespoon worcestershire sauce

A few drops of tabasco sauce (or to taste)

1 heaped teaspoon dijon mustard

+

1 teaspoon salt flakes, plus extra to season

Per serve

energy	protein	tot. fat	sat	poly	mono	carb	sugars	fibre
1370 kJ 330 Cal	27 g	13 g	5 g	2 g	6 g	18 g	10 g	8 g

NUTRITION BLOCKS PER SERVE

 **2** PLANT    **1** PROTEIN   **1** CARB   **1** FAT

Lamb and red bean cocotte

A cocotte is just a casserole, but it makes it sound so much more enticing! I'm a sucker for hearty meals on a winter's night and this one hits the mark—but does so without the kilojoules of most cold-weather fare. Beans are such a great addition to casserole style meals; they add slow-release carbs, plant protein, stacks of fibre and nutrients such as folate.

Serves 4 Time 2 hours DF GF NF

Preheat the oven to fan-forced 180°C (350°F/Gas 4).

Coat the lamb in 1 tablespoon of the extra virgin olive oil. Heat a flameproof casserole dish over high heat, add the lamb (working in three batches so as not to overcrowd the pan) and cook for about 5 minutes or until evenly browned. Remove each batch from the dish and set aside to rest.

Heat the remaining oil in the dish over medium heat. Add the onion, garlic, carrot, celery, thyme and rosemary, and gently sauté for 4–5 minutes until soft.

Return the meat to the dish and add the tomatoes, wine and stock. Bring to the boil, cover with the lid and place in the oven. (Alternatively, cook over low heat on the stovetop for 2 hours covered with the lid. Stir occasionally to ensure the casserole does not catch on the bottom.)

After the meat has been cooking for 1 hour, add the beans and check there is enough liquid. Add a splash of water if it looks a little dry.

Bring a saucepan of water to the boil. Add the sweet potato, bring back to the boil, then reduce the heat to a simmer and cook for about 15 minutes or until tender. Drain well and then mash until smooth. Add a little salt and black pepper to taste. Cover to keep warm until ready to serve.

When almost ready to serve, bring a saucepan of water to the boil over high heat. Put the broccoli in a steamer, cover with the lid and place on top of the pan. Cook for 2 minutes, or until *al dente*. (Alternatively, place the broccoli in a microwave-proof bowl with a little water, cover and microwave on High for about 2 minutes.)

Sprinkle the cocotte with the oregano (or parsley) and serve with the mashed sweet potato and the steamed broccoli.

Note You can buy kidney beans dry or ready cooked in tinned form. I usually buy the latter for convenience. If you wish to prepare your own beans, place them in a bowl, cover with water and leave to soak overnight. The next morning discard the soaking water, rinse well and transfer to a large pot. Cover with fresh water and bring to the boil. Reduce the heat to simmer and then cook for a couple of hours until soft. Adding a splash of extra virgin olive oil to the pot helps to improve the texture. Only add salt at the end of cooking or once using them in a dish.

1 brown onion, finely diced

2 garlic cloves, finely chopped

2 carrots, diced

2 celery stalks, diced

1 teaspoon thyme leaves (or ¼ teaspoon dried)

1 teaspoon chopped rosemary (dried if you prefer)

400 g (14 oz) tinned tomatoes (buying them whole they are more flavourful than ready chopped)

Freshly ground black pepper

200 g (7 oz/1 head) broccoli, cut into florets

1 teaspoon fresh oregano leaves (or flat-leaf/Italian parsley)

360 g (12¾ oz) lean lamb, diced

400 g (14 oz) tinned red kidney beans, drained and rinsed (see note)

500 g (1 lb 2 oz) sweet potato, unpeeled, scrubbed and chopped

2 tablespoons extra virgin olive oil

+

125 ml (4 fl oz/½ cup) red wine

250 ml (9 fl oz/1 cup) beef stock (preferably homemade, see page 126, or good quality store-bought)

Pinch of salt

Per serve

energy	protein	tot. fat	sat	poly	mono	carb	sugars	fibre
1880 kJ 450 Cal	32 g	15 g	3 g	2 g	8 g	36 g	16 g	16 g

NUTRITION BLOCKS PER SERVE

3 PLANT 1 PROTEIN 1 CARB 1 FAT

Mustard herb roast beef

This is one of my go-to recipes I turn to when we have friends over and I need to feed lots of people—you can use a whole fillet rather than half for this. It's also brilliant for a Sunday night family dinner and you then have leftover meat for lunches through the week. Beef fillet is lean and so you do need to be careful not to overcook the meat. Slice and serve with roast root veggies and a big green salad, or steamed greens to complete your Dr Joanna Plate.

Serves 6   Time 40 minutes   DF GF NF

Preheat the oven to fan-forced 180°C (350°F/Gas 4). Line a baking tray with baking paper.

Trim any large pieces of visible fat from the beef and brush the extra virgin olive oil over the meat. Heat a frying pan over high heat and sear the beef on all sides for about 4–5 minutes to seal. Remove from the pan.

Chop all of the herbs very finely and spread out over a chopping board. Smear the mustard all over the seared beef and roll in the herbs until coated. Place on the prepared baking tray and roast for 15 minutes for rare, 20 minutes for medium–rare or 25–30 minutes for well done (I don't recommend this as it will make the meat tougher—this dish is best served medium–rare). Remove from the oven, cover with foil and allow to rest for 10 minutes. Slice and serve.

Handful basil, leaves picked

Handful flat-leaf (Italian) parsley, leaves picked

2 tablespoons thyme leaves

1 tablespoon rosemary leaves

½ whole beef fillet (about 540 g/1 lb 3 oz) (see note)

2 teaspoons extra virgin olive oil

+

125 g (4½ oz/½ cup) dijon mustard

Notes Those on higher energy levels, simply choose more serves of this dish to match your Protein Block allocation.

Beef is an excellent source of haem iron, which is better absorbed than the non-haem iron we get from plant foods. A beef serve of 100 g (3½ oz) provides 2.2 mg of iron—that's 12 per cent of the daily need for pre-menopausal women and 28 per cent that for men and post-menopausal women. A regular-sized steak is larger than this, so you can see that beef can substantially boost your iron intake.

Marbled beef such as wagyu may be favoured by chefs—the fat melts through the meat while cooking helping to keep it moist—but nutritionally this is not the best choice. The red meat our hunter-gatherer ancestors ate was from wild animals that had lower fat and saturated fat, and higher omega-3 fats compared to domesticated animals we eat today. I recommend choosing grass-fed beef (sometimes labelled pasture-fed) to get a meat closer to the meats we ate in the past.

Per serve

energy	protein	tot. fat	sat	poly	mono	carb	sugars	fibre
620 kJ 150 Cal	21 g	6 g	2 g	1 g	3 g	1 g	0 g	2 g

NUTRITION BLOCKS PER SERVE

0 PLANT   1 PROTEIN   0 CARB   0 FAT

Poultry

Duck ragu with wholegrain pappardelle

While there's a trend these days to blame carbs for all our woes, the Italians have been eating pasta for hundreds of years without getting fat. The key lies in the balance of foods on the plate and the portion size. Visit Italy and you'll see that they have pasta as a first or middle course and not as an enormous bowl. Enjoy with a lovely green salad to boost your Plant Blocks.

Serves 4 Time 1 hour 30 minutes NF

Preheat the oven to fan-forced 180°C (350°F/Gas 4).

Heat a flameproof casserole dish over medium–high heat. Place the duck breasts, skin side down, in the hot pan and render the fat for a few minutes. (This means to fry off the fat under the skin.) Once you have at least 1 tablespoon of liquid duck fat, remove the duck breasts from the pan, cut the skin off the meat and discard.

Using 1 tablespoon of the duck fat, reduce the heat to medium–low, add the onion, garlic, rosemary, thyme, celery and carrot and cook for 4–5 minutes until the vegetables are soft but not browned.

Add the tomatoes and stock to the dish and stir to combine. Return the duck breasts to the pan with the mushrooms. Cover the dish with the lid and cook in the oven for 1 hour, or until the duck meat is tender. Remove from the oven.

Using two forks shred the duck meat, then add back to the dish and mix through the sauce. Remove and discard any herb stems. Add a splash of water if the sauce needs loosening. Taste and season with a pinch of salt if necessary and a good grind of fresh black pepper. Stir in the parsley.

Cook the pasta according to the packet instructions. (Most wholegrain pasta varieties will take a little longer to cook. However, some have been par-cooked to shorten the cooking time.)

Either toss the pasta through the sauce or pour the sauce over the pasta in the bowls. Scatter over the parmesan and serve.

Note In my opinion duck is an under-used meat—it is a popular meat in China where it has been farmed for thousands of years—and I rate it highly from a nutritional, taste and environmental perspective. It's usually thought of as a fatty meat, but in fact the fat is almost all directly under the skin and separable from the meat. Furthermore, the fat itself is predominately super-healthy monounsaturated fat and highly stable for cooking. Compared to chicken breast, duck meat has almost 80 per cent more iron and 65 per cent more zinc. It's also rich in the B group vitamins thiamin, niacin and riboflavin.

1 small brown onion, finely chopped

2 garlic cloves, finely chopped

1 rosemary sprig

1 thyme sprig

2 celery stalks, finely diced

1 carrot, finely diced

400 g (14 oz) tinned whole roma (plum) tomatoes, chopped (buying them whole they are more flavourful than ready chopped)

100 g (3½ oz) button mushrooms

Freshly ground black pepper

2 tablespoons chopped flat-leaf (Italian) parsley, to serve

2 x 200 g (7 oz) duck breasts, skin on

2 tablespoons shaved parmesan cheese

300 g (10½ oz) wholegrain pappardelle pasta

1 tablespoon duck fat rendered from the duck breast skin (see note)

+

250 ml (9 fl oz/1 cup) chicken stock (preferably homemade, see page 113, or good quality store-bought)

Pinch of salt

Per serve

energy	protein	tot. fat	sat	poly	mono	carb	sugars	fibre
1950 kJ 470 Cal	30 g	13 g	4 g	2 g	5 g	51 g	5 g	11 g

NUTRITION BLOCKS PER SERVE

2 PLANT **1** PROTEIN **2** CARB **½** FAT

Turkey rissoles with chilli, garlic and ginger

These rissoles are a crowd pleaser, whether serving for a family mid-week dinner or a weekend barbecue when you have friends over. In fact, if you're entertaining you can make them smaller to serve on cocktail sticks as a canapé, perhaps with a bowl of sweet chilli sauce for dipping. For a family meal I like to serve them with baked sweet potato chips (see page 135) and a salad of whatever veggies I have in my fridge.

Serves 4 Time 20 minutes DF GF NF

Heat 2 teaspoons of the extra virgin olive oil in a small frying pan over medium heat. Add the onion and sauté for a few minutes until translucent, taking care not to let it burn. Add the garlic, ginger and chilli and sauté for a minute or so more.

Combine the mince, onion mixture, parsley, salt and plenty of black pepper in a mixing bowl. Use your hands to ensure an even mix of ingredients. Then divide the mixture into 8 pieces and mould each into a rissole shape—running cold water over your hands first helps to stop it sticking. Flatten each rissole slightly and set aside on a sheet of baking paper. At this stage you can cook them straight away, or cover with plastic wrap and store in the fridge to cook within 24 hours, or you can freeze them for 4–6 months.

When ready to cook heat a chargrill pan (this gives nice char lines on your rissoles), a frying pan or the barbecue to a medium heat. Drizzle with the remaining oil, add the rissoles and cook for 2–3 minutes on each side or until cooked through. Be careful not to have the heat turned up too high or you'll burn the outside of the rissole before the centre is cooked. If need be you can pop the lid over the pan to assist cooking if your rissoles are thicker.

Serve with a gorgeous big green salad as additional Plant Blocks along with baked sweet potato chips, boiled waxy potatoes or mashed cannellini beans as your smart carb.

Note Many people ask me about whether it is safe to fry in extra virgin olive oil and the answer is a resounding yes, provided you are using a good quality extra virgin olive oil. Here in Australia we have among the best quality oils in the world and over 95 per cent of that produced is extra virgin. Our oils have smoke points of 200–220°C (400–425°F) making frying perfectly safe. In addition, we know that monounsaturated fats are extremely stable in cooking and the antioxidants present help to protect the oil from oxidation. No other oil has such a vast number of phytochemicals and beneficial attributes.

¼ red onion, finely diced

2 garlic cloves, crushed or finely chopped

1 tablespoon finely grated ginger

1 red chilli, finely chopped

Handful flat-leaf (Italian) parsley (or coriander/cilantro), leaves picked and finely chopped

Freshly ground black pepper

500 g (1 lb 2 oz) lean minced (ground) turkey

1 tablespoon extra virgin olive oil (see note)

+

¼ teaspoon iodised salt

Per serve of two rissoles

energy	protein	tot. fat	sat	poly	mono	carb	sugars	fibre
910 kJ 220 Cal.	20 g	14 g	4 g	2 g	7 g	2 g	<1 g	1 g

NUTRITION BLOCKS PER SERVE

1 PLANT **1** PROTEIN **0** CARB **0** FAT

* The nutrition analysis does not include the green salad serving suggestion.

Tarragon chicken ricotta parcels

I love using filo pastry. It's light, really tasty and has none of the fat, especially the trans fats, found in other commercial pastries. Instead, I add my own healthy fat with a little extra virgin olive oil and the end result always goes down well. I have recently cultivated a herb garden and simply throwing a handful of fresh herbs into a dish makes a world of difference. My kids wolf these down and it's one of the few times I can get them to eat spinach!

Serves 4   Time 35 minutes   NF

Preheat the oven to fan-forced 180°C (350°F/Gas 4).

Combine the chicken strips, tarragon, spinach and ricotta in a bowl and season with salt and black pepper.

Layer 2 sheets of filo on your work surface, spraying or brushing with a little extra virgin olive oil between sheets. Then put a quarter of the chicken mixture onto one end, fold over the edges, add more oil around the edges and then roll up to make a parcel. Brush the top with the beaten egg and sprinkle with black sesame seeds. Repeat three more times to make 4 parcels.

Bake the parcels in the oven for about 20 minutes or until golden on top and crispy.

Cut each parcel diagonally in half and serve with the rocket and tomatoes drizzled with the remaining oil and a squeeze of lemon.

1 tablespoon chopped tarragon

90 g (3¼ oz/2 cups) baby English spinach leaves, washed

Freshly ground black pepper

140 g (5 oz) rocket (arugula)

12 cherry tomatoes, halved

1 lemon, cut into quarters

300 g (10½ oz) skinless chicken breast fillet, cut into small strips (see note)

230 g (8½ oz/1 cup) fresh full fat ricotta cheese

1 free-range or organic egg, beaten with a fork

8 sheets frozen filo pastry, thawed

2 tablespoons extra virgin olive oil

1 teaspoon black sesame seeds

+

¼ teaspoon iodised salt

Note A good reason to choose chicken over other meats is that it has a relatively small environmental footprint. As our populations grow, how we feed us all without destroying our planet becomes top of the priority list. There is much credence in choosing to eat more smaller birds and animals, and fewer big methane-producing animals that contribute to global warming.

I do recommend you buy free-range or organic chicken, for both taste and animal welfare considerations. I also urge you to buy and use the whole bird as much as possible. In the era of low fat eating we were all urged to eat only the breast. It is indeed the leanest part of the bird and in some recipes, such as the above, I prefer to use it. However, the brown meat from the leg and thigh is much higher in nutrients such as iron and zinc … not to mention what waste there would be if all of us only ever bought breast meat!

From a nutritional perspective all cuts of chicken are excellent protein choices for your Dr Joanna Plate. Chicken is an especially rich source of niacin and has good levels of riboflavin, phosphorus, magnesium, and in the brown meat, zinc and iron.

Per serve

energy	protein	tot. fat	sat	poly	mono	carb	sugars	fibre
1500 kJ / 360 Cal	28 g	18 g	6 g	2 g	9 g	22 g	5 g	3 g

NUTRITION BLOCKS PER SERVE

2 PLANT   **1** PROTEIN   **1** CARB   **1** FAT

Pan-roasted duck breast with roast sprouts and veggie mash

The meat-eaters among us should all be diversifying our protein intake to include more smaller animals and birds, such as duck. The meat is actually very lean as the fat doesn't marble through the muscle. The fat sits in a layer under the skin so it's easy to separate if you want to. I like to cook duck with the skin on as this keeps the meat nice and moist. A little fat will be absorbed, but less than you might think, and, in fact, duck fat is high in healthy monounsaturated fats.

Serves 4 Time 1 hour 30 minutes DF GF NF

Whisk the marinade ingredients together in a bowl. Transfer to a small non-metallic dish and add the duck breats, skin side up. Cover with plastic wrap and put in the fridge to marinate for at least an hour. (It is better to marinate as long as you can, even overnight.)

Place the carrot, parsnip and sweet potato in a saucepan, cover with water, bring to the boil, then cook for 15–20 minutes until the veggies are tender. Drain well and mash with a pinch of salt and plenty of black pepper. Cover and set aside until ready to serve.

Meanwhile, preheat the oven to fan-forced 180°C (350°F/Gas 4). Line a baking tray with baking paper.

While the root vegetables are cooking, heat a frying pan over low heat. You won't need to add any fat to the pan as there is plenty of fat just under the skin of the duck. Pat dry the duck fillets, reserving the marinade, and pan fry, skin side down for at least 5 minutes. This will render the duck fat and crisp the skin.

Once the skin is crisp, remove it from the meat, turn the fillet over and cook for a couple more minutes. Add the marinade ingredients to the pan and cook for a further 2 minutes, spooning the marinade over the meat.

Remove the pan from the heat, cover with the lid and wrap the top with a tea towel (dish towel) to keep the heat in. Let the duck rest for 5–10 minutes—this will finish off the cooking process and allow the duck to retain its juices.

While the duck is resting, cut the brussels sprouts in half and toss with the cherry tomatoes and the extra virgin olive oil. Spread out on the prepared tray, season with a pinch of salt and roast for about 10 minutes until the tomatoes start to burst.

Slice the duck breast and drizzle with the duck marinade juices. Serve with the veggie mash and the roast tomatoes and sprouts.

Note Brussels sprouts are notably high in vitamins A, C and E, folate and potassium. The trick is to not overcook them! Overcooked sprouts are soggy and sulphurous smelling—not appealing at all!

2 carrots, cut into chunks

1 parsnip, cut into chunks

Freshly ground black pepper

16 brussels sprouts, blanched (see note)

16 cherry tomatoes

4 x 135 g (4¾ oz) duck breasts

420 g (15 oz) sweet potato, unpeeled, scrubbed and cut into chunks

1 tablespoon extra virgin olive oil

+

Pinch of salt flakes

Pomegranate-tamari marinade

1 teaspoon finely grated ginger

1 rosemary sprig

1 tablespoon pure maple syrup

2 tablespoons pomegranate molasses

1 teaspoon sesame oil

+

Pinch of salt flakes

60 ml (2 fl oz/¼ cup) tamari

Per serve

energy	protein	tot. fat	sat	poly	mono	carb	sugars	fibre
1850 kJ 440 Cal	32 g	18 g	4 g	3 g	10 g	31 g	20 g	11 g

NUTRITION BLOCKS PER SERVE

 3 PLANT   1 PROTEIN   1 CARB   1 FAT

Mediterranean baked chicken and veggies

This is one of my mid-week go-to meals when I don't want any fuss. For a dish that is so simple it really is delicious and goes down well with everyone in the family. The other big bonus is that there is only one pot to wash up at the end. For those on higher energy levels simply increase the serve size, or double the recipe. I sometimes also add steamed brown rice to fill up the kids while I happily eat more of the veggies.

Serves 4   Time 40 minutes   DF GF NF

Preheat the oven to fan-forced 180°C (350°F/Gas 4).

Put the onion, capsicum and zucchini in a casserole dish and mix together well. Scatter with the garlic slices and the chilli, then lay the chicken pieces on top. Drizzle over the extra virgin olive oil, squeeze over the lemon juice, sprinkle with the salt and plenty of black pepper.

Cover with foil and bake in the oven for 20 minutes or until the chicken is almost cooked and the veggies have softened.

Remove from the oven, lift out the chicken breasts and set aside. Add the broccoli, asparagus, cherry tomatoes and borlotti beans to the dish and mix gently. Pop the chicken breasts back on top, replace the foil and bake in the oven for a further 10 minutes.

Remove the foil and scatter with the herbs. Serve immediately.

1 red onion, cut into fat wedges (see note)

1 red capsicum (pepper), cut into 8 pieces

1 large or 2 small zucchini (courgettes), cut into thick slices

3 garlic cloves, thinly sliced

1 red chilli, sliced

Juice of 1 lemon

Freshly ground black pepper

180 g (6½ oz) broccoli, cut into florets

8 asparagus spears

12 cherry tomatoes

Handful flat-leaf (Italian) parsley, leaves roughly chopped

Handful basil, leaves roughly torn

400 g (14 oz) skinless chicken breast fillet, cut into 4 pieces

400 g (14 oz) tinned borlotti beans, drained and rinsed

2 tablespoons extra virgin olive oil

+

Pinch of salt flakes

Note You might never have considered onion a superfood, but they most certainly are. Onions are part of the family of veggies called alliums—these also include leeks, garlic, bulb spring onion (scallion), spring onions and French shallot. These vegetables have been associated with a lower risk of several cancers, including cancer of the stomach, colon, oesophagus, pancreas, breast, prostate and brain.

Per serve

energy 1500 kJ 360 Cal | protein 32 g | tot. fat 17 g | sat 3 g | poly 2 g | mono 11 g | carb 18 g | sugars 6 g | fibre 10 g

NUTRITION BLOCKS PER SERVE

 3 PLANT    **1** PROTEIN   **1** CARB   **1** FAT

Balinese nasi goreng with chicken

I love Bali, and the dish that is recognised and loved by everyone for breakfast, lunch or dinner on that Indonesian island is Nasi goreng. I've created my own healthier version here using brown rice and loading it up with vegetables to make it a fabulously tasty *Get Lean* recipe. I hope you enjoy it as much as I do. Feel free to change up the protein in this dish. Instead of the chicken you could add barbecued prawns, sliced grilled steak or even a piece of fish.

Serves 4   Time 60 minutes   DF GF NF

Preheat the oven to fan-forced 180°C (350°F/Gas 4).

Place the brown rice in a saucepan and add 750 ml (26 fl oz/3 cups) of water. Bring to the boil over high heat and then reduce the heat to simmer. Cover with the lid and cook for about 45 minutes until the rice is cooked (the time may vary depending on the variety of rice). Once cooked turn off the heat and leave to sit with the lid on.

To make the marinade, combine all the ingredients in a bowl and mix well. Put the chicken in a casserole dish and pour over the marinade, ensuring you coat the meat all over. Bake for 30 minutes or until the chicken is golden and crispy on the outside.

When the chicken and rice are almost cooked, heat 1 tablespoon of the extra virgin olive oil in a frying pan over medium heat. Add the shallots, garlic and anchovies and cook for 2–3 minutes or until the anchovies have almost melted down and the shallots are softened.

Drain any remaining liquid in the brown rice and then add the rice to the pan. Stir to coat the rice with the anchovy–garlic flavours. When you hear the rice slightly popping, add the kecap manis, carrot, spinach, spring onion, coriander and chilli, if using. Stir through and allow to cook for a couple of minutes to just soften the veggies.

Heat the remaining olive oil in a separate frying pan over medium heat. Break the eggs into the pan, turn the heat down to low and cook for 4–5 minutes or until the egg white is set, but the yolk remains runny. Putting the lid on the pan for the last minute helps set the white without having to flip the egg so it looks beautiful on the finished dish.

Shred the chicken and stir through the nasi goreng along with any of the cooking juices. Divide among four plates and serve topped with the fried egg and a wedge of lime.

Note For coeliacs who need a strictly gluten-free diet, ensure you buy a gluten-free soy sauce (these are now available) or use tamari in its place, and double check the label on the kecap manis.

2 French shallots, thinly sliced

2 garlic cloves, crushed

1 carrot, grated or julienned

150 g (5½ oz) English spinach, leaves washed and roughly chopped

2 spring onion (scallions), thinly sliced

Handful coriander (cilantro), leaves picked

1 red chilli, sliced (optional)

1 lime, cut into quarters

400 g (14 oz) skinless chicken breast fillets

6 anchovies in olive oil, drained

4 free-range or organic eggs

200 g (7 oz/1 cup) brown rice (Alternatively use microwavable packs of ready-cooked brown rice to serve 4)

2 tablespoons extra virgin olive oil

+

2 tablespoons kecap manis (Indonesian sweet soy sauce, available at leading supermarkets and Asian food stores, see note)

Ginger soy marinade

2 garlic cloves, crushed

1 teaspoon finely grated ginger

+

250 ml (9 fl oz/1 cup) chicken stock (preferably homemade, see page 113, or good quality store-bought)

1 tablespoon soy sauce (see note)

1 tablespoon Shaoxing rice wine (Chinese cooking wine, available at leading supermarkets and Asian food stores)

Per serve

energy	protein	tot. fat	sat	poly	mono	carb	sugars	fibre
2050 kJ 490 Cal	35 g	17 g	4 g	2 g	9 g	47 g	8 g	4 g

NUTRITION BLOCKS PER SERVE

2 PLANT   1 PROTEIN   2 CARB   1 FAT

Chicken and chickpea curry with pumpkin and spinach

A really good Indian curry is hard to beat, but in restaurants and takeaways they can be really greasy, energy dense and lacking in plant food—far removed from traditional South Asian fare. In this recipe I've cheated and used a ready-made curry paste—but if you have more time, try making your own (see note). It's well worth the effort. This dish shows you curries can be deliciously spicy and flavoursome, while still being light on kilojoules.

Serves 4 Time 35 minutes DF GF NF

Heat the extra virgin olive oil in a saucepan over medium heat. Add the onion and cook for 3–4 minutes until the onion softens. Add the curry paste and gently fry for a couple of minutes until you smell the aromas. Add 60 ml (2 fl oz/¼ cup) of water and stir to combine.

Add the chicken and pumpkin and stir to coat with the curry paste. Add the tomatoes, stock and coconut milk and bring to a simmer. Reduce the heat to low and cook gently for 20 minutes or until the pumpkin is just tender.

Stir in the chickpeas and spinach and cook for 2 minutes, stirring occasionally, or until the spinach has just wilted. Serve immediately.

1 brown onion, thinly sliced

55 g (2 oz/¼ cup) red curry paste (see note)

220 g (7¾ oz) butternut pumpkin (squash), peeled and diced

400 g (14 oz) tinned whole tomatoes (buying them whole they are more flavourful than ready chopped)

200 g (7 oz) baby English spinach leaves, washed

400 g (14 oz) chicken thigh fillets, visible fat trimmed, diced

400 g (14 oz) tinned chickpeas, drained and rinsed

1 tablespoon extra virgin olive oil

80 ml (2½ fl oz/⅓ cup) coconut milk

+

250 ml (9 fl oz/1 cup) chicken stock (preferably homemade, see page 113, or good quality store-bought)

Note You can make your own curry paste by heating a small frying pan over medium heat. Add 1 tablespoon each of coriander seeds, cumin seeds and mustard seeds to the pan and dry-fry them for 1–2 minutes or until you smell the aromas. Transfer to the small container of a Vitamix and add 1 tablespoon of grated ginger, 3 crushed garlic cloves, 1 finely chopped red chilli, a teaspoon of ground turmeric, a teaspoon of ground cinnamon and 60 ml (2 fl oz/¼ cup) of light-flavoured extra virgin olive oil. Blend on level 10 for 30 seconds or until you have a smooth paste. Alternatively, you can crush the roasted spices using a mortar and pestle and then mix with the other ingredients by hand. Transfer the paste to a jar and drizzle a little extra oil over the top to seal. This will then keep in the fridge for 3–4 weeks.

Per serve

energy	protein	tot. fat	sat	poly	mono	carb	sugars	fibre
1610 kJ 380 Cal	29 g	17 g	6 g	3 g	7 g	25 g	9 g	8 g

NUTRITION BLOCKS PER SERVE

2 PLANT **1** PROTEIN **1** CARB **1** FAT

Roast chicken with mung bean dhal stuffing

Thanks go to my mum for this idea of using mung bean dhal as a stuffing for chicken. It's a delicious low GI twist to a traditional meal. Spoon any extra stuffing that doesn't fit into the cavity of the chicken into a loaf (bar) tin and bake alongside the chicken. Perfect for a family Sunday dinner. Don't be put off by the time for this recipe. Most of this is used during roasting when you can be off doing something else.

Serves 6 Time 2 hours 15 minutes DF GF NF

Place the mung beans, turmeric, cumin and pepper in a saucepan with 500 ml (17 fl oz/2 cups) of water. Bring to the boil and then reduce the heat and simmer for 30 minutes. Drain and set aside.

Heat the extra virgin olive oil in a frying pan over medium heat, then add the onion, garlic and capsicums, and sauté for a couple of minutes until soft.

Add the sautéed ingredients to the mung bean mixture, along with a pinch of salt. Beat the egg and stir through the cooked mung beans to bind the stuffing.

Preheat the oven to fan-forced 180°C (350°F/Gas 4).

Stuff the chicken with the mung bean mixture and squeeze the lemon juice over the chicken. Grind some black pepper over the top.

Cover the chicken with foil and bake in a roasting tin for 1 hour.

Once the chicken has been cooking for 1 hour, add the carrot, squash, zucchini and beetroot to the tin and cook for a further 20 minutes under the foil.

Remove the foil to brown the chicken, toss the veggies and cook for a further 20 minutes.

Steam the broccoli, green beans and brussels sprouts just as you are getting ready to serve. These will only take a couple of minutes. Do not overcook them—they should still be slightly crunchy.

Carve the chicken and serve with a spoonful of the stuffing and a generous half plate combination of roast and steamed veggies. Garnish with the coriander and parsley. Spoon the juices from the roasting tin over the meat as a light gravy and serve.

Note You'll find mung beans in the dried peas and beans section of the supermarket or in health food stores. They are used often in Indian cuisine to make dhal and hence we've used Indian spices here. I love to use them as the smart carb in a meal as they are fabulous for fibre, while delivering slow-release carbs and a good dose of plant protein.

¼ teaspoon ground turmeric

¼ teaspoon ground cumin

Freshly ground black pepper

1 onion, finely diced

1 garlic clove, crushed

½ red capsicum (pepper), diced

¼ yellow capsicum (pepper), diced

Juice of 1 lemon

3 large carrots, roughly chopped

6 baby (pattypan) squash, roughly chopped

2 large zucchini (courgettes), roughly chopped

2 beetroot (beets), roughly chopped

200 g (7 oz/1 head) broccoli, chopped into florets

250 g (9 oz/2 cups) sliced green beans

340 g (12 oz) brussels sprouts

1 tablespoon coriander (cilantro), leaves chopped

1 tablespoon chopped flat-leaf (Italian) parsley

1 whole free-range or organic chicken (1.5 kg/3 lb 5 oz)

1 free-range or organic egg

225 g (8 oz/1 cup) dried mung beans (see note)

1 tablespoon extra virgin olive oil

+

Pinch of iodised salt

Per serve

energy	protein	tot. fat	sat	poly	mono	carb	sugars	fibre
1914 kJ 460 Cal	36 g	23 g	6 g	12 g	12 g	18 g	15 g	14 g

NUTRITION BLOCKS PER SERVE

 3 PLANT   **2** PROTEIN  **1** CARB   ½ FAT

Turkey and sun-dried tomato meatloaf

I absolutely love meatloaf but I never buy them as I don't know the quality of the meat used, or what else has been added. This recipe is a real winner and works equally well warm from the oven for dinner, or sliced cold for lunch the next day. I love to serve it warm with boiled or roast kipfler potatoes and mixed steamed greens drizzled with extra virgin olive oil and lemon, or cold with a simple salad, or as my protein filling for a sandwich or wrap.

Serves 4 Time 1 hour 15 minutes DF NF

Preheat the oven to fan-forced 180°C (350°F/Gas 4).

Put the eggs in a saucepan of water and bring to the boil over medium–high heat. Once the water is boiling, cook for 8 minutes then drain and refill the pan with cold water to help cool the eggs. Once cool enough to handle, peel and set aside.

Meanwhile, place the garlic, onion, sun-dried tomatoes, parsley and bread into the large container of a Vitamix or food processor. Blitz until the mixture resembles soft breadcrumbs. Combine this mixture in a bowl with the turkey mince, tomato relish, cayenne pepper, salt and black pepper, using your hands to combine the mixture well.

Grease (with the extra virgin olive oil) and line a 22 x 11 x 7 cm (8½ x 4¼ x 2¾ inches) loaf (bar) tin with baking paper. Fill the mixture half way up the sides of the tin. Place the whole boiled eggs on top of the mixture, spaced out down the centre, then place the rest of the mixture over the top of the eggs, ensuring they are totally covered. Press down gently so the mixture is evenly distributed.

Bake for 1 hour, or until the meatloaf is lightly golden on top and firm to the touch.

Remove the meatloaf from the oven and allow to cool slightly in the tin for 10 minutes before turning out. Cut into thick slices and serve. Otherwise allow to cool completely before covering and storing in the fridge for 3–4 days.

½ garlic clove
½ red onion
50 g (1¾ oz) sun-dried tomatoes
2 tablespoons roughly chopped flat-leaf (Italian) parsley
¼ teaspoon cayenne pepper
Freshly ground black pepper

2 free-range or organic eggs
500 g (1 lb 2 oz) minced (ground) turkey (see note)

2 slices wholegrain bread

1 teaspoon extra virgin olive oil

+
2 tablespoons tomato relish or chutney
¼ teaspoon iodised salt

Note Turkey is an excellent choice as your protein food when putting together a meal. Overall the meat is pretty lean, particularly when you remove the skin, although if cooking the drumsticks or a whole bird I would always cook with the skin on to prevent the meat from drying out. Although the breast is leaner, like chicken the brown meat contains considerably more iron and zinc. Turkey is also a terrific source of vitamin B6, niacin and phosphorus, and is an important source of the antioxidant mineral selenium, which is often low in our diets.

Per serve

energy	protein	tot. fat	sat	poly	mono	carb	sugars	fibre
1240 kJ 300 Cal	35 g	7 g	2 g	3 g	2 g	20 g	11 g	4 g

NUTRITION BLOCKS PER SERVE

½ PLANT 1 PROTEIN 1 CARB 0 FAT

Apricot chicken with couscous

Apricot chicken is a classic family dish, although it can be very sweet if tinned, sweetened apricot nectar is used. Instead, I've used dried apricots, along with fresh herbs and spices here for a healthy alternative. For a modern take, the chicken is served with a wonderful Middle Eastern style wholegrain couscous with eggplant, coriander and almonds. The combination is, I promise you, totally delicious.

Serves 4 Time 30 minutes DF*

Heat half the stock in a small saucepan over high heat. Once simmering, add the dried apricots, turn off the heat and allow to soak for about 5 minutes.

Heat 2 teaspoons of the extra virgin olive oil in a large frying pan over medium–high heat. Add the chicken pieces and cook for 3–4 minutes, turning frequently, until brown on all sides. Remove from the pan and set aside.

Heat the remaining olive oil in the pan, turning the heat down a little, add the onions and gently sauté for a few minutes until soft and translucent. Stir in the garlic and ginger and sauté for another minute. Add the thyme and curry powder and stir to combine. Then add the remaining stock and bring to a simmer.

Using a Vitamix on level 10, or food processor, blitz the apricots with the soaking liquid to form a purée. Add this to the pan and stir to combine.

Return the chicken pieces to the pan and stir into the sauce. Simmer for a further 10 minutes.

Meanwhile, bring a saucepan of water to the boil and pour in the couscous. Bring to a simmer and allow to cook for about 4 minutes, or until *al dente*. (If you want, you can use stock to cook the couscous for more flavour.) Once cooked, drain in a sieve and set aside.

Heat the extra virgin olive oil in a small frying pan over medium heat. Add the onion and eggplant and gently sauté for 3–4 minutes, stirring regularly, until the onion has softened and the eggplant has turned a slightly golden colour.

Add the cooked couscous, coriander, almonds, a generous grind of black pepper and the salt. Mix well and taste to check the seasoning. Adjust as necessary.

Serve the couscous with the apricot chicken, a simple green salad, and if you like, top with a dollop of natural yoghurt.

Note You'll find whole-wheat Israeli or pearl couscous at good health food stores and grocers, or at a Middle Eastern store if there is one in your area. If you can't find it, just use wholegrain regular couscous instead, stocked by most supermarkets, and check the cooking instructions.

40 g (2½ oz) dried apricot halves (roughly 6 whole apricots)

2 brown onions, halved then sliced

1 garlic clove, crushed

1 teaspoon thyme leaves

1 teaspoon curry powder

1 teaspoon finely grated ginger

500 g (1 lb 2 oz) skinless chicken breast fillets, cut into chunks

80 g (2¾ oz) natural yoghurt, to serve (optional, not for dairy-free diets of course)

1 tablespoon extra virgin olive oil

+

500 ml (17 fl oz/2 cups) chicken stock (preferably homemade, see page 113, or good quality store-bought)

Eggplant almond couscous

1 red onion, thinly sliced

½ eggplant (aubergine), finely diced

2 large handfuls coriander (cilantro), leaves roughly chopped

Freshly ground black pepper

140 g (5 oz) whole-wheat Israeli or pearl couscous (see note)

1 tablespoon extra virgin olive oil

2 tablespoons roughly chopped dry-roasted almonds

+

Pinch of salt flakes

Per serve

energy	protein	tot. fat	sat	poly	mono	carb	sugars	fibre
1790 kJ 430 Cal	36 g	15 g	2 g	2 g	10 g	32 g	9 g	9 g

NUTRITION BLOCKS PER SERVE

 **2** PLANT **1** PROTEIN **1** CARB **1** FAT

* The nutrition analysis does not include the green salad serving suggestion.

Macadamia chicken with green pea and broccoli mint smash

This one is sure to become a family favourite. The crunchy nut and seed topping is divine with the chicken, but the real winner is the smash. Even the kids ask for extra veggies when I serve them this way! Bigger eaters can simply take two pieces of chicken (with each piece counting as 1 Protein Block and 1 Fat Block). You could further boost the plant content by adding steamed leafy greens or a simple green leaf salad.

Serves 4   Time 45 minutes   GF

Preheat the oven to fan-forced 180°C (350°F/Gas 4). Line a baking tray with baking paper.

Cut the potatoes in half, toss them in a bowl with the extra virgin olive oil and spread out on the prepared baking tray. Roast for 30–40 minutes until a lovely golden colour.

Using a food processor or Vitamix, use the pulse setting to gently grind the nuts, seeds, garlic, lemon zest, spices, tarragon and parmesan until the mixture resembles breadcrumbs—don't over-blend or you'll end up with a paste.

Cut the chicken breasts horizontally to give you 4 chicken fillets. Place the chicken fillets in a casserole dish or on a baking tray lined with baking paper. Spoon the crumb mixture over the chicken, pressing softly to form a crust topping, then scatter over the rosemary. Pop the dish into the oven alongside the potatoes to roast for 15 minutes or until golden on top and cooked through.

Meanwhile, to make the pea smash, bring a saucepan of water to the boil over high heat. Put the broccoli and peas into a steamer, cover with the lid and place on top of the pan. Cook for 2–3 minutes, or until soft enough to mash. (Alternatively, place the peas and broccoli in a microwave-proof bowl with a little water, cover and cook on High for 3 minutes.)

Strain any water from the vegetables, then mash roughly with a fork. Mix through the mint and basil, crumble over the goat's cheese and stir to just combine. Season with a pinch of salt and plenty of black pepper and serve warm with the crusted chicken and roast potatoes.

Note Don't worry about the fat content in this dish as it is almost all coming from those fabulously healthy nuts and seeds, along with a little extra virgin olive oil. This makes the overall recipe low in saturated fats, while you get the benefits of those good unsaturated fats. The fibre content is also boosted by the topping and the veggies, giving you a healthy 10 g per serve.

2 rosemary sprigs, leaves picked

1 garlic clove

Grated zest of ½ lemon

2 teaspoons ground coriander

1 teaspoon ground cumin

1 tablespoon tarragon, finely chopped

200 g (7 oz/1 head) broccoli, chopped

140 g (5 oz/1 cup) frozen peas

2 handfuls mint, leaves roughly chopped

6 basil leaves, finely shredded

Freshly ground black pepper

2 tablespoons grated parmesan cheese

2 x 200 g (7 oz) skinless chicken breast fillets

40 g (1½ oz) goat's cheese (or labne)

400 g (14 oz) small potatoes in their skins (chat or kipfler are ideal)

1 tablespoon extra virgin olive oil (see note)

40 g (1½ oz/¼ cup) raw macadamia nuts

30 g (1 oz) raw almonds

2 tablespoons sunflower seeds

2 tablespoons sesame seeds

1 teaspoon chia seeds

+

Pinch of salt flakes

Per serve

energy	protein	tot. fat	sat	poly	mono	carb	sugars	fibre
2030 kJ 480 Cal	38 g	28 g	5 g	5 g	15 g	16 g	3 g	10 g

NUTRITION BLOCKS PER SERVE

2 PLANT   **1** PROTEIN   **1** CARB   **1** FAT

Vegetarian

Baked falafels with tzatziki dip

Falafels are traditional Middle Eastern fare and they are delicious when done well. However, usually they are deep-fried, and not in the best quality oils. They also tend to contain a little white flour and are not therefore gluten free. So this is my falafel makeover. I've used lupin flour to bind them instead of white flour and have baked them rather than deep-frying. You can buy lupin flour online and from good health food stores.

Serves 4   Time 1 hour 45 minutes   DF GF NF V

Put the chickpeas, onion, garlic, lemon juice, spices, parsley and tahini into a food processor bowl and blend for 30 seconds or until combined. Take care not to over-process as you want the mix to have a little texture rather than become a paste.

Transfer to a mixing bowl and mix through the lupin flour with a spoon. Cover and refrigerate for at least an hour. (The mix can be kept in the fridge for 3–4 days until you are ready to cook.)

Preheat the oven to 180°C (350°F/Gas 4). Line a baking tray with baking paper.

Using wet hands (this helps prevent the mixture sticking), take a spoonful of mixture and shape it into a ball, roughly the size of a walnut, then roll it in sesame seeds. Repeat until you have used all of the mixture—this will make roughly 12 falafels.

Place the falafels onto the prepared baking tray and drizzle with the extra virgin olive oil. Roll them to coat in the oil and then slightly flatten with your fingers or a spatula. Bake in the oven for 45 minutes, turning halfway through cooking to crisp up evenly on both sides.

Meanwhile, make the tzatziki by simply combining the yoghurt, grated cucumber, crushed garlic, mint and lemon juice in a small bowl. Refrigerate until ready to serve.

Serve the falafels hot from the oven with the tzatziki dip on the side.

½ onion, cut into quarters

1 garlic clove

Juice of ¼ lemon

½ teaspoon cumin seeds

½ teaspoon coriander seeds

¼ teaspoon ground cardamom

Handful flat-leaf (Italian) parsley

400 g (14 oz) tinned chickpeas, drained and rinsed

1½ tablespoons lupin flour (see note)

1 tablespoon tahini

2 tablespoons sesame seeds

2 tablespoons extra virgin olive oil

Tzatziki

¼ Lebanese (short) cucumber, finely grated with skin on

½ garlic clove, crushed

Handful mint, leaves finely chopped

Juice of ¼ lemon

130 g (4½ oz/½ cup) natural yoghurt

Note Lupin is a legume, but is unusual in that it has a low carbohydrate content (less than 10 per cent dry weight) and is higher in protein than almost all other plant foods. It is also superbly rich in both soluble fibre and resistant starch, both of which feed the good bacteria in your gut. This makes lupin a winner for gut health. The combination also means that when substituted for grain flours in a recipe such as this, you lower the GI and the available carbohydrate, while boosting protein and fibre.

Per serve

energy	protein	tot. fat	sat	poly	mono	carb	sugars	fibre
1300 kJ / 310 Cal	14 g	19 g	3 g	4 g	10 g	18 g	6 g	9 g

NUTRITION BLOCKS PER SERVE

½ PLANT   1 PROTEIN   0 CARB   2 FAT

Tex-Mex tofu soft tacos

My family love Mexican-style food and we regularly have tacos or fajitas with various fillings and combinations. The best way to serve them is to pop everything in the middle of the table so that everyone can make their own. Here I've used tofu in place of meat and, if you have a vegan in the group, they can simply omit the yoghurt. Corn tortillas should be gluten free, but do check the ingredients list on the packet—they should be made entirely from corn.

Serves 4 Time 20 minutes GF NF V

Preheat the oven to fan-forced 160°C (315°F/Gas 2–3). Drain the tofu, slice and press gently between two pieces of paper towel to remove the excess moisture.

Combine the cumin, oregano, paprika and chilli in a bowl. Crumble the tofu slices into the spice blend and stir to coat.

Wrap the tortillas in foil and pop them into the oven to warm.

Heat 2 teaspoons of the extra virgin olive oil in a frying pan over medium–high heat. Add the onion and capsicum and sauté for 2 minutes. Add the remaining oil and the spiced tofu. Cook for 3 minutes until heated through. Season to taste with a pinch of salt and black pepper.

Divide the lettuce, tofu mixture, tomato and avocado across the warm tortillas. Top each with a dollop of yoghurt, and serve with lime wedges and a scattering of coriander. Alternatively, pop everything in bowls in the middle of the table and each person can make up their own.

1 teaspoon ground cumin
2 teaspoons dried oregano
2 teaspoons sweet paprika
¼ teaspoon chilli flakes
Freshly ground black pepper
1 brown onion, diced
1 red capsicum (pepper), diced

600 g (1 lb 5 oz) firm tofu (see note)

1 tablespoon extra virgin olive oil

+
Pinch of salt flakes

To serve

1 small cos (romaine) lettuce, shredded
1 tomato, diced
2 limes, cut into wedges
Handful coriander (cilantro) leaves

80 g (2¾ oz) natural yoghurt

4 large or 8 mini corn tortillas

½ avocado, diced

Note Tofu is made by coagulating soy milk and then pressing together the resulting curds. It's a terrific source of protein and the soy bean is one of few plants that contain all of the essential amino acids. This makes it ideal for vegetarian and vegan diets. Tofu also provides good amounts of iron and zinc, B group vitamins, magnesium, phosphorus and the antioxidant mineral selenium. All up it's a pretty impressive nutrition package, worthy of any diet. A tofu serve of 100 g (3½ oz) provides 500 kJ (120 Cal), 12 g protein, 7 g fat (mostly as polyunsaturated fat), no carbohydrate and 3.5 g of fibre.

Per serve

energy	protein	tot. fat	sat	poly	mono	carb	sugars	fibre
1975 kJ 470 Cal	24 g	25 g	4 g	9 g	11 g	29 g	7 g	15 g

NUTRITION BLOCKS PER SERVE

3 PLANT 1 PROTEIN 1 CARB 1 FAT

Almond and chickpea burgers with tarragon yoghurt

We can all benefit from having at least one vegetarian meal per week—'meatless Monday' is a movement dedicated to this and I think it's a wonderful initiative. But if you are vegetarian, then this combination of nuts, legumes, seeds and grains delivers a perfect balance of protein with all the essential amino acids. It's rich in good fats and with the smart carbs coming from the wholegrain roll and chickpeas, it's a low GI meal that will keep you fuller for longer.

Serves 4   Time 40 minutes   V

Cut the stems from the beetroot, leaving 2–3 cm (about ¾–1¼ inches) of stem—this ensures the beetroot retain their gorgeous colour. Scrub the skins to remove any dirt, but leave the skins on. Place the beetroot in a saucepan and cover well with water. Place over high heat and bring to the boil. Reduce the heat to low, cover with the lid and simmer for 20–30 minutes until tender. (The larger the beetroot the longer they will take to cook.) Drain and run under cold water to cool enough to touch. Using your fingers, peel off the skins (wear food-grade rubber gloves to prevent staining of your hands). Slice and set aside.

While the beetroot is cooking, make the almond and chickpea patties. Blitz the garlic, basil, spring onions, chickpeas, flaxseed and almonds in a food processor or Vitamix at level 10, using the tamper to push the ingredients down into the blades. Turn out the ground mixture onto a plate, divide into 4 and roll into burger shapes.

Heat the extra virgin olive oil in a frying pan and add the patties. Cook for 2–3 minutes on each side until golden and warmed through.

To make the tarragon yoghurt, mix the yoghurt, lemon juice and tarragon together in a bowl. Season with black pepper to taste.

Serve the patties in the wholegrain rolls spread with the mashed avocado, and top with the sliced tomato, lettuce and beetroot. Drizzle with the tarragon yoghurt dressing and enjoy!

Note Beetroot has rarely been listed on typical superfood lists, but that is all likely to change. Recent research has shown that this beautifully vibrant purple root vegetable can significantly lower your blood pressure, and it's one of the best sources of dietary nitrates. These are converted to nitric oxide in the body, which in turn helps to relax blood vessels and lower blood pressure. Beetroot is also an excellent source of folate, essential for protecting DNA from oxidative damage through our lifespan, and for creating healthy new cells. You'll also get a good dose of fibre from them, and they seem to boost the detoxification processes in the body. All up they are a pretty worthwhile addition to your diet.

2 beetroot (beets) (alternatively, use tinned sliced beetroot, see note)

1 garlic clove, crushed

Handful basil, leaves picked

2 spring onions (scallions), sliced

Freshly ground black pepper

1 tomato, sliced

60 g (2¼ oz) lettuce, shredded (or rocket/arugula or baby English spinach leaves)

400 g (14 oz) tinned chickpeas, drained and rinsed

4 wholegrain rolls (about 50 g/1¾ oz each)

1 tablespoon flaxseed (linseed)

40 g (1½ oz/¼ cup) raw almonds

½ avocado, mashed

1 tablespoon extra virgin olive oil

Tarragon yoghurt

½ lemon, juiced

1 tablespoon chopped tarragon

100 g (3½ oz) natural yoghurt

+

1 tablespoon balsamic vinegar

Per serve

energy	protein	tot. fat	sat	poly	mono	carb	sugars	fibre
1640 kJ 390 Cal	16 g	17 g	3 g	5 g	8 g	37 g	9 g	11 g

NUTRITION BLOCKS PER SERVE

 **2** PLANT   **1** PROTEIN   **1** CARB   **1** FAT

Quinoa, eggplant and bocconcini croquettes

These croquettes are deliciously crunchy on the outside, but soft on the inside with the added bonus of the melting bocconcini centre. Serve them with a gorgeous mixed green salad, sprinkled with a few sunflower seeds or pepitas (pumpkin seeds). Don't worry about the saturated fat in this recipe as it's almost all in the cheese and the latest research has been positive with regards to dairy fat when accompanied by the protein and calcium also found in dairy.

Serves 4   Time 1 hour 30 minutes   NF V*

Preheat the oven to fan-forced 180°C (350°F/Gas 4). Line a baking tray with baking paper. Prick the eggplant with a sharp knife all over the skin. Place the eggplant, whole, on the prepared tray and bake for 1 hour or until softened. The skin should look slightly wrinkled. Remove from the oven and set aside to cool.

While the eggplant is in the oven, put the quinoa in a saucepan and cover with water. Drain in a sieve and repeat. This washes away the bitter compounds, called saponins, on the surface. Return to the pan and add 170 ml (5½ fl oz/⅔ cup) of water. Bring to the boil, then reduce the heat to a simmer and cook for about 15 minutes until the water has been absorbed and the quinoa is cooked.

Meanwhile, place the sweet potato in a separate saucepan and cover with water. Place over high heat and bring to the boil, then reduce the heat and simmer for 10–15 minutes until soft. Drain well and then mash. Set aside to cool.

Cut the eggplant in half and scoop out the flesh. Roughly chop the flesh. Discard the skin. Place the eggplant, quinoa, sweet potato mash, garlic, parsley, cumin, salt and pepper in a large bowl and mix together well. Roll into 8 patties, placing half a bocconcini ball in the centre of each patty.

Mix the breadcrumbs in a bowl with the grated parmesan. Crumb the patties, dipping them into the cornflour then the beaten egg, then the breadcrumb and cheese mixture.

Heat the extra virgin olive oil in a deep frying pan over high heat until the oil starts to glisten. Gently place the patties into the hot oil, in batches, and fry for 2 minutes before flipping over and frying the other side until they are golden brown. Place on a plate lined with paper towel and keep warm in the oven while you cook the remaining croquettes.

Serve the croquettes with a simple green salad dressed with lemon juice and extra virgin olive oil.

Note The oil in this recipe is used to cook and not all is consumed. You'll find about half of the oil will be absorbed by the croquettes and so this is the amount I have used for the nutrition analysis below.

1 eggplant (aubergine)

2 garlic cloves, finely chopped or crushed

2 tablespoons chopped flat-leaf (Italian) parsley

1 teaspoon ground cumin

Freshly ground black pepper

4 bocconcini balls

1 tablespoon grated parmesan cheese* (vegetarians, see note page 93)

1 free-range or organic egg, beaten with a fork

65 g (2¼ oz/⅓ cup) quinoa

200 g (7 oz) sweet potato, peeled and cut into chunks

2 slices wholegrain bread, processed into breadcrumbs

30 g (1 oz/¼ cup) cornflour (cornstarch)

60 ml (2 fl oz/¼ cup) extra virgin olive oil (see note)

+

1 teaspoon iodised salt

Per serve

energy	protein	tot. fat	sat	poly	mono	carb	sugars	fibre
1530 kJ 370 Cal	17 g	19 g	8 g	2 g	9 g	28 g	4 g	4 g

NUTRITION BLOCKS PER SERVE

1 PLANT   1 PROTEIN   1 CARB   1 FAT

* The nutrition analysis does not include the green salad serving suggestion.

Mrs Mac's lentil loaf

Mrs Mac is my mum and this is her recipe that she hand-wrote into a recipe journal my family gave me for my birthday a few years ago. The first time I made it, I couldn't quite believe how good it was! You can serve this hot from the oven, or cold at a later date, with a wonderful mixed salad for a complete vegetarian meal. Don't be put off by the time it takes. This includes over an hour of cooking in the oven, and the preparation time is actually only about 15–20 minutes.

Serves 6   Time 1 hour 40 minutes   NF V*

Wash the lentils and put them into a saucepan with the stock and bay leaf. Bring to the boil, reduce the heat and simmer for 20–30 minutes until the lentils are soft and cooked through. Remove the bay leaf and drain.

Preheat the oven to 180°C (350°F/Gas 4).

Put the bread slices into a food processor, or Vitamix on level 5 using your tamper to push down into the blades, and blitz into breadcrumbs.

Finely dice the onion, mushrooms, capsicums and garlic. Heat the extra virgin olive oil in a frying pan over medium heat and sauté the veggies for 4–5 minutes until softened, but take care not to burn.

Remove the pan from the heat and add the cooked lentils along with the breadcrumbs, coriander, lemon juice and zest, and half of the cheese. Mix well to combine, season with plenty of black pepper and taste before adding a little salt if needed. Add half of the beaten egg and, only if you think the mixture needs to be softer, add the other half of the egg. You want the mixture to be moist but not sloppy.

Line a 22 x 11 x 7 cm (8½ x 4¼ x 2¾ inches) loaf (bar) tin with baking paper. Spoon the mixture into the prepared tin and bake in the oven for 1 hour. It should be firm to touch at this point. Sprinkle the remaining cheese over the top and pop it back into the oven for 10 minutes.

Remove the lentil loaf from the oven and allow to cool slightly in the tin for 10 minutes before turning out. Cut into thick slices and serve. Otherwise allow to cool completely before covering and storing in the fridge for up to 5 days.

1 dried bay leaf
1 brown onion
125 g (4½ oz) button mushrooms
½ red capsicum (pepper)
½ yellow capsicum (pepper)
1 garlic clove
2 tablespoons finely chopped coriander (cilantro) leaves
Juice and grated zest of 1 lemon
Freshly ground black pepper

90 g (3¼ oz) red lentils
90 g (3¼ oz) green lentils
170 g (6 oz) strong cheddar cheese*, grated (see note)
1 free-range or organic egg, beaten with a fork

4 slices wholegrain bread

1 teaspoon extra virgin olive oil

+

400 ml (14 fl oz) vegetable stock (preferably homemade, or good quality store-bought)
¼ teaspoon iodised salt

Note* To make this recipe suitable for vegetarians, you can purchase a cheddar-style hard cheese made with rennet obtained from micro-organisms. These will be clearly labelled as vegetarian.

Per serve

energy	protein	tot. fat	sat	poly	mono	carb	sugars	fibre
1360 kJ 320 Cal	21 g	13 g	7 g	1 g	4 g	27 g	4 g	8 g

NUTRITION BLOCKS PER SERVE

1 PLANT   1 PROTEIN   1 CARB   0 FAT

Mediterranean chickpea stuffed sweet potatoes

Stuffed baked potatoes were all the rage when I was growing up, but they seem to have faded from fashion. So I'm bringing them back with, of course, an injection of extra nutrition! I love to use orange sweet potatoes as these have a few extra phytonutrients over regular potato varieties. The filling is a plant-powered mix of Mediterranean ingredients including chickpeas, sun-dried tomatoes and olives.

Serves 4 Time 1 hour 10 minutes GF NF V

Preheat the oven to 180°C (350°F/Gas 4). Line a baking tray with baking paper.

Scrub the sweet potatoes, prick with a fork and place on the prepared tray. Cover with foil and bake for 45 minutes. Uncover and bake for a further 15 minutes or until very soft when pierced with the tip of a knife.

Meanwhile, heat the extra virgin olive oil in a saucepan over medium heat. Add the onion and garlic and sauté for 3 minutes or until softened. Add the passata, oregano, sun-dried tomatoes, olives and chickpeas to the pan. Bring to the boil then reduce the heat to low and simmer for 20 minutes until slightly thickened. Add a little water if the sauce is getting too thick. Stir through the spinach just before serving so that it just wilts.

Slice the roasted sweet potatoes lengthways, nearly all the way through, leaving the base intact. Fill with the chickpea mixture, crumble the feta over the top and scatter over the basil. Serve.

1 brown onion, diced

2 garlic cloves, diced

500 ml (17 fl oz/2 cups) tomato passata (puréed tomatoes)

2 teaspoons dried oregano

4 tablespoons chopped sun-dried tomatoes

4 tablespoons chopped kalamata olives

150 g (5½ oz) baby English spinach leaves, washed

Handful basil leaves

400 g (14 oz) tinned chickpeas, rinsed and drained (see note)

80 g (2¾ oz) feta cheese

4 x 200 g (7 oz) small sweet potatoes, unpeeled (or 2 larger sweet potatoes cut in half, see note)

1 tablespoon extra virgin olive oil

Notes Although the total carbohydrate in this meal is a little higher, you're only counting 1 Carb Block—the sweet potato. The chickpeas also provide some carbohydrate, but we're counting them as our Protein Block for this meal. Rest assured the overall kilojoule count is right on track, the overall carbs remain moderate and the meal is nutrient-rich with an impressive 14 g of fibre to boot. You can bake the sweet potatoes in advance and keep them in the fridge. Then all you need do is reheat them and top with the filling to serve.

Per serve

energy	protein	tot. fat	sat	poly	mono	carb	sugars	fibre
1930 kJ 460 Cal	17 g	17 g	5 g	3 g	8 g	54 g	26 g	14 g

*All sugars naturally present.

NUTRITION BLOCKS PER SERVE

3 PLANT **1** PROTEIN **1** CARB **1** FAT

Roast veggie tart with quinoa crust

This is one of my favourite *Get Lean, Stay Lean* recipes. I wanted to create a pastry that was easy to make and really tasty using only ingredients from the *Get Lean* pantry. This quinoa crust hits the bullseye. It's also gluten free so suitable for coeliacs or those of you with gluten sensitivity. It is higher in fat, but it's mostly monounsaturated fat—exactly what we want—and unlike commercial pastries has no trans fats or refined white flour.

Serves 6   Time 1 hour   GF NF V*

Preheat the oven to 180°C (350°F/Gas 4). Line a baking tray with baking paper.

Toss the beetroot, zucchini, pumpkin, onion and sweet potato with 1 tablespoon of the extra virgin olive oil, a pinch of salt and a good grind of black pepper. Spread out on the prepared tray and roast for about 30 minutes or until the veggies are tender. (See note.) Remove from the oven and allow to cool slightly.

While the veggies are roasting, make your pastry case. Using a food processor or a Vitamix on level 6 combine the quinoa, extra virgin olive oil, parmesan and mustard. Blitz for a couple of minutes until the mixture resembles dark flecky sand. (If you are using a food processor the result will not be as fine as using a Vitamix. The alternative is to use quinoa flour, although this will not give the same crunchy texture—you'll have a more traditional pastry-smooth texture.) Press the quinoa crumbs into a 20 cm (8 inch) round springform cake tin, evenly around the sides and base. Blind bake for 10–15 minutes until slightly golden in colour.

While the vegetables and crust are baking, heat 1 teaspoon of olive oil in a frying pan over medium heat. Add the leek and thyme and gently sauté for 2–3 minutes until the leek is soft. Season with a good grind of black pepper.

Whisk the eggs and milk together in a bowl.

Once the quinoa crust is ready, spread the leeks on the base of the quinoa crust, then pour the egg mixture over the top. Place back in the oven for 15 minutes or until just set. You can tell this by gently moving the tin—if the middle of the custard wobbles, it needs a few more minutes.

Remove the tart from the oven and leave it to cool slightly—this gives the custard time to set firmly. Top with the roasted vegetables and dollops of creamy feta. Serve at room temperature with a leafy green salad dressed with extra virgin olive oil and lemon.

Note When roasting the vegetables just keep in mind the consistency of size and cooking time. Some vegetables cook faster than others.

1 beetroot (beet), peeled and cut into 8 wedges (see note)

1 large zucchini (courgette), sliced

60 g (2¼ oz) jap or butternut pumpkin (winter squash), cut into bite-sized chunks

1 red onion, cut into 8 wedges

Freshly ground black pepper

½ leek, white part with only a little of the green, thinly sliced

½ teaspoon thyme leaves

40 g (1½ oz) parmesan cheese*, grated (vegetarians, see note page 93)

6 free-range or organic eggs

60 ml (2 fl oz/¼ cup) low fat milk

30 g (1 oz) feta cheese

70 g (2½ oz) sweet potato, unpeeled, scrubbed and cut into bite-sized chunks

200 g (7 oz/1 cup) quinoa (or use quinoa flour for a smoother crust if you prefer)

125 ml (4½ fl oz/½ cup) extra virgin olive oil, plus 1 tablespoon extra to roast the veggies and 1 teaspoon to fry the leeks

+

1 teaspoon wholegrain mustard

Pinch of salt

Per serve

energy	protein	tot. fat	sat	poly	mono	carb	sugars	fibre
1800 kJ 430 Cal	15 g	30 g	7 g	4 g	18 g	24 g	0 g	4 g

NUTRITION BLOCKS PER SERVE

 PLANT   PROTEIN   CARB   FAT

* The nutrition analysis does not include the green salad serving suggestion.

Veggie quinoa stir-fry with garlic and ginger

Quinoa is a really versatile ingredient—I like to cook up a bigger batch and keep it in my fridge or freezer ready to add to dishes such as this. It's a terrific addition to a vegetarian diet as it has a higher protein content and boasts better iron, zinc and other nutrients than most true grains. The addition of edamame beans boosts the protein content of this meal further, giving the final dish a pretty good level of 18 g per serve. To make it vegan friendly, omit the oyster sauce.

Serves 4 Time 30 minutes DF GF NF V

Put the quinoa in a saucepan and cover with water. Drain in a sieve and repeat. This washes away the bitter compounds, called saponins, on the surface. Return to the pan and add 500 ml (17 fl oz/2 cups) of water. Bring to the boil, then reduce the heat to a simmer and cook for about 15 minutes until the water has been absorbed and the quinoa is cooked. Turn the heat off but leave the lid on.

Heat the extra virgin olive oil in a wok or frying pan over medium heat. Add the onion, garlic, ginger and chilli, if using, and fry for 2–3 minutes until softened.

Add the squash, capsicums and beans to the pan, turn the heat up to high and stir-fry for 1–2 minutes before adding the bok choy, mushrooms and edamame beans. Stir-fry tossing the veggies around the wok for a further 2–3 minutes. Add the tamari, rice wine, oyster sauce and sesame oil and stir to combine.

Fluff the quinoa with a fork and add to the wok. Toss to combine. Divide between bowls and sprinkle with the pepitas. Serve immediately.

Note Quinoa is cooked and eaten as a grain alternative, but it is in fact a seed. You'll often see it called a pseudo-grain for that reason, similar to amaranth. It boasts an impressive nutritional profile. Compared to brown rice, quinoa has 75 per cent more fibre and double the protein, plus it provides all of the essential amino acids—the building blocks of protein. By comparison most commonly eaten grains tend to be low in the amino acid lysine, essential for muscle growth and repair. This makes quinoa an especially good choice for vegetarians. It's rich in several B group vitamins required to turn the food you eat into energy to fuel your body. It is also low GI, making it an excellent smart carb choice for your Dr Joanna Plate.

1 brown onion, sliced

2 garlic clove, finely chopped

1 tablespoon finely grated ginger

2 red chillies, chopped (optional)

8 baby (pattypan) squash, cut into quarters

1 red capsicum (pepper), sliced

1 yellow capsicum (pepper), sliced

100 g (3½ oz) green beans, trimmed

4 bok choy (pak choy), cut lengthways into quarters

8 oyster or shiitake mushrooms, sliced (or any other type of mushroom of your choice)

150 g (5½ oz/1 cup) edamame beans, (you can buy these frozen in major supermarkets or Asian food stores— defrost before using; alternatively, use tinned soy beans)

200 g (7 oz/1 cup) quinoa (see note)

1 tablespoon extra virgin olive oil

1 teaspoon sesame oil

2 tablespoons pepitas (pumpkin seeds)

+

2 tablespoons tamari

2 tablespoons Shaoxing rice wine (Chinese cooking wine, available at leading supermarkets and Asian food stores)

1 tablespoon oyster sauce (be sure to choose a gluten-free one if you are strictly gluten free)

Per serve

energy	protein	tot. fat	sat	poly	mono	carb	sugars	fibre
1560 kJ 370 Cal	18 g	14 g	2 g	4 g	6 g	39 g	8 g	11 g

NUTRITION BLOCKS PER SERVE

3 PLANT   **0** PROTEIN   **1** CARB   **1** FAT

Veggie san choy bau

Whether you're a vegetarian or not, you must try this dish. It's a delicious way to increase your plant food intake, and makes for a light fresh starter (serving 8) or as a main vegetarian meal (serving 4). Combining lentils, quinoa and veggies, flavoured with garlic and ginger, and topped with crunchy sesame seeds, it's low GI, a good source of plant proteins and packed with nutrients. It's particularly fibre-rich with 11 g per serve.

Serves 4 Time 30 minutes DF GF NF V Ve

Put the quinoa in a saucepan and cover with water. Drain in a sieve and repeat. This washes away the bitter compounds, called saponins, on the surface. Return to the pan and add 250 ml (9 fl oz/1 cup) of water. Bring to the boil, then reduce the heat to a simmer and cook for about 15 minutes until the water has been absorbed and the quinoa is cooked.

Place the lentils, tamari and 375 ml (13 fl oz/1½ cups) of water in a saucepan. Bring to the boil then reduce the heat and simmer uncovered for 5 minutes. Remove from the heat and set aside to rest, covered, for a further 5 minutes.

Heat the extra virgin olive oil in a large frying pan over medium heat. Add the ginger, garlic and all the vegetables, except the lettuce, and sauté for 3–5 minutes until softened.

Add the cooked vegetable mixture to the lentils along with the sesame oil and mix well. Set aside to cool for 5 minutes and then stir through the coriander.

Spoon the cooked quinoa into the lettuce leaves and top with the lentil mixture. Sprinkle with the toasted sesame seeds and serve.

1 teaspoon finely grated ginger

2 garlic cloves , finely chopped

3 spring onions (scallions), sliced

1 red capsicum (pepper), finely diced

2 celery stalks, finely chopped

1 carrot, diced

100 g (3½ oz) button mushrooms, finely chopped

1 tablespoon roughly chopped coriander (cilantro) leaves

12 baby cos (romaine) lettuce leaves

205 g (7¼ oz/1 cup) split red lentils

100 g (3½ oz/½ cup) quinoa

1½ tablespoons tamari

1 tablespoon extra virgin olive oil

2 teaspoons sesame oil

1 tablespoon toasted sesame seeds (see note)

See recipe photo on page 47.

Note Sesame seeds contain a wonderful array of minerals. They are particularly rich in manganese and copper, and also provide significant levels of calcium, iron, magnesium, phosphorus and zinc. Sesame oil is traditionally used as a cooking oil in much of India and throughout Asia. It has an almost equal mix of polyunsaturated and monounsaturated fats, with only a small amount of saturated fat. It also contains vitamin E which helps to protect the fats from oxidative damage. Do look for cold pressed sesame oil as the regular process uses high heat and often chemical solvents to refine the oil. This affects the flavour and the nutritional qualities of the oil.

Per serve

energy	protein	tot. fat	sat	poly	mono	carb	sugars	fibre
1370 kJ 325 Cal	18 g	11 g	2 g	4 g	5 g	35 g	5 g	11 g

NUTRITION BLOCKS PER SERVE

 **2** PLANT **1** PROTEIN **1** CARB **1** FAT

Mushroom stroganoff

Mushrooms work really well as a replacement for meat as they have a good texture and umami flavour. This stroganoff is filling, satisfying and utterly delicious, whether you are a vegetarian or not! Although the yoghurt is the only official protein food choice in the dish, the mushrooms actually provide most of the protein, with smaller amounts coming from the rice, broccoli and kale. It's a lovely example of how we can easily meet our protein requirements from plant foods.

Serves 4 Time 50 minutes (less if using pre-cooked rice) GF NF V

Place the rice in a saucepan along with 500 ml (17 fl oz/2 cups) of water. Place over high heat and bring to the boil. Reduce the heat to low until just simmering, cover with a tight-fitting lid and cook for 40 minutes. Then turn off the heat leaving the lid on and sit for a further 10 minutes. The rice will continue to steam to finish cooking.

When the rice is almost ready, trim and discard the mushroom stems, slice the caps into 5 mm (1/4 inch) thick slices.

Heat the extra virgin olive oil in a large frying pan over medium–high heat. Add the onions, thyme and mushrooms and toss to combine. Sauté for 7–10 minutes until the mushrooms are golden and soft. Add the tomato paste to the pan and cook for 30 seconds.

Add the stock, tamari and dijon mustard and bring to a simmer. Add the kale and stir until wilted.

Dissolve the cornflour in 60 ml (2 fl oz/1/4 cup) of water and add to the pan, stirring constantly. Cook for about 3 minutes until the sauce is thick and glossy. Remove from the heat and swirl through the yoghurt and parsley.

While the mushrooms are cooking, bring a saucepan of water up to the boil. Place the broccoli in a steamer, cover with the lid and place over the pan. Steam for about 2 minutes until just tender, but still a lovely bright green colour. (Alternatively, place the broccoli in a microwave-proof bowl with a little water, cover and microwave on High for about 2 minutes.)

Fluff the brown rice with a fork and serve with the stroganoff and broccoli.

Note Mushrooms are a pretty amazing food. I classify them as veggies and, therefore, in the plant section of our plate, but that's not botanically accurate. In fact, mushrooms are not veggies at all—as fungi they get a classification all to themselves. They are rich in many micronutrients including the B group vitamins riboflavin, niacin, vitamin B6, pantothenic acid and biotin, along with the minerals copper, chromium and selenium. All this for less than 100 kJ (24 Cal) a cup. Mushrooms are also one of only a few foods to provide vitamin D.

800 g (1 lb 12 oz) portobello or large field mushrooms (see note)

1 brown onion, diced

1 teaspoon dried thyme

2 tablespoons no added salt tomato paste (concentrated purée)

120 g (4¼ oz) kale, shredded

Handful flat-leaf (Italian) parsley, leaves chopped

200 g (7 oz/1 head) broccoli, cut into florets

130 g (4½ oz/½ cup) Greek-style yoghurt

135 g (4¾ oz/⅔ cup) brown basmati rice (or use pre-cooked microwavable packet rice to serve 4)

1½ tablespoons cornflour (cornstarch)

2 tablespoons extra virgin olive oil

+

500 ml (17 fl oz/2 cups) vegetable stock (preferably homemade, or good quality store-bought)

2 teaspoons tamari

2 teaspoons dijon mustard

Per serve

energy	protein	tot. fat	sat	poly	mono	carb	sugars	fibre
1680 kJ 400 Cal	18 g	14 g	3 g	2 g	7 g	48 g	12 g	11 g

NUTRITION BLOCKS PER SERVE

 3 PLANT   **1** PROTEIN **1** CARB   **1** FAT

Sweet treats

Custard filo tart with caramelised figs

This is a dessert that really will feel like a treat without blowing your Daily Blocks count. I'm a big fan of filo pastry as it has none of the ugly processed fats found in most commercial pastries, plus it's light, low in kilojoules and cooks up to give a crispy totally yum mouthfeel. I've teamed it with my childhood favourite—homemade custard—and one of my adult favourite fruits, figs. For this recipe you will need a 12-hole muffin tin.

Serves 12 Time 30 minutes NF V

Preheat the oven to fan-forced 180°C (350°F/Gas 4).

Whisk together the scraped vanilla seeds, cornflour, semolina, xylitol, egg and milk in a saucepan. Place the pan over medium heat and cook for about 10 minutes stirring often until the mix becomes a custard consistency. Pour the custard into a dish, cover with plastic wrap, and refrigerate until required. (You can make the custard ahead of time if you wish.)

Get your muffin tin ready. Working quickly, lay 1 sheet of filo pastry on your work surface and brush with extra virgin olive oil. Cut the sheet into 6 equal portions. Lay a second piece out and also cut into 6 equal portions. Place 1 dry filo rectangle slightly diagonally on top of 1 of the oiled rectangles. Place the 2 filo pieces into one of your muffin tin holes, to make a pastry case. Continue to fill all 12 muffin holes.

Remove the custard from the fridge and scoop approximately 1 tablespoon of the custard into each pastry case. (See note.)

Gather all the edges of the overhanging pastry and gently scrunch the tops together to seal the parcels.

Bake in the oven for 10–15 minutes until the pastry is slightly golden around the edges.

Meanwhile, cut the figs in half and lightly brush the cut side with extra virgin olive oil. Put the figs in a frying pan over medium–high heat and gently brown the flesh for about 4–5 minutes until golden.

Serve two fig halves alongside the custard filo tarts.

½ vanilla bean, split lengthways and seeds scraped (or ½ teaspoon natural vanilla extract)

12 figs

1 free-range or organic egg
330 ml (11¼ fl oz/1⅓ cups) full cream milk

1½ tablespoons cornflour (cornstarch)
2 tablespoons semolina
4 sheets frozen filo pastry, thawed

1 tablespoon extra virgin olive oil (light flavoured)

+
45 g (1½ oz/⅓ cup) xylitol (see note on page 212, or an erythritol–stevia mix, see note on page 226)

See recipe photo on page 13.

Note You won't need all of the custard you make for these 12 tarts. But keep the rest in your fridge for 5–6 days to use fresh for another night. It's delicious cold or reheated and served simply with fresh fruit.

Per serve

energy	protein	tot. fat	sat	poly	mono	carb	sugars	fibre
300 kJ 75 Cal	2 g	3 g	<1 g	3 g	1 g	10 g	5 g	2 g

NUTRITION BLOCKS PER SERVE

 1 PLANT   **0** PROTEIN   **½** CARB   **0** FAT

Choc orange almond bliss balls

Bliss balls are all the rage, but most recipes call for loads of coconut oil and I'm yet to be convinced of this particular fat. Plus, I have to confess that I really don't love the taste of it. So I wanted to give you a chocolatey bliss ball that truly was good for you and wouldn't bust your kilojoules out the park for the day (just warning you, many other versions really do). A serve of two bliss balls has under 700 kJ (160 Cal)—perfect for a snack with a cup of tea or coffee. (See note.)

Serves 10   Time 1 hour   DF GF V Ve

Using a food processor or Vitamix on level 10, blitz the dates and orange juice to a thick paste. Add the almond meal, cocoa powder, salt and orange zest and pulse until well combined.

Tip the mixture onto a piece of baking paper, form into a log roughly 25 cm (10 inch) long, roll up in the paper and refrigerate for 30 minutes until firm.

Cut the log into 20 pieces (or use a 1 tablespoon measure to portion) and roll into balls. Roll the balls in the extra almond meal or chopped flaked almonds. Serve.

These balls will keep in the fridge for a week or in the freezer for 4–6 months.

200 g (7 oz) dates, pitted

Grated zest of 1 orange and 60 ml (2 fl oz/ ¼ cup) of the freshly squeezed juice

30 g (1 oz/¼ cup) pure cocoa powder

150 g (5½ oz/1½ cups) almond meal, plus 2 tablespoons extra (or chopped flaked almonds)

+

Pinch of salt flakes

Note The ingredients list in this recipe is wonderfully simple and essentially these are just orange and cocoa–flavoured almond meal. The sweetness comes from the dates (and so all naturally present sugars), and the fat is also all naturally present in the almonds.

Per serve

energy	protein	tot. fat	sat	poly	mono	carb	sugars	fibre
685 kJ 160 Cal	4 g	9 g	<1 g	2 g	6 g	14 g	13 g	3 g

NUTRITION BLOCKS PER SERVE

 **0** PLANT   **0** PROTEIN   ½ CARB   ½ FAT

Dark choc berry muffins

Muffins have to be a favourite snack for most of us, but unfortunately café-bought versions are usually enormous, loaded with refined starch and sugar, have almost no fibre and use the wrong types of fat. I'm not much of a baker, but with two kids who need lunchbox snacks, I have perfected the art of creating a healthy muffin! You can add any fruit combo you like— once you master the basic recipe, experiment and the options are limitless!

Serves 12 Time 40 minutes NF V

Preheat the oven to fan-forced 180°C (350°F/Gas 4). Line a 12-hole muffin tin with non-stick muffin cases.

Sift the flour and baking powder into a bowl.

In a separate bowl, whisk together the eggs, buttermilk, honey and extra virgin olive oil.

Pour the wet ingredients into the dry and mix gently to combine, but take care not to over-mix or you'll end up with heavier muffins. Gently fold through the berries and dark chocolate chips.

Spoon the mixture into the muffin cases and bake in the oven for about 25 minutes or until the muffins are a golden brown colour and a skewer inserted into the centre comes out clean. Transfer to a wire rack to cool. Serve.

- 260 g (9¼ oz/about 1 cup) fresh or frozen berries, thawed (mixed or whatever type you like)
- 2 large free-range or organic eggs
- 185 ml (6 fl oz/¾ cup) buttermilk (or a mix of natural yoghurt and milk)
- 300 g (10½ oz/2 cups) wholemeal (wholewheat) flour (see note)
- 2 teaspoons baking powder
- 90 g (3¼ oz/¼ cup) honey
- 60 ml (2 fl oz/¼ cup) extra virgin olive oil (light flavoured)
- 40 g (1½ oz) no added sugar dark chocolate, chopped into small chips

Notes I like to use all wholemeal flour, but admittedly you get a lighter result if you mix half and half with white plain (all-purpose) flour. If your family is not used to wholemeal, this might be the way to gently edge them towards the healthier version.

These muffins freeze well, so pop any that won't be used in the next couple of days into individual freezer bags and store in the freezer for a few months. This also helps to stop you eating more than you intend!

Per serve

energy	protein	tot. fat	sat	poly	mono	carb	sugars	fibre
820 kJ 195 Cal	5 g	8 g	2 g	1 g	4 g	24 g	9 g	4 g

NUTRITION BLOCKS PER SERVE

 0 PLANT **0** PROTEIN **1** CARB  **½** FAT

Gluten-free coconut raspberry muffins

Coconut flour is a relatively new ingredient to many of us, including me, but I'm enjoying playing around with it. What you will notice is that it behaves completely differently from wheat flour, therefore you can't simply substitute it one-for-one in recipes. You'll also notice that the batter in this recipe is very runny, but it needs to be as coconut flour is highly absorbent. If the mixture is not wet enough the end muffin will be dry and crumbly.

Serves 4 Time 40 minutes DF GF NF V

Preheat the oven to 180°C (350°F/Gas 4). Line 4 muffin holes with non-stick muffin cases.

Sift the coconut flour, baking powder and salt into a bowl. Add the raspberries and mix together well, ensuring that the flour coats the raspberries and none are sticking together.

In a separate bowl, whisk together the eggs, extra virgin olive oil, honey and vanilla extract or seeds.

Tip the dry ingredients into the wet and stir gently to combine. (The mixture will be much runnier than a usual wheat flour muffin mix.) Divide the mixture between the muffin cases.

Bake for about 30 minutes or until the muffins are golden brown on top and a skewer inserted into the centre comes out clean. Remove from the oven and transfer to a wire rack to cool.

- 130 g (4 oz/½ cup) fresh or frozen raspberries
- 3 large free-range or organic eggs
- 1 tablespoon honey
- 35 g (1¼ oz/¼ cup) coconut flour (see note)
- 2 tablespoons extra virgin olive oil

+

¼ teaspoon gluten-free baking powder

Pinch of salt flakes

¼ teaspoon natural vanilla extract (or ¼ vanilla bean, split lengthways and seeds scraped)

Note Coconut flour is really a by-product of coconut milk production. Coconut flesh is pressed to release the coconut milk and it is the leftover flesh that is dried and then ground to make coconut flour. It is best used with lots of eggs—a good guide is 35 g (1¼ oz/¼ cup) of coconut flour to 3 eggs—and oil of some sort to give a moist end product.

Nutritionally, I like it. It provides some plant protein, it's low in carbohydrates and therefore reduces the glycaemic load of a recipe when substituted for some of the wheat flour, and it's really high in fibre with 2 tablespoons providing almost 10 g.

Per serve

energy	protein	tot. fat	sat	poly	mono	carb	sugars	fibre
800 kJ 190 Cal	6 g	13 g	3 g	2 g	8 g	9 g	9 g	6 g

NUTRITION BLOCKS PER SERVE

 0 PLANT  **0** PROTEIN ½ CARB **1** FAT

Rhubarb and apple quinoa nut crumble

Rhubarb crumble was a favourite in our house growing up, so I wanted to create a healthier version in line with the *Get Lean, Stay Lean* food philosophy. I've replaced the traditional buttery, sugary topping with a crumble of almonds, coconut, sesame and quinoa flakes. This recipe has no added sugar—the sweetness comes entirely from naturally present sugars. The crumble looks nicest cooked in individual ramekins, and that will also help you stick to just one serve!

Serves 6 Time 50 minutes DF GF V Ve

Preheat the oven to fan-forced 180°C (350°F/Gas 4).

Put the rhubarb, apples, dates, orange juice, cinnamon, star anise and vanilla bean in a saucepan over medium–low heat and stew for 10 minutes until the fruit is soft. Turn off the heat and leave to cool. Remove the solid spices.

Mix the almond meal, coconut, quinoa flakes, sunflower seeds, black sesame seeds and extra virgin olive oil together in a bowl.

Portion the stewed fruit among individual ovenproof ramekins or one 1.5 litre (52 fl oz/6 cup) capacity baking dish, then top with the crumble.

Bake in the oven for 20–30 minutes until the topping is golden brown and the fruit is bubbling.

Serve with a dollop of natural yoghurt, or a coconut yoghurt alternative for dairy-free diets.

600 g (1 lb 5 oz) rhubarb, chopped (see note)

4 green apples, peeled, cored and chopped

6 dates, pitted and chopped

125 ml (4 fl oz/½ cup) orange juice

½ teaspoon ground cinnamon

1 star anise

½ vanilla bean, split lengthways and seeds scraped (or ½ teaspoon natural vanilla extract)

50 g (1¾ oz/½ cup) quinoa flakes

50 g (1¾ oz/½ cup) almond meal

1 tablespoon shredded coconut (or you can use desiccated coconut for a finer texture)

1 tablespoon sunflower seeds, roughly chopped

1 teaspoon black sesame seeds

1 tablespoon extra virgin olive oil

Note Rhubarb is actually a vegetable, but we eat it like a fruit. It's rich in fibre and low in kilojoules. It's also very low in sugar and total carbohydrates, hence it's extremely tart if you cook it without adding any fruit for the sugar content. It's rich in vitamin K, is a good source of manganese and has useful levels of calcium. The purple colour comes from small but significant levels of several carotenoids, including lutein and zeaxanthin known to be important for eye health.

Per serve

energy	protein	tot. fat	sat	poly	mono	carb	sugars	fibre
890 kJ 210 Cal	5 g	10 g	2 g	2 g	5 g	22 g	16 g	6 g

NUTRITION BLOCKS PER SERVE

1 PLANT **0** PROTEIN **1** CARB **½** FAT

Flourless blood orange and almond maple cake

This is such a simple cake recipe, yet you won't believe how beautiful it tastes. I use blood oranges when they are in season. If you can't get hold of any, simply use navel oranges instead. The almonds have been roasted before grinding them to give a deeper depth of flavour. You don't have to do this and can simply use almond meal instead if you prefer. The recipe as it stands is dairy free, but it is delicious served with a spoonful of Greek-style yoghurt.

Serves 6   Time 2 hours 15 minutes   DF GF V

Put the oranges in a saucepan and cover with water. Place a piece of baking paper over the top of the oranges—this helps keep the oranges from bobbing on the water surface. Gently bring to the boil, then reduce the heat to a simmer. Simmer for 1 hour.

Preheat the oven to fan-forced 180°C (350°F/Gas 4). Brush a round 22 cm (8½ inch) springform cake tin with the extra virgin olive oil and line with baking paper.

Drain the oranges and slice in half, removing any pips. Using a food processor or a Vitamix on level 10, blitz the oranges to a paste.

Add the eggs and blitz again. Then add the maple syrup and baking powder, and mix together well.

Pour the mixture into the tin and bake in the oven for about 1 hour. To test that the cake is ready, insert a skewer into the centre of the cake and if it comes out clean the cake is cooked. Remove from the oven and leave to cool in the tin.

Remove the cake from the tin, decorate with fresh blood orange segments, whole almonds and mint leaves, and serve.

4 blood oranges, skin on, plus extra orange segments to serve

Mint leaves, to serve

6 large free-range or organic eggs

175 g (6 oz/½ cup) pure maple syrup

1 teaspoon baking powder

1 teaspoon extra virgin olive oil to grease the baking tin

250 g (9 oz) flaked almonds, pan-roasted, then ground (alternatively, you can use almond meal, see note)

Handful whole almonds, to serve

Note Using nut meal in place of flour keeps the cake gluten free and since nuts are already high in fat you don't need to add additional butter or oil as with a traditional cake. This, of course, also ensures you have all good fats present. You do, however, need to be careful with your portion size, as nut meal is energy dense—not always easy with a delicious cake! Just be sure to cut each quarter of the cake into a further four slices to keep your kilojoules appropriate for a snack.

Per serve

energy	protein	tot. fat	sat	poly	mono	carb	sugars	fibre
680 kJ 130 Cal	6 g	10 g	1 g	2 g	6 g	10 g	10 g	3 g

NUTRITION BLOCKS PER SERVE

 **0** PLANT   **0** PROTEIN   **½** CARB   **1** FAT

Dark chocolate pomegranate brownies

Both dark chocolate and pomegranate are super rich in beneficial antioxidant compounds, so together they make a pretty powerful duo! Regular brownie recipes use white flour, but here I have used a combination of homemade almond meal and lupin flour instead. You can of course use bought almond meal if you prefer, but by making your own you ensure the freshness of the nuts, you utilise the skins as well adding to the nutrition, and it costs less.

Serves 12   Time 1 hour   DF GF V Ve

Preheat the oven to fan-forced 180°C (350°F/Gas 4). Line a 31 x 20 cm (12½ x 8 inch) baking tin or tray with baking paper.

Put the almonds into a blender or Vitamix on level 5 or 6 and blitz for a few seconds until the nuts resemble breadcrumbs. Do not over-blend or you'll end up with almond butter! Pour the resulting almond meal into a mixing bowl.

Remove all the arils (seeds) from the pomegranate into a bowl, collecting any juice, then put both the arils and juice into the blender or Vitamix on level 10—no need to rinse first—and blitz until puréed.

Half fill a small saucepan with water and bring to the boil over high heat, then turn down the heat until the water is just simmering. Break the chocolate into pieces in a small glass bowl and place this over the simmering water, stirring occasionally until it is all melted. Ensure the base of the bowl doesn't touch the water.

Whisk the eggs in a clean mixing bowl, then add the puréed pomegranate, the pomegranate molasses, maple syrup, vanilla seeds or extract, extra virgin olive oil and melted chocolate. Use a balloon whisk to combine all the ingredients.

Sift the lupin flour and baking powder into the mixing bowl containing the almond meal and mix to combine.

Add the wet mixture to the dry and combine well, ensuring there are no lumps of flour. Pour into the prepared tin, shaking the tin a little to even the mixture out.

Bake in the oven for 30 minutes or until a skewer comes out clean when inserted in the centre.

Remove from the oven and leave to cool for a few minutes in the tin, before turning out onto a wire rake. Once completely cool cut into 12 squares.

Enjoy these brownies on their own with your coffee or tea, or serve them as a dessert drizzled with a little extra pomegranate molasses, fresh pomegranate arils and, if not dairy free, a dollop of natural yoghurt.

Note Pomegranates are rich in vitamin C, fibre and polyphenols credited in helping the prevention of heart disease and cancer.

1 pomegranate (see note)
1 vanilla bean, split and seeds scraped lengthways (or 1 teaspoon natural vanilla extract)

3 free-range or organic eggs
60 g (2¼ oz/½ cup) lupin flour

70 g (2½ oz) pomegranate molasses
90 g (3¼ oz/¼ cup) pure maple syrup
1 teaspoon gluten-free baking powder

160 g (5½ oz/1 cup) raw almonds (or you can use almond meal)
100 g (3½ oz) dark chocolate (85 per cent cocoa)
2 tablespoons extra virgin olive oil (preferably light flavoured)

Per serve

energy	protein	tot. fat	sat	poly	mono	carb	sugars	fibre
830 kJ 200 Cal	7 g	13 g	3 g	2 g	7 g	12 g	10 g	4 g

NUTRITION BLOCKS PER SERVE

 **0** PLANT   **0** PROTEIN   **1** CARB   ½ FAT

* The nutrition analysis does not include the serving suggestions.

Carrot, coconut and date cakes

Cakes are usually made with the wrong types of fat and too much added sugar and refined white flour. But they needn't be. These delicious little cakes are made with wholemeal flour, a low energy natural sweetener instead of sugar and super healthy extra virgin olive oil as the fat. The result is completely yum. For most people, I recommend keeping snacks to around or under 800 kJ (190 Cal) and so one of these cakes is bang on target.

Serves 12   Time 45 minutes   DF V

Preheat the oven to 180°C (350°F/Gas 4). Line a 12-hole muffin tin with non-stick muffin cases.

Using an electric stand mixer with the K beater attachment, combine the xylitol and extra virgin olive oil for 1 minute or until blended well. Sift the mixed spice, flour and bicarbonate of soda and add to the mixture.

Add the eggs, one at a time, with the mixer on a slow speed, alternating with the grated carrot. Then add the coconut and the chopped dates.

Spoon the mixture, three-quarters full, into the muffin cases.

Bake for 30 minutes or until the cakes are springy and a skewer inserted into the centre of a cake comes out clean. Remove from the oven and leave to cool on a wire rack.

These cakes are best eaten within 2–3 days. They do freeze well so pop the extras into individual bags and store in the freezer for a few months.

3 teaspoons mixed spice

300 g (10½ oz) carrots, grated

110 g (3¾ oz) dates, pitted and chopped

3 large free-range or organic eggs

200 g (7 oz) stoneground wholegrain flour

60 ml (2 fl oz/¼ cup) extra virgin olive oil (light flavoured)

50 g (1¾ oz/⅔ cup) shredded coconut (or desiccated but shredded gives more texture)

+

90 g (3¼ oz) xylitol (see note, or an erythritol–stevia mix, see note on page 226)

2 teaspoons bicarbonate of soda (baking soda)

Note I don't buy into the current sugar hysteria—a little sugar in an otherwise healthy diet is fine. However, clearly the more we can reduce added sugars the better. So in this recipe we have used a sugar alcohol (it's not alcoholic) xylitol in combination with the natural sweetness of dates and carrots. Xylitol occurs naturally in the fibres of many fruits and vegetables, and is extracted from corncobs and hardwoods for commercial sale. We even make a small amount of xylitol in our bodies as part of normal metabolism. It has very few kilojoules, is tooth friendly and has about the same sweetness as table sugar. It works really well in baking, but do be warned that it has a laxative effect if you consume too much of it. Those following a low FODMAPs diet for managing IBS should not use xylitol. You'll find xylitol in some pharmacies and major supermarkets.

Per serve

energy	protein	tot. fat	sat	poly	mono	carb	sugars	fibre
760 kJ 180 Cal	4 g	9 g	3 g	<1 g	4 g	19 g	8 g	4 g

NUTRITION BLOCKS PER SERVE

0 PLANT   **0** PROTEIN   **1** CARB   **½** FAT

Banana, amaranth and walnut bread

In Sydney banana bread is everywhere, from cafés to service stations, so clearly we love it. But I think the name is misleading us into assuming it's a healthy snack. It really ought to be called banana cake and a typical slice can provide you with upwards of 2000 kJ (480 Cal)! This revamp is just as delicious but is *Get Lean, Stay Lean* worthy. That doesn't mean you can eat the whole loaf, but a slice in the afternoon with a cup of tea fits deliciously into your menu plan.

Serves 12 Time 1 hour 20 minutes V

Preheat the oven to 180°C (350°F/Gas 4) and lightly brush or spray a 22 x 11 x 7 cm (8½ x 4¼ x 2¾ inches) loaf (bar) tin with extra virgin olive oil.

Using an electric stand mixer with the K beater attachment, mix together the extra virgin olive oil and xylitol. Add the eggs, one at a time, with the beater on slow. Add the bananas whole, as the machine will do the mashing for you. Next add the flours, mixed spice and yoghurt and mix together well. Then gently stir in the walnuts.

(If you don't have an electric mixer, whisk together the oil, xylitol and eggs. Mash the bananas with a fork and add to the mixture along with all the other ingredients. Mix well to combine.)

Pour the mixture into the prepared tin, drizzle with the maple syrup and dress with the extra walnuts.

Bake in the oven for 1 hour or until golden brown and a skewer inserted into the centre comes out clean.

Remove from the oven and leave to cool for 10 minutes in the tin. Remove from the tin onto a wire rack to cool completely. Slice and serve fresh or lightly toasted.

3 ripe bananas

1 teaspoon mixed spice

3 free-range or organic eggs

200 g (7 oz/¾ cup) natural yoghurt

70 g (2½ oz/½ cup) amaranth flour (see note)

150 g (5½ oz/1 cup) wholemeal (whole-wheat) self-raising flour (or add 2 teaspoons baking powder to plain/all-purpose wholemeal flour)

1 tablespoon pure maple syrup

60 ml (2 fl oz/¼ cup) extra virgin olive oil, plus extra to grease the tin

30 g (1 oz/¼ cup) chopped walnuts, plus extra to decorate

+

60 g (2¼ oz/¼ cup) xylitol (see note opposite, or an erythritol–stevia mix, see note on page 226)

¾ teaspoon bicarbonate of soda (baking soda)

Note Amaranth is a pseudo-grain similar to quinoa. While it's less common today and may be new to you, it's an ancient grain and was a staple food of the Aztecs. Compared to other grains amaranth stands out for its protein content—it has almost double the protein of brown rice. In addition, it has a good balance of amino acids—the building blocks of proteins. Most grains are low or lacking in lysine, but amaranth provides this essential amino acid. This makes it a particularly good choice for vegetarians and vegans. You'll find amaranth flour in good health food stores.

Per serve

energy	protein	tot. fat	sat	poly	mono	carb	sugars	fibre
770 kJ 180 Cal	5 g	9 g	2 g	2 g	4 g	20 g	7 g	3 g

NUTRITION BLOCKS PER SERVE

0 PLANT **0** PROTEIN **1** CARB **½** FAT

Festive frozen yoghurt log

For those of us in the Southern Hemisphere, a traditional Christmas pudding just doesn't cut it. So I wanted to come up with an alternative that was equally festive, embraced those traditional flavours, but appealed on a hot Christmas afternoon. I've used ricotta and Greek-style yoghurt, combined with festive fruits and frozen mango—although you can also use fresh if you prefer. Serve with fresh cherries or mixed berries—and don't feel you have to wait until Christmas!

Serves 12   Time 10 minutes + 5 hours freezing   GF V

Line a 20 x 11 x 7 cm (8 x 4¼ x 2¾) loaf (bar) tin with baking paper.

In a mixing bowl beat the ricotta, vanilla seeds or extract and maple syrup until well combined. Stir in all the other ingredients and pour into the tin. Cover with a sheet of baking paper and then wrap with a sheet of foil.

Place in the freezer for at least 5 hours to set. Remove from the freezer 5 minutes before serving. Slice with a knife (it helps to run your knife under hot water first) and serve with a handful of fresh cherries.

1 vanilla bean, split lengthways and seeds scraped (or 1 teaspoon pure vanilla extract)

185 g (6 oz/1 cup) frozen diced mango (or fresh)

75 g (2½ oz/½ cup) craisins (sweetened dried cranberries)

15 g (½ oz/¼ cup) finely shredded mint leaves

Grated zest of 1 lime

400 g (14 oz) fresh full fat ricotta cheese

520 g (1 lb 2½ oz/2 cups) Greek-style yoghurt (see note)

175 g (6 oz/½ cup) pure maple syrup

30 g (1 oz/¼ cup) pistachio nut kernels

100 g (3½ oz) dark chocolate

Note Yoghurt is simply fermented milk and it probably came about as a method of making milk last longer. In doing so there were unexpected side effects and they were beneficial. Many cultures (excuse the pun) around the world from Nepal and India to the Middle East and Europe have long considered yoghurt a medicinal food and for good reason. The probiotic bacteria present may confer many of the health benefits.

Yoghurt is rich in top quality protein, an excellent source of calcium and gives you a serious boost in several B group vitamins including riboflavin, and minerals magnesium and zinc.

But of course not all yoghurts are the same. They have different levels of fat, added sugars, may have fruit and other additions, and some are thickened with gums or have other additives. Always read the ingredients list to know exactly what you are getting. Your absolute best options are natural yoghurts with live cultures, and nothing else in the ingredients list.

Per serve

energy	protein	tot. fat	sat	poly	mono	carb	sugars	fibre
910 kJ 215 Cal	6 g	10 g	6 g	1 g	3 g	25 g	25 g	1 g

NUTRITION BLOCKS PER SERVE

1 PLANT   **0** PROTEIN   **2** CARB   **1** FAT

Drunken strawberries with citrus yoghurt and dark chocolate

This is such an easy dessert recipe, yet it's completely delicious and looks fancy enough to serve to your guests when you're entertaining. Neither will it break the bank for kilojoules and so you can enjoy this one whenever you feel the need for a sweet ending to your meal. When fresh berries are not in season you can defrost frozen berries to use instead. Any other berries or cherries will also work beautifully.

Serves 4   Time 10 minutes   GF NF V

Mix the berries together in a container and pour over your liqueur of choice. Cover with the lid and leave to marinate in the fridge for at least an hour.

Heat a frying pan over medium heat. Place the shredded coconut into the pan, shaking intermittently, and dry-fry for 1–2 minutes. Remove the coconut from the pan once it starts to turn golden in colour. (It's important to remove the coconut from the hot pan, as it will continue to brown with the residual heat from the pan otherwise.) Set aside to cool.

Mix together the yoghurt, lime juice and a grind of black pepper in a bowl. Set aside.

Divide the berries between four glass dishes. Pour over the yoghurt mixture. Sprinkle with the chocolate, coconut flakes and lime zest. Serve immediately.

125 g (4½ oz) fresh strawberries (or frozen, defrosted), sliced

125 g (4½ oz) blueberries (or frozen, defrosted)

Juice and grated zest of 1 lime

Freshly ground black pepper

70 g (2½ oz/¼ cup) natural yoghurt

2 tablespoons shredded coconut

2 tablespoons shaved dark chocolate

+

60 ml (2 fl oz/¼ cup) liqueur (such as Chambord, Cointreau or Frangelico, see note)

Note For an alcohol-free alternative you can use freshly squeezed orange juice.

Per serve

energy	protein	tot. fat	sat	poly	mono	carb	sugars	fibre
650 kJ 155 Cal	3 g	8 g	6 g	0 g	2 g	12 g	10 g	2 g

NUTRITION BLOCKS PER SERVE

 **0** PLANT   **0** PROTEIN   **0** CARB   ½ FAT

Drinks

Beetroot, apple and ginger smoothie

Beetroot is rich in nitrates that relax your blood vessels and in turn reduce your blood pressure. Here I've combined cooked beetroot with apple and carrot to add sweetness, and lemon, ginger and mint for a wonderful complexity of flavour. The result is a refreshing, super heart-healthy and nutrient-rich smoothie. It's rich in fibre, folate, potassium, beta-carotene, several other phytonutrients and even has a nice dose of iron and zinc from the beets.

Serves 1   Time 2 minutes   DF GF NF U Ve

Put all the ingredients into a Vitamix or high-speed blender with 250 ml (9 fl oz/1 cup) of water and the ice on top. Blitz for about a minute or until completely smooth, using the tamper if required to push the ingredients down into the blades. Pour into a glass and enjoy.

1 cooked beetroot (beet) (or you can use raw if you prefer, see note)

½ carrot

½ apple, cored

1 teaspoon finely grated ginger

1 lemon slice

Handful mint

+

Handful ice

See recipe photo on page 36.

Note To cook beetroot, scrub the skins and trim the stalks leaving a couple of centimetres intact (otherwise you lose more of the wonderful purple colour). Place in a saucepan, cover with water and bring to the boil over high heat. Reduce the heat to low and simmer for 20–30 minutes. Drain and when cool enough to handle remove the skins with your fingers. Cooked beetroot will keep in the fridge for up to 5 days. Alternatively, you can buy beetroot ready cooked in the refrigerated section of the supermarket or grocers.

Per serve

energy	protein	tot. fat	sat	poly	mono	carb	sugars	fibre
580 kJ 140 Cal	4 g	0 g	0 g	0 g	0 g	25 g	25 g	10 g

*All sugars naturally present.

NUTRITION BLOCKS PER SERVE

2 PLANT **0** PROTEIN **0** CARB **0** FAT

Oat and cashew breakfast smoothie

While I highly recommend sitting down to a breakfast you eat with cutlery and have to chew—that helps to turn down your appetite cues—sometimes you need something on the run. Or perhaps you just don't feel like solid food in the morning and a nutritious drink is more your thing. In either event this smoothie will hit the mark. It has a perfect balance of low GI carbs, it's high in protein with 20 g and has all good fats coming primarily from the nuts and seeds.

Serves 1 Time 2 minutes V

Put all the ingredients into a Vitamix, or high-speed blender, finishing with the frozen fruit on the top (this helps to push the other ingredients down into the blades). Blend for a minute or until completely smooth. Enjoy straight away or take with you in a portable drink container.

- 75 g (2½ oz/about ½ cup) fresh or frozen mixed berries
- 50 g (1¾ oz) frozen pineapple chunks (about 1 round slice)
- 250 ml (9 fl oz/1 cup) light milk (or full cream if you prefer, but note this will increase the kilojoules)
- 2 tablespoons natural yoghurt
- 25 g (1 oz/¼ cup) rolled (porridge) oats
- 20 g (¾ oz) raw cashew nuts (see note)
- 10 g (¼ oz) chia seeds

Note Compared to other common nuts, cashews (along with pine nuts) top the charts for iron and zinc. Consuming them with vitamin C-rich fruit, as I have done here, improves the uptake of iron. This is especially important if you are a vegetarian.

Cashews also provide some protein, with a 30 g (1 oz) handful supplying about 5 g. They provide some fibre, are terrific for magnesium and the fats present are predominantly super-healthy monounsaturated fats.

Per serve

energy	protein	tot. fat	sat	poly	mono	carb	sugars	fibre
1890 kJ 450 Cal	20 g	20 g	5 g	5 g	8 g	43 g	28 g	10 g

NUTRITION BLOCKS PER SERVE

 1 PLANT 1 PROTEIN  1 CARB 1 FAT

*If made with full cream milk this pushes the kilojoules up to 2140 kJ (510 Cal). All sugars naturally present.

Natural protein berry smoothie

I just don't get the current obsession with protein powders, unless you're an athlete. While I agree with a higher protein intake to help in getting and staying lean, this can easily be achieved for almost all of us with whole foods. This smoothie uses the high quality protein of dairy, mixed with antioxidant-rich berries and the probiotic benefits of natural yoghurt. It's the perfect snack to get you over the mid-afternoon energy slump and keep hunger pangs at bay until dinner.

Serves 1 Time 5 minutes GF NF V

Put all the ingredients in a Vitamix or high-speed blender and blitz for about a minute until completely smooth. Pour into a glass and enjoy.

In summer you can also pour this mix into ice block (popsicle) moulds and freeze to make fabulous high protein ice blocks!

75 g (2 oz/about ½ cup) fresh or frozen mixed berries (see note)

100 g (3½ oz) natural yoghurt

200 ml (7 fl oz) light milk (or full cream if you prefer, but note this will increase the kilojoules)

See recipe photo on page 40.

Note Berries are pretty much impossible to overeat since they are low in kilojoules. The fabulous purple, blue and red colours of berries comes from the wealth of antioxidants present, primarily anthocyanins, a sub-group of flavonoids. These compounds have been shown in scientific studies to help protect our heart and blood vessels, protect blood components such as LDL cholesterol from oxidative damage, reduce age-related oxidative damage so we look and feel younger, and they have an anti-inflammatory effect in the body. They have even been shown to be beneficial for brain health, improving memory and slowing cognitive decline as we age.

Per serve

energy	protein	tot. fat	sat	poly	mono	carb	sugars	fibre
760 kJ 180 Cal	15 g	3 g	2 g	0 g	<1 g	21 g	21 g	3 g

NUTRITION BLOCKS PER SERVE

1 PLANT **1** PROTEIN **0** CARB **0** FAT

*If made with full cream milk this pushes the kilojoules up to 920 kJ (230 Cal). All sugars naturally present.

Green smoothie with kale, pineapple and coconut

Nothing makes you feel quite as healthy as a green smoothie. I used to think these were too hardcore, even for me, but since I started giving them a go, I admit to being a convert. Make the bulk of the smoothie vegetable based, with a little fruit for taste, and you have a winning combo with a serious nutrient boost. Swap your afternoon cappuccino and muffin for this and I promise you, you'll be bouncing off the walls with vitality!

Serves 4 Time 10 minutes DF GF NF V Ve

Put all the ingredients, except the lemon slices, including the ice cubes, into a Vitamix or high-speed blender and blitz for about a minute or until completely smooth.

Serve with a slice of lemon and a few extra ice cubes. If you don't like the 'bits' you can strain them out or use a juicer, however, the 'bits' do add fibre so I recommend you get used to them!

½ celery stalk

20 g (¾ oz) kale (see note)

5 cm (2 inch) piece cucumber

Juice of ½ lemon

Handful mint

160 g (5½ oz/1 cup) fresh or frozen pineapple pieces

250 ml (9 fl oz/1 cup) coconut water, chilled

Lemon slices, to serve

+

Handful ice cubes

Note Kale is one of the most nutritious veggies you can eat. It's particularly rich in carotenoids that can be converted to vitamin A in the body. A single cup of chopped kale provides you with over 200 per cent of your daily-recommended amount of vitamin A!

It is one of the best sources of the carotenoids lutein and zeaxanthin. These are known to play an essential role in eye health and a high dietary intake is associated with a reduced risk of age-related macular degeneration and cataracts.

Per serve

energy	protein	tot. fat	sat	poly	mono	carb	sugars	fibre
1450 kJ 35 Cal	1 g	0 g	0 g	0 g	0 g	7 g	7 g	1 g

*All sugars naturally present.

NUTRITION BLOCKS PER SERVE

3 PLANT **0** PROTEIN **0** CARB **0** FAT

My go-to green smoothie

This is the smoothie I make most often. It's all plant food and so has a seriously low number of kilojoules, yet delivers some serious nutrition. It has B group vitamins for energy, folate for cell protection, vitamin C for immune function and healthy skin, antioxidants galore for anti-ageing and it even has almost 2 mg of iron. All up it's a fantastic addition to your daily *Get Lean, Stay Lean* menu plan.

Serves 1 Time 5 minutes DF GF NF V Ve

Put all the ingredients into a Vitamix or high-speed blender with 250 ml (9 fl oz/1 cup) of water and the ice on top. Blitz for about a minute or until completely smooth.

½ celery stalk

½ Lebanese (short) cucumber

20 g (¾ oz) baby English spinach leaves

1 thin slice of lemon

6 mint leaves

Small handful flat-leaf (Italian) parley leaves

80 g (2¾ oz/½ cup) fresh or frozen pineapple pieces (see note)

+

A few ice cubes

Note You might not think of a pineapple automatically when we list superfoods, but there's more to this tropical fruit than you might realise. A cup of pineapple chunks provides you with over 60 per cent of your RDI for vitamin C. Since we know vitamin C aids in the absorption of plant iron, adding some pineapple to smoothies like I have done here, or to a legume or quinoa salad will boost your uptake of iron from these foods.

I always chop up my pineapple soon after purchase so they are ready to eat immediately. I keep one tub in the fridge for using fresh over the next few days and pop the rest, ready in ice cube-sized chunks, into zip-lock bags in my freezer. These are ideal for then using in your smoothie and frozen dessert recipes.

Per serve

energy	protein	tot. fat	sat	poly	mono	carb	sugars	fibre
260 kJ 60 Cal	2 g	0 g	0 g	0 g	0 g	10 g	10 g	5 g

NUTRITION BLOCKS PER SERVE

 3 PLANT  **0** PROTEIN **0** CARB **0** FAT

*All sugars naturally present.

Acai cocoa smoothie

Acai is touted as a superfood and with good reason; it has impressive antioxidant power on account of the high numbers of phytochemicals present in the fruit. Here I've teamed it with another antioxidant-rich plant food, cocoa. Neither are very sweet, they're actually a little bitter, so I've added frozen pineapple for some natural sweetness. The end result tastes decadent yet it's bursting with nutrients. For a dairy-free alternative, use soy or oat milk in place of dairy milk.

Serves 2   Time 5 minutes   GF NF V

Put all the ingredients into a high-speed blender or Vitamix and blitz for about a minute or until completely smooth. Divide between two glasses and serve immediately.

100 g (3½ oz) frozen acai purée

80 g (2¾ oz/½ cup) fresh or frozen pineapple chunks

1 tablespoon pure cocoa powder

500 ml (17 fl oz/2 cups) light milk (or full cream if you prefer, but note this will increase the kilojoules)

+

1 teaspoon xylitol (see note on page 212, or an erythritol–stevia mix, see note, optional)

A few ice cubes

Note Stevia is a natural sweetener extracted from the leaves of a plant native to South America. It is tooth friendly, kilojoule free, and won't raise your blood glucose. Bear in mind that most stevia you buy is mixed with erythritol, a sugar alcohol like xylitol. In fact, only about one per cent of the product is stevia. This makes it more like sugar in the way it can be used. Erythritol is also natural and usually well tolerated by the body, but may have a laxative effect if you use too much. Those with irritable bowel syndrome may want to avoid it.

Per serve

energy	protein	tot. fat	sat	poly	mono	carb	sugars	fibre
660 kJ 160 Cal	11 g	4 g	1 g	<1 g	<1g	19 g	19 g	2 g

NUTRITION BLOCKS PER SERVE

1 PLANT   1 PROTEIN   0 CARB   0 FAT

*If made with full cream milk this pushes the kilojoules up to 1020 kJ (240 Cal). All sugars naturally present.

Banana, prune and almond milk smoothie

You won't believe how three ingredients, whipped together in your blender, can taste this good. Honestly, this feels like a special treat, yet is simply frozen banana and prunes, blended with almond milk. Prunes are one of my favourite dried fruits because they are so rich in antioxidants.

Serves 1   Time 5 minutes   DF GF V Ve

Put all the ingredients into a Vitamix or high-speed blender and blitz for about a minute or until completely smooth. Divide between two glasses and serve immediately.

- 1 frozen banana (see note)
- 4 pitted prunes
- 500 ml (17 fl oz/2 cups) unsweetened almond milk

Note Bananas are a pretty fantastic natural snack, served up in their own biodegradable packaging. A medium banana provides about a third of your vitamin C, 13 per cent of your potassium, 12 per cent of your magnesium, 10 per cent of your riboflavin and 10 per cent of your folate for the day— all for only 350 kJ (80 Cal). The carbs are not much higher than many other fruits, with a medium-sized fruit providing around 18 g. Furthermore those carbs are slowly absorbed, giving bananas a low GI of 52.

When bananas are still firm and slightly green, they are high in resistant starch. This is a type of fibre that is gold star fuel for the 'good' bacteria in the gut.

Freeze ripe bananas, removing the skin and stringy parts first, to use in smoothies or to make frozen desserts.

Per serve

energy	protein	tot. fat	sat	poly	mono	carb	sugars	fibre
580 kJ 140 Cal	3 g	<1 g	0 g	0 g	0 g	27 g	27 g	5 g

*All sugars naturally present.

NUTRITION BLOCKS PER SERVE

 PLANT   **0** PROTEIN   **0** CARB   FAT

Almond chai latte

A really good cup of chai is hard to beat and nutritionally it gets top marks. The combination of tea leaves and spices gives you an impressive array of phytochemicals. Unfortunately, most café versions of chai are made with a pre-made powdered mix and not authentic at all. These mixes tend to be heavily sweetened with refined sugar and aside from the taste not being the same, many of those valuable phytochemicals are lost in processing. This recipe is the real thing.

Serves 2   Time 5 minutes   DF GF NF V Ve

Place all the ingredients in a saucepan over medium heat and bring to a gentle simmer—do not boil. Simmer for a couple of minutes to allow the flavours to infuse.

Remove from the heat, strain and pour into two cups. Serve immediately.

For a strong chai, steep the spices and tea for an extra 3 minutes after turning off the heat. Then strain and reheat briefly before serving.

1 cinnamon stick

4 whole cloves

2 cardamom pods, lightly crushed

1 slice ginger

2 black or green tea bags or 3 teaspoons black or green loose-leaf tea (for a caffeine-free chai, replace black tea with rooibos)

2 teaspoons honey

625 ml (21½ fl oz/2½ cups) almond milk (see note)

Note Almond milk is made principally with water and ground almonds (albeit a very small amount—usually only 2–3 per cent). Almond milk is terrific for vegans and for anyone who can't or doesn't want to consume dairy milk. It's also low in kilojoules, about the same as skim milk, but lacks the protein of dairy milk. It's also lactose- and gluten-free.

The fat in almond milk is predominantly monounsaturated fats that can help you to reduce fat around the middle and they are good for your overall health. Just bear in mind drinking almond milk will not deliver the same health benefits as eating a full handful of nuts every day.

Per serve

energy	protein	tot. fat	sat	poly	mono	carb	sugars	fibre
580 kJ 140 Cal	2 g	9 g	1 g	3 g	4 g	12 g	12 g	1 g

NUTRITION BLOCKS PER SERVE

 **0** PLANT   **0** PROTEIN   **½** CARB   **½** FAT

*All sugars naturally present.

Hot spiced cocoa

Feeling like you need a chocolate hit? This recipe is magic in a cup. Pure cocoa powder
is a mixture of the cocoa solids left after cocoa butter is extracted from the cacao bean.
It has the slightly bitter but wonderfully chocolatey taste, but without the energy density of
chocolate. It's also rich in a group of antioxidants called flavonoids. Some of these are
lost in processing, so the less processed powders are better for you.

Serves 1 Time 5 minutes GF NF V

Combine the milk, cocoa powder and spices in a small saucepan. Place
over medium heat and whisk the cocoa powder into the milk as it heats.
Allow the flavours to mingle for a few minutes, then serve in a warm
mug. I like to leave the spices floating, but if you prefer you can remove
these prior to drinking.

1 teaspoon pure cocoa powder (see note)

1 cinnamon stick

1 star anise

Grating of nutmeg

250 ml (9 fl oz/1 cup) light milk (or full
cream if you prefer, but note this will
increase the kilojoules)

Note Cocoa consumption has been associated with a number of health
benefits, including lower blood pressure, improved blood cholesterol
profiles, improved blood vessel health and overall may reduce the risk of
heart disease.

Cocoa powder retains many of the beneficial antioxidants and is an easy
way of adding cocoa into your diet without the kilojoules (or sugar in
most) chocolate. Look for raw cocoa powder to maximise the antioxidants
present, but be ready for a more powerful cocoa taste!

Per serve

energy	protein	tot. fat	sat	poly	mono	carb	sugars	fibre
520 kJ 120 Cal	10 g	3 g	2 g	0 g	1 g	13 g	13 g	<1 g

NUTRITION BLOCKS PER SERVE

0 PLANT   **1** PROTEIN   **0** CARB   **0** FAT

*If made with full cream milk this pushes the kilojoules up to 760 kJ (180 Cal). All sugars naturally present.

Index